dance of a fallen monk

Also by George Fowler

Feed Your Soul

dance *of a* fallen monk

a journey to spiritual

enlightenment

George Fowler

ANCHOR BOOKS
DOUBLEDAY
NEW YORK   LONDON   TORONTO   SYDNEY   AUCKLAND

AN ANCHOR BOOK

PUBLISHED BY DOUBLEDAY

a division of Bantam Doubleday Dell Publishing Group, Inc.
1540 Broadway, New York, New York 10036

ANCHOR BOOKS, DOUBLEDAY, and the portrayal of an anchor
are trademarks of Doubleday, a division of Bantam Doubleday
Dell Publishing Group, Inc.

Dance of a Fallen Monk was originally published in hardcover by
Addison-Wesley in 1995. The Anchor Books edition is published
by arrangement with Addison-Wesley.

Library of Congress Cataloging-in-Publication Data

Fowler, George, 1929–
Dance of a fallen monk / by George Fowler.
p. cm.
Originally published: Reading, Mass. : Addison-Wesley Pub. Co.,
© 1995.
1. Fowler, George, 1929–   . 2. Spiritual biography.
3. Ex-monks—Biography. 4. Ex-clergy—Biography. I. Title.
[BL73.F68A3 1996]
291.4'092—dc20
[B] 96-2605 CIP

ISBN 0-385-48407-0
First Anchor Books Edition: July 1996

10 8 6 4 2 1 3 5 7 9

It's difficult to take "fallen" seriously when

where you've landed is with those who dance deep

in the heart of a Light-filled Universe.

~~~~~~~~~~~~~~~~~~~~

Dedicated to all who dare to long for such a fall.

Contents

dance of a fallen monk

Preface

This book is more about a path than about me. It's the story of all who walk—or want to walk—the road to inner wholeness but who find themselves, as I did, struggling against negative odds and surrounded by unhelpful circumstances. It's meant to encourage people to let their hearts dance. And not to take as long about it as I did!

I've learned that healing and wholeness mean more than just getting by. They mean getting by securely, confidently. They mean freedom not only from feelings of guilt for what we've done amiss, but even more from the psychological guilt of feeling bad about ourselves. I've come to realize that true healing is a freedom marked by mirth at being authentic and alive in a Technicolor universe. The only adequate expression of true wholeness, true healing is dancing in our hearts.

In the end, I've found high happiness, even ecstasy. Along the way, though, there were problems, pains, mistakes . . . and far too little intimacy. If I were doing it all over again, I'd make my move to freedom earlier. This book has been written to tell everybody—and me—how I'd do that and why.

An abbot, an admiral, a Roman cardinal, and a long queue of relatives will say I've blundered often. I agree, but never for the reasons they give. I see my life as a study in blundering, what it is and what it isn't.

There were years of silence along the way. There were female, then male, then female lovers. There were upset church managers and memorably spiritual monks. And then a wonderful assortment of equally memorable, equally conscientious military friends.

I've had twenty-seven years of formal education, but, in the words of Thomas Aquinas when, late in life, he compared his learning to what he had learned in meditation, a lot of my study turned out to be straw. I spent my first fifty years in self-hatred, and all of that turned out to be silly. I've even danced with cancer, and that turned out to be a gift. Most of all, though, and last of all, I've found myself dancing with a freedom and joy that border on bliss.

I lived as a silent monk for seventeen years and twelve as a priest. There were fifteen as a manager in the "military industrial complex," a few as a Catholic chaplain, and two as a Protestant chaplain. Through it all, with very little regret, I've been a pain in the lower dorsal areas of organized religion's anatomy.

The search that I launched on the prairies of Montana, intensified in the mountains of Utah, and pursued in many different places has been consistent throughout. It came into first focus during a night of panic in the Philippines when I was eighteen, and from that point on I never seriously veered from conscious steps upon it.

The only thing I've ever truly wanted from life is to be okay. I got more than I asked for, because human okayness, it turns out, includes bliss. This book chronicles how I found more wholeness than I'd dreamed of. It traces how the focusing of my goal became more and more spiritual as life went on—and had less and less to do with institutional religion.

After the dark things in my life had had their way with me for half a century, I finally learned that we can come to inner and outer security despite flagrant disregard of society's sacred rules for a successful career. I learned that we can do this while deliberately, even uproariously, ignoring the greater part of what churches thump their Book about as being essential for a meaningful, spiritual, and happy life.

I spent years grubbing around the globe for something to eat, having all the while a pocket filled with priceless stones. Or, in the metaphor of Meister Eckhart in the fourteenth century West and of Buddhists before him in the East, I was a man riding an ox looking for an ox to ride on.

As truthfully as the rights of others and memory allow, this is the story of how I found the ox.

Peace to Those Who Enter

A thunderstorm that had been tagging me across northern Utah finally caught my borrowed '48 Chevy in the mountains east of Ogden and promptly swamped the talents of its windshield wipers. It was about midnight as I pulled over to the side of an abysmally dark and unfamiliar canyon road. Whether or not I was lost, I felt lost—not at all sure I'd made the correct turns at several recent forks in the road. I was alone, confused, and, since this is going to be a truthful telling, a lot more scared than I'd like to remember in myself as a young man of twenty.

Only minutes before I'd been so sure I was on the right road, not only to the monastery I was visiting for the first time, but to the rest of my life I planned to spend there. As the not noticeably friendly powers of the universe threatened me from just outside a flimsy box of metal and glass, I filled with familiar doubts and whatever new ones could find room. Was my father, then, right after all? Was this trip to "that goddamned Catholic monkey cage" as big a mistake as he said?

Like most of the world, he understood Trappist monks and their lifestyle not at all. When I told him I wanted to be a monk in order to be intimate with God, he didn't have the foggiest idea of what I was talking about. I gave him their literature, but all it did was provide him more detailed reasons to wonder why in God's name any young man would choose such a life. The Trappist order of monks had its origin in a seventeenth-century reform of an eleventh-century reform of a venerable sixth-century Benedictine monasticism.

Dad wondered loudly why Trappists didn't reform yet one more time and join the human race.

Until the late 1960s, Trappist monks never spoke out loud to each other except in a few, clearly identified situations, such as in the confessional, during classes, and to their abbot and spiritual director. They explained that they wanted no earthly conversation to interrupt the one they were having—or aiming to have—with God. They had no recreation of any sort, no radio, no television, no newspapers, and were never allowed to visit their families, even at the death of a parent. To keep their flesh in line, they whipped themselves with knotted cords each Friday, never rose later than 2 A.M.—1:30 on Sundays and 1:00 on days of major liturgy, and began their Lent not six weeks before Easter, but on September 14 of the previous year. At no time did they eat eggs, fish, or meat, and they lived most of the year on one meal a day made up of boiled vegetables and unbuttered bread.

Most confounding to outsiders was the reasoning that drove this harshness: the pressing hunger for the closest possible union with God. Few nonmonks saw the connection. The church told Trappists that theirs was the best life; anyone who lasted in a Trappist abbey had to be passionately convinced the church was right.

My father was equally passionate that the complete program was pathological on all points.

Alone in my car in a suddenly surreal canyon, I wondered if the storm raging around me was sent by God to keep me from a stupid decision—or by Satan to keep me from a good one. Was I running from life as I knew I'd often done before? The crashing and howling midwifed all kinds of questions, but made it impossible to work on any answers.

As soon as I pulled over to the side of the road, I locked the car doors. Today, a lifetime later, I know there were still enough medieval fears in me that it wasn't the beings who wouldn't or couldn't be out in that weather I was fearing, but those who I still believed could and by preference would. I don't remember if I consciously thought about demons then, but I did lock the doors.

I arrived in that midnight canyon of strange shapes and leaping shadows fully primed for any terrors that might come crashing down upon me. The whole show was straight out of hell, even if recognizable a half hour later as nothing more than one of Utah's high-end electrical storms. Maybe my reaction was Dante's fault. A few weeks earlier we'd been dissecting his *Inferno* in college. But it's more likely that what set me up was the two years I'd been meditating on what my new Catholic church painted as the landscape of the damned. If I was going to be a celibate priest, I stood warned: from here on out I could use my penis for peeing and absolutely nothing else. In fledgling efforts at what the church considered "purity," I had quickly learned that whenever sexual hunger came visiting, eternal fire is a far more effective bouncer than icy showers.

Caged in a Wasatch canyon, my pounding heart was rocking my body as severely as the storm was rocking my car. I was experiencing a visible, audible portrayal of what the raw fury of God could be like, the God who will, the church said, thus forever treat those who stumble on what it proudly proclaimed to be a narrow and pit-filled celibate pathway. I heard my father's voice, my father confessor's voice, my church's voice, even what I took to be God's voice. I had not yet learned to listen for my own.

Eventually, of course, both storm and crisis passed, and, to my youthful relief, I survived. It turned out I had taken all the correct turns and before long was stopping once again, this time in the monastery parking lot. As I caught my first glimpse of the abbey's bell tower, I felt warm in the certainty that the Mormon's Utah weather had been conniving with my Protestant ancestors (and still-protesting parents) to keep me away from a place where God clearly wanted me to spend the rest of my life.

The clouds opened in evident benediction as I emerged from the car. A bright moon quickly transformed the surroundings into a fairyland of freshly washed trees, sparkling stones, and shining buildings. The brief walk to the gatehouse was heady beyond anything I'd known. Everything so clearly promised a magical first visit and a magical lifetime as a monk. Over the entrance in huge letters readable in the fresh moon, Latin words spoke to me personally, summarizing as well as any could why I'd come: *Ingredientibus Pax*—"Peace to Those Who Enter." I hoped so.

Flowing with an undiminished but now softer adrenaline, piously, courageously, I *knew* so. I was as blissful as a young man can be when I rang the bell at the huge wooden doors of the gatehouse.

As the brother night porter who answered the bell led me to the guest house, the monastery grounds inside the gate turned out to be as starkly but distinctly beautiful as I had been led to expect. They had some of the severe beauty of a Montana prairie about them. I was not prepared, however, for the shabby and outright dank room to which the porter silently led me. It was spotless, but that's all that can be said for it. When he left me, without once raising his eyes to mine, and without uttering a single word, I wondered if his silence and slight departing bow were prescribed rites of the monastic great silence of the night or embarrassment at the kind of lodging he was offering me. My first impression inside a monastery was by no means as enthusiastic as it had been outside.

After only an hour in bed—I couldn't call it sleep—I was jolted by the abbey bell rousing the monks to what I would later learn they called the night office portion of their choir duty. Half asleep, I got back into my clothing and wandered down a long hallway to the guests' balcony in the abbey church. From there I watched the monks begin their day of chant and prayer at 2:20 A.M.

My emotions that early July morning in 1949 seemed to surpass one another as they successively appeared. I was on the tail of a kite, flapping with each new event that blew past. It was going to be many years before I would be able to crawl up onto the kite itself and achieve any stability in the ride.

When the choir's ancient voice began pouring over me, I felt the strongest emotion of all. Watching the heavily robed men move through their cadenced ritual of bows and prayer, I was carried back to medieval times and could hardly believe it was to be my good fortune one day to join them.

And join them I eventually did, there in their mountain choir.

In later years as I stood with them in that same choir, now in my own great robes and by then knowing a large part of the chant by heart, I would often see a young aspirant kneeling back where I myself had knelt that first morning. I would long to talk to him. My heart ached to play father to him. I almost wanted to warn him, not precisely to go away and not join—something, after all, that I myself honestly loved—but . . . well, there are so many paths to fulfillment beyond the way of a Trappist monk. I never had an opportunity to talk to any of them, and I wouldn't have done so in any case. We all have a right to our own adventures, our own choices, our own process. I'd been permitted mine, and those who came after me had to be allowed theirs. But there was so much I could have told them to help them make their decisions. Did they truly know what they were doing in wanting to be a Trappist?

For about two hours that first morning, a carefully cadenced monotone recitation, punctuated regularly by Gregorian plainsong, washed over me like warm, relentless waves from an ocean of pure light. I remember being disappointed that even though I was by then a good student of Latin, I could only here and there catch a meaningful word. *God* and *father* and *son* now and then, but that was about it. But this made little practical difference because I didn't have to translate the words to know, to *feel,* that these monks of perpetual silence were talking to God in a very special, very intimate way.

Then, as abruptly as it had begun and beautiful though it was, the chanting stopped. The monks filed out of the church to go, as I would learn later, some to offer Mass at the abbey's many altars, and others to their desks and studies in a room they called their scriptorium, their writing room. There they pursued whatever they pursued until returning once again for more chanted prayer about 5:30 A.M.

In the hope of getting some badly needed sleep, I returned to my room. I was greeted by a valiant twenty-five-watt bulb illuminating it with about as much energy as I was by then feeling, but with a self-affirmation I could only envy. A note tacked to my door told me that guests would be served breakfast at seven. That permitted me, at best, about a third of the sleep I needed.

I sat on the edge of the narrow, squeaky bed as the chill of the damp night and my own weariness finally overtook me. All moonlight magic was gone. I swung once again, this time from soaring ecstasy to equally intense irritation. Every doubt I had already answered about myself, my fitness, my willingness for monastic life came flooding back to me. My unpacked bag lay only inches away as I considered getting into my car and driving down out of the mountains to the nearest hotel in Ogden seventeen miles away. Had it really come to this—a dismal, damp little room? Were those men *really* happy under those layers and layers of clothing with their forever zipped-up penises? My God, they couldn't even talk to one another. Everything around me suddenly seemed cheap. I was particularly put off by the flimsy homemade door of my room that felt as if it were made of cardboard.

And then I broke out laughing. It was the sight of my only companion, the small light bulb, that broke the spell. Twenty-five watts—maybe that was symbolic of what I had to begin with. It reflected the wattage of my own self-estimate. The pint-sized bulb struck me as happy doing its thing, giving the little it had to give. No complaints, no flickering, no questions. "I could learn a lesson," I preached to myself as I undressed and climbed back under the covers. The temptation to pick up and leave was gone. It would not return for another eighteen years.

Later, in the morning, I was glad I had stayed when I met Father Bartholomew, the man who in another twelve months would become my novice master for two years. A quiet man with a gentle smile and simple piety, he would see me through many troubled times in the years to come. Thirty-five years later, long after I had come and gone from the monastery, I wrote him a letter of gratitude for his goodness. His reply was warm and typical: "I always knew you were a good person deep down." About the same time another priest at the monastery, the abbot, to whom I had also written, chose not to reply.

On the last day of my week-long visit, I met Brother Matthew. He made me doubly grateful I had not left that first night.

My encounter with this Irish immigrant gentleman of Black-and-Tan days happened simply enough. I was sitting on a small log bench beneath an obliging maple, deep in one of the magic, contemplative moments with which my visit had been so full, when through a crack in a big wooden gate I noticed an elderly, brown-clad brother moving amid some flowers. The serious-looking gate sported an even more serious-sounding sign warning visitors that they were not to pass through it out of the guests' garden and into what it announced was a Papal Enclosure—Reserved to the Monks.

The initial mystery of the place had worn off, and I was feeling a certain sense of saltiness in the presence of green-as-grass guests who had arrived only that morning. I stood up, postured my most authoritative tallness, and strode over to the forbidden gate. I pushed it open with what I hoped looked like a deep knowing and, suddenly more unsure, cautiously approached the old brother. I had yet to talk to one of the "real" monks (as distinct from the two the abbot had appointed to deal with guests). I was anxious to meet one of the *non*talking monks before leaving the next morning. Who knows, I thought, he might even speak to me. To my surprise—and to what I realized in later years would have been the abbot's indignant and certainly angry dismay—he did.

He returned my greeting simply and gently, without a trace of hesitation or affectation. As far as he was concerned, I must have

seemed just another of God's creatures moving amid the flowers
with whom he was communing at the moment.

I can still see his well-worn hands working slowly, reverently,
in the garden as we spoke. Here he gently removed a dead leaf,
there a dried blossom. Once he leaned to a weed and, hesitating an
instant before pulling it, softly spoke to it, almost in apology, saying something to the effect that it really should be growing out in
the fields with its brothers and sisters and not here in a garden of
flowers. Once he moved an inchworm from a bud to a leaf.

After small talk about flowers and weather, I answered his direct question: yes, I was at the abbey in the hope of being admitted
as a novice. At that point I met the real Brother Matthew.

"The problem is," he said, glancing over at me, "you come here
looking for a beginning that's already past."

I was instantly dismayed, disappointed. Surely this kindly old
monk wasn't going to be another of those counterfeit gurus, like
some of the priests at my college and most preachers I'd ever heard.
They are the ones who delight in clever wordiness, the syrupy in-
consequence of which they hope will be taken as too profound
for clear understanding.

He sensed my difficulty and smiled as he went on. "You come,
as I once did, looking for a bit of guidance, some special secret
that will open to you the world of joyful peace and closeness to
God. But the truth is that you've already got what you're looking
for." He stopped as though what he had said was to be taken as
self-evident.

Musing on it today, I still see the old brother's gentle presence
as he spoke those words of quiet wisdom—and with what I sensed
might just be an impish amusement at breaking his Trappist rule
of silence. Some spirits allow themselves to be bigger than little
rules. Some are even free enough to enjoy the delinquency.

All these years later I can still quote, almost verbatim, the words
he added. I didn't understand them much at the time, but my intuition was far ahead of my understanding and it must have sensed
they were important enough to store for a later day.

"That's the secret, my young brother," he continued, "the 'al-readyness' of it all. You have nothing whatsoever to gain. Nothing is off in the future or out there that you can acquire. In having God, you have all spiritual goals and all spiritual perfection already. Sooner or later we all have to quit looking and start realizing. We waste so many years looking. . . ." His voice trailed off in what seemed a guiltless nostalgia.

Today I realize that what the old brother told me there amid the flowers summarizes all there is to say about the spiritual life, all there is to say about transcendent consciousness, about religion itself. Maybe he, too, wanted to play father to a visiting young man and was trying to tell me it wasn't at all necessary to become a monk to find what I was looking for.

We talked long, too long. I had quit glancing about to see if I'd been discovered in a place forbidden to "seculars" and apparently personally guarded by one who was still my pope. When the old brother finally asked what time I had on my wristwatch, he realized he was late for vespers. He winked as he told me the abbot would give him a penance for that. I walked with him to the door of the abbey church and apologized for having made him late and obliged to do penance for something that was my fault. He leaned back out of the doorway just long enough to break the rule of silence one more time.

"When you already have whatever there is to have, young friend," he whispered, "you can't get upset just because an abbot chooses to get upset, now can you."

Then, raising a finger, "Remember, it's *already* yours."

I either wasn't hearing or didn't understand. But I would. Both.

2

First Guru

That was in 1949. I'm writing this in 1994.

One year after my late-night arrival at the monastery known as Trinity Abbey, I was accepted as a monastic candidate. Five years later I made the five solemn vows as a Trappist and became a full-fledged monk. I remained one for twenty years, seventeen of them in the mountains of Utah and three as a monastic priest on leave from my abbey and working for the archbishop of San Francisco.

After eight years of study in the monastery, I was ordained a priest. The abbot then appointed me one of the priests designated to hear confessions of monks and visitors and to provide spiritual direction to those who might ask for it.

This new responsibility occasioned my getting to know Brother Matthew—the same brother who had broken silence with me among the roses thirteen years before—in a more intimate manner than is normally possible in a perpetually silent community. One Sunday afternoon in 1962, shortly before vespers, he asked me in simple monastic sign language if I would be his spiritual director. I agreed, but I realized that while I could now and then provide him the theological clarification he might request, he would forever remain master in matters of spirituality.

That was how our close friendship continued until he died in the mid-sixties. Close friendship means something significantly different in a Trappist monastery than what most understand by that term. No long conversations, weeknight poker games, or Saturday-afternoon beers. No shared family pictures or letters from home; no discussion of favorite books or even the latest sermon. Certainly no fishing trips or vacations taken together.

Nevertheless, Brother Matthew and I had got off to a good start the day we met, and over the years his eyes never lost their special twinkle—almost as if forever remembering that we shared a bit of devilment all our own—when we exchanged our prescribed slight bows upon passing in the cloisters. I don't know if he thought of me as a son, but perhaps the best way to describe my feelings for him is that they were those of a son. He, of course, was calling me "Father" in the confessional . . . but I could as easily have called him "Dad." We knew a closeness and warmth that was sustained by nothing but five minutes of conversation a week, plus a shared respect for something bigger than little rules of silence or the abbot's latest demand for one tight observance or another.

He was the gentlest of men, and he several times remarked that I was a particularly insightful and warmhearted confessor. Our relationship, however, was much more than a mutual admiration society. In a desert of human emotions, one learns quickly to appreciate whatever bit of gentle appreciation there is to be had. During our sessions we probably drew as close to each other as Trappist monks can.

When monks die, they are wrapped in their robes and, without coffins, buried within a few hours of death. As Brother Matthew lay on his bier in the abbey church just prior to being carried to his grave, I removed the rosary the infirmarian had entwined between his fingers. I could imagine the old brother's mirth as I performed this deed while a few monks kneeling in prayer beside his body looked on in scandalized, helpless dismay. Making rosaries had been his specialty, and I took this beauty he had made for himself years before, replacing it with a beat-up one of my own. I wanted a keepsake of this fine man who had become such a friend. I have long since given up praying the Rosary, but today there it is, passing its days in a velvet-lined walnut jewelry box alongside cuff links, studs, class rings, and other vanities. Relic of a world more distant than anything Star Trek's Captain Jean-Luc Picard ever dreamed of. I leave it where I will see it each time I open the box. It makes me smile. It reminds me of the old brother's dependable sense of perspective and quiet amusement. Each time, too, I look back with my own amusement at the other monks' shock the day I stole a rosary, an example of something Matthew and I spoke of more than once: stuffy propriety mistaken for religion. Even for spirituality.

This understated old master had something important to contribute to my life and had done so within five minutes of our meeting amid the flowers: "It's already yours," he had told me, and it was a bit of guidance I would meet again years later when reading the mystics. But the story of my earliest spiritual awakening had actually begun four years before when another friend had appeared in my life and had shared his own special awareness with me.

I met that earlier guru on a frozen December evening in 1945, at what started out to be just another supper at Mrs. Maclean's Restaurant. I was eating there and not at home with my family because three years before that, in my high school sophomore year, and with my father's reluctant permission, I had abandoned the family ranch and moved to town. Now a senior, I lived without cost at the town's fire station in the station keeper's room. It was lonely there by myself, but it had its advantages when I wanted to bring a girl home or preferred that no one see me in the inebriated condition in which I often made it to bed at 4:00 or 5:00 A.M. And it had also been lonely on the family ranch, after all.

I made payment for the room by keeping the town's red fire engine polished, and, if I happened to be in when the siren sounded atop city hall, by opening the station doors and starting the truck's engine. The volunteer firemen saw great advantage in having the truck warmed and ready to roll when the first of them arrived after an alarm.

When Mrs. Maclean found out I was living next door to her restaurant, where she knew there was no kitchen, she offered to let me eat three meals a day at her place, six days a week (closed on Sundays) for fifteen dollars a week. Not a bad deal, even in 1945. I was earning twenty-five dollars a week as soda jerk and stock clerk at Drake's, one of the town's two drugstores and a favorite high-school hangout. With free rent, fifteen dollars a week for meals, and clothing provided by my parents, I had ten dollars a week left over. Savings didn't even cross my mind. When Cokes cost a nickel and movies thirty-five cents, that was lots of money to play with.

And that is exactly what my friends and I did, almost always with the help of alcohol, from our junior year in Conrad High School on. Most of us were A students except in those classes, like second-year Latin, that we decided to ignore. We turned to alcohol to improve things, even creating a supersecret club we called the CIO, Conrad's Intoxication Organization. I was elected treasurer with the obligation to keep the club in cash by badgering members to pay arbitrary dues as empty coffers—and beer kegs— might demand. Unchallenged by school, bored with our hometown, we partied in the hills, in the lone bar of nearby Brady (population about fifty), in one another's homes when parents were away, and—our special delight—in a Sunday School room behind the walk-in baptismal pool of a local church. There were no alert school counselors to go to in those days, but we wouldn't have consulted them even if they had been there.

I had been a good student in grammar school and was a good one in high school, if grades alone define a good student. I was, with none of that ambiguity, a distinctly unhappy one.

Self-rejection—what I knew then only as hatred for my body— had dominated me for as long as I could remember. It got worse and harder to live with during high school when it was evident that all my friends were turning into men. At least, that was how I saw it. When some of my buddies began to sport hair on their chests, I took the deepest nosedive of all. I had red hair and despised red hair. Was embarrassed by lily-white skin and freckles and had a double portion of each. I envied fellow students their tanned summer hides and what appeared to me to be the most enviable possessions in the world: bulging deltoids, triceps, biceps, and muscled, hairy legs.

Years later, studying graduate psychology, I wondered at how I pulled even passing grades in high school with my obsessive degree of imagined bodily inferiority and its offspring, depression. Life was more than uncomfortable. It was painful, minute by minute, and it would remain so until more than halfway through my time in the abbey in my mid-thirties. Only then did it change for me substantially.

Supper at Mrs. Maclean's on the evening I met my first spiritual teacher started out like any other, but it was to be the best supper I'd ever had.

There never seemed to be more than six or seven patrons in the place at one time. It was tiny, seating fifteen at most. Mrs. Maclean made a go of it by attracting a steady stream of locals who knew of her remarkable cooking, enjoyed the family-style atmosphere, and ate there with some regularity. On this special evening in 1945, there were only a family of three at one table and myself and a young man, new in town, at the counter. Conrad had only fifteen hundred inhabitants in those days, and it was immediately known by everyone when someone new arrived. He sat a few stools away from me, around the corner of the counter. I could see his face clearly as he reacted to the conversation Mrs. Maclean and I were having.

Even had he ignored us, we could not have ignored him. He was striking, outstandingly good looking. Somewhat older than myself, trim, athletic, self-possessed, quiet, outgoing. His smile and twinkling eyes crowned what seemed to me, and obviously to Mrs. Maclean, the presence of a prince.

It was predictable that our effusive hostess would soon enough corral her new guest into the conversation. He picked it up easily when she did. He told us he was in town on a job with a state-contracted engineering company and would be around for another six months or so. His name turned out to be an unusual one, Adeodatus Nikos.

When Mrs. Maclean learned he had rented one of the small cabins, also without kitchens, down on the south edge of town, she made him the same offer she had given me, fifteen dollars a week for six days of meals. He accepted readily.

All I knew at first was that I felt good about the prospect of having a companion for my meals. Especially this one. I didn't know then that my life had just taken a turn.

Datus (rhymes with "taught us")—the shortened name he asked us to call him—was twenty-five. That made him eight years my senior, but it wasn't his age that impressed me. Even the most admired jocks at school couldn't hold a candle to his build and good looks. Only later and with his help did I come to realize that what was so attractive to me about him were not his muscular physique and handsome face, but his easy poise and self-presence. He looked the way I always wanted to look, yes. More important, he evidently felt about himself the way I had always wanted to feel about myself.

New customers called for Mrs. Maclean's attention, and Datus and I finished our meal and moved together out onto the icy sidewalk. I had been planning on a 7:00 P.M. movie at the Orpheum directly across the street, and Datus said he had nothing planned and "would I mind?" Mind!

Those were the days of double features, and I remember *Casablanca* was playing with some readily forgotten comedy. My responses to the double fare were varied: concentration, a few opinions, laughter, some (I hoped) unobserved tears.

My new companion reacted as spontaneously as I did, and by the time the first feature was over, it was clear we had a lot in common. I doubt if I dared hope yet that we would become good friends, but I do remember being eager for the second movie to end.

My answer to his first question back on the street was honest. "No, I don't have studies waiting for me." I never did. High school didn't ask much of me, and I didn't give it more than it asked. Besides, it was Saturday night, and who ever heard of studying on weekends. Sure, I'd be glad to go to his place for cocoa. I was so loaded with admiration that I would have lied about studies and shared a cup of hemlock to spend more time with him.

This was just the beginning of cocoa with Datus. We drank gallons of it before our time together was over.

It was only about six blocks from the theater to his cabin on the edge of town—fifteen hundred inhabitants make for a *small* town. We talked easily about the movies as we walked, and I noticed he was studying me casually and openly all the way. It struck me that while I was a bit uneasy, I was not as uneasy under his scrutiny as I had always been under that of others. From the start, Datus didn't hook into my feelings of inadequacy. A lifelong self-embarrassment seemed to be losing itself in the warmth of his presence.

Datus's cabin was neat, his bed made. Off in one corner, he had a small table with a hot plate—which, in purest Sydney Greenstreet, he told me broke the manager's rules—and in another a large assortment of pillows. Beside his bed was a bookcase of stacked apple boxes containing, it seemed to me, an astonishing number of books for someone not still in school.

He had a small stash of snacks and what I would come to learn was a bottomless supply of cocoa. While he brewed, I busied myself looking through his library. There were books on electricity, mechanical drawing, oriental religions, meditation, something by or about Mary Baker Eddy, and others I have forgotten. Meditation was still as mysterious to me as Hinduism, Buddhism, and Christian Science. My mulling through his books was an act of nervousness, not informed interest.

His frigid cabin was only slowly cooperating with the small gas heater he lit when we arrived, and I welcomed the hot cocoa. When he handed me my cup, Datus also gave me the first glimpse of a spontaneous charm I would experience again and again in the months to come.

Cocoa in hand, I sat on one of the two chairs in the room, expecting him to sit on the other. Instead, he walked across the room and, as easily as he would have sat on a sofa, folded his legs under him and sank into his pillows. Without interrupting our flow of words, his eyes twinkled and he flashed a smile as he patted the pillows for me to come join him.

3

First Friend

From the beginning, the relationship Datus and I knew had most of the earmarks of a gay love affair. Only we weren't gay. At least he wasn't. Whether I was, am, used to be, should be, could be, is part of the story remaining to be told in this book. At this point it's enough to report that Datus and I never once had any overt sexual encounter. To that degree, at least, our relationship was not homosexual. But I add with no reluctance that in later years I sometimes thought "too bad." Our love certainly ended up with everything else going for it.

No sex, but did we love each other? Most certainly. Profoundly. Intimately, deeply, with an overpowering inner passion. I came to love Datus as much as brother could love brother. And I never wanted for indicators that the feeling was returned in kind.

Since then, gay men have happily—*most* happily—reminded all men who are secure enough to listen, gay or straight, that they can and may love each other. Male couples, like any other couples, may or may not be genitally involved. Do they or don't they isn't a criterion with which to judge whether love is real.

My own first experiment in sexual preference was to come two years later. What I looked for and needed from my new friend at this time was not more sex, but precisely what he began to give me that first evening: a love I couldn't doubt. He recognized in me the person I'd not yet begun to realize I was. Famine of the heart pressed me infinitely more than my fairly well-fed high-school libido.

Datus and I talked about sex several times. The results were always the same. I was astonished at his attitudes, and he at mine. He astounded me by the ease with which he treated what for me was a topic (and certainly an experience) loaded with guilt and doubt. He couldn't understand why I belabored what for him was so straightforward. I remember listening in dumb silence once when, to illustrate his point, he told me that he simply masturbated when he felt like it. He saw it as a simple act of self-care and love for himself, as free of moral consideration as urinating or brushing teeth. He said he'd had sex with girls in high school and college when circumstances seemed right, and that was that. One evening he even shared with me what he didn't realize I already knew, that he occasionally had afternoon love-making rendezvous with one of our mutual acquaintances in Conrad.

I smile as I imagine what he would have thought had he known me a few years later, after I let Catholicism fill my absorbent mind with a few thousand of its own sexual inhibitions honed into finer and finer absurdities—and legislation—by centuries of crusty career celibates in Rome.

Had people in Conrad realized the degree of intimacy that developed between Datus and me, they undoubtedly would have shipped me back to the ranch and him back to wherever he came from. As it was, they didn't suspect anything, and we were discreet enough that they saw nothing they could misinterpret. Besides, homosexuality was hardly thought of, much less presumed, in rural Montana of the 1940s. Mexican sugar-beet workers had been rumored to "satisfy each other," as farmers put it, but these laborers had been caught growing marijuana among the beets, so "What can we expect?" Obviously "no white person" would ever think of using marijuana and, equally obvious, "no white person would . . .well, do that *other* thing that some Mexican workers are said to do."

As a young man I was sensitized early to the possibility of being ridiculed as "queer" when a horse-obsessed young lady who disliked me as much as I disliked horses once rather contemptuously asked if *that* was the reason why I liked classical music. Worse still, she footnoted, I refused to go hunting jackrabbits and gophers and (where had my family gone wrong?) even played the violin.

Dad never seemed to have any questions about my sexual orientation until much later, when I announced plans to become a monk. He found out once about one of my amorous exploits with a girl in high school and seemed rather proud of me. His only remark at the time was that I should be careful not to "knock up" any of my girlfriends. He warned me countless times about the evils of masturbation, but he seemed indifferent to any "normal sex." Only once, as I recall, did he warn me about "queers," when he found out I had accepted a ride from a stranger in Great Falls, a nearby seeming metropolis of fifty thousand. Being queer, like masturbation, he elaborated, was something I should avoid lest I grow up to be—his favorite tag for ultimate failure—"no goddamn good."

The frequency with which dad warned against "self-abuse" imprinted deeply on my young mind. Probably because he said it only once, I saw his alert about homosexuals as just another of his trademark bigotries. There was only one black man in Conrad, Rastus, the shoeshine man at Matt Kirsch's barber shop, and everybody liked him. Dad, however, openly called this elderly, universally friendly, always smiling gentleman a "goddamn nigger" and never gave any sign of wondering if his words were fair. I decided early that *anything* Dad told me about those he called spicks, Japs, waps, Krauts, kikes, kooks, pollaks, niggers, Catholics, and most of our neighbors' wives was to be ignored. I laughed each time he named a new milk cow after still another of our neighbors' wives, but I never found what he said about those women very amusing. I knew and liked every one of them.

I was unprepared for Datus's gesture to come sit next to him on his pillows. Not from wondering if it was a come-on, but simply from surprise. It had been only three hours and I was already feeling a closer, easier, more honest warmth from him than I'd yet known. I hesitated only an instant. Then I smiled with a hope and trust new to me and moved across the room to sit beside him, close again as in the movies.

Telling personal history, even with a good memory and honest intentions, is precarious business. When and how much does later insight and history bleed back into the incident being described? How much of what I tell of this first evening with Datus actually happened then? How much is from later exchanges with him, from insights years later for which he only planted the seed?

We moved in and out of serious talk and laughter on our first evening together as if we had known each other forever. He may have taken it all for granted. I didn't. If a young man of seventeen can, in one brief evening, move from despair to hope, I managed it. I remember watching the clock on his table, wishing the damn thing would slow down.

I can still at times hear Datus's rich and gentle voice. There was always a smile in it somewhere. It seemed to me to underline the logic and good sense my youthful but fairly bright mind was recognizing in everything he said. He made a profound impact on me as we bantered and as he patiently answered my shamelessly dogged questions about his books. I smile at the compulsive spin I was in as I write of this a lifetime later, aware now that I didn't know enough then to ask him even one intelligent question about religion, philosophy, meditation. My conversation was an avalanche because I was confused by my sudden turn of fortune. I didn't know how to handle this totally new kind of easy intimacy.

Nervous or not, my questions were genuine and did express a sincere and huge appetite. I didn't know what I was hungering for or exactly what it was that Datus had, but I knew I wanted some. He sensed that, respected my tangled curiosity and handled it patiently.

I spent much of the evening watching his face, half expecting to see a patronizing, mocking air. Contempt maybe, or at least a tiring. None appeared. Instead, all I saw was a warm, involved

Greek godliness, a gentle friendliness that had absolutely no precedent in my life.

Two thoughts obsessed me. How could any one person be so good looking and so charming, and why would such a person be interested in someone like me? I didn't have to wait long to find out.

In the midst of my frantic act, a new kind of smile spread over Datus's face. Before I could wonder if he was at last tiring of me, he reached out and placed a hand on my cheek in such a way that his thumb fell naturally across my lips. In mock seriousness, he leaned toward me and in a loud whisper said, "All these questions! It's time *I* get to know something about *you.*" He paused for the full effect of his hand and words to register. Then: "I'll be glad to share everything in my books, but now tell me about yourself."

My shields were penetrated, facade down. But old habits die hard, and I laughed nervously as I ricocheted off some banality or other and tried to carry on in generalities. Again the hand on my face, the finger across my lips—this time without words, just his best smile, arched brows, and a tilt of his head in waiting expectation.

"He really does expect me to talk about myself!"

"George," he said, finally bailing me out and answering my thoughts, "I listened to you in Mrs. Maclean's tonight and watched you during the movies. You're a sensitive guy, a bright guy. I'm not going to let you out of here without knowing more about you" — a pause to make sure I'd heard, and then an aside to lighten it all up—"especially if I have to eat my meals with you for the next few months."

There's an ancient spiritual principle, "When the disciple is ready, the master will appear." I've seen it proved in my life and the lives of others many times over. On a snowy December night in 1945, long before I'd ever heard of it, I experienced its truth for the first time. A master honed precisely to my needs had just arrived.

4

Point of Departure

Somehow or other Datus had arrived at our first evening together with a striking inheritance of genes and a singular conditioning in self-confidence. Somehow or other I had not. I can only guess what path got him there in his enviable form, but I understand my own fairly well.

There was nothing wrong with my genes, but it took me another twenty-five years to realize that. In 1945, I was still complaining about them and damning all four of my grandparents for handing me a slight frame and an untannable skin that embarrassed me beside the muscular builds and browned hides of my friends on the high school's varsity teams.

My mother's parents came from a village in the far north of Norway. A surviving document describes them as popular newlyweds who dismayed fellow townsfolk by their decision to catch a ship to America in the 1890s. That Viking spirit, though, even had I known of it in high school, wouldn't have diluted the disgust I felt for the complexion they passed down to me. All I thought about the two withered and seemingly ancient grandparents they had become by the time I knew them was why hadn't they learned English well enough so I could understand them and why did anybody have to be so incredibly white.

My father's side of the family was equally without melanin. English immigrants to Massachusetts in the 1600s, my father's immediate line of Fowlers were New York farmers by the time of the American Revolution. They remained loyal to their king during the war, and in 1783 saw their Long Island farms confiscated and their families forced onto deportation ships in New York harbor. In 1986 I visited the land grants they received for their troubles from the British crown in New Brunswick. Set between long arrays of Fowler grants was a double grant to Benedict Arnold. My father's people were right up there in guts with my mother's Norwegian Vikings, and, depending on the latest definition of what's politically correct, the company they kept was gutsy or traitorous along with them. But nowhere in any of this inheritance did I see the slightest hope of getting a tan.

In the 1880s, Grandfather left his Loyalist roots in Canada and came back to the United States for the gold mines of Last Chance Gulch, now Helena, Montana. By 1898, he had gold in his pockets as he took his new wife to settle north of what is now Great Falls, on the Missouri River. They built a two-story ranch house, still standing, which his children and I as one of his grandchildren knew from childhood as home.

Grandfather's first son died in infancy and lies buried on the ranch. His only surviving son became my father.

In many ways my father inherited the best of his aggressive family. It showed up in unstoppable energy, a noteworthy creativity in ranching, and an almost universal conviviality. Unfortunately, it also appeared in a shameless store of courageously outspoken bigotries of which he alone was proud.

I doubt if Grandfather ever understood his son even a little. Dad's gregariousness and loud partying were matched at the opposite end of the spectrum by a quiet-spoken, retiring, English-Canadian gentility Grandfather never lost. While my father owned car after car, and stretched every one of them to its limit, Grandfather, by choice, never learned to drive. Dad used alcohol freely, slowing not even during the years of Prohibition. The only time Grandfather ever took a drink, family tradition has it, was once when, deep in a winter flu, he asked his son if he thought a wee sip of home brew would help him recover. It did. Neither man bothered much with church, but while Grandfather communed with his prairie surroundings and the wild birds and animals, my father saw almost everything that moved on the prairie primarily as a target. No church for him meant no inwardness of any sort, except self-hatred and despair.

Dad's problems traced not to his father, but to his mother. She was an immigrant from Edinburgh, Scotland, making her way across the United States for a ship to the South Pacific as a Presbyterian missionary when grandfather met her, irresistibly wooed her, and then married her. After a couple of apparently happy years at the turn her adventure had taken, the romance wore off, and she spent the rest of her life in bitterness—angry in the best self-righteous style of her high Presbyterian tradition that a wicked man, her husband, had done the work of the Devil by enticing her away from her divine calling. She died before I was born, but her image came up again and again in our home. My father and his younger sister, feisty Aunt Myra, were sometimes heard arguing loudly about which of them their mother had hated most.

Whether or not Grandmother Fowler was actually the tyrant my father remembered is not so important as the fact that that is how he carried her memory, like burning acid, in his heart. Once in a rare moment of confidence he told me of the protracted beatings she gave him as an adolescent, beatings from which there was no recourse. Grandfather seems to have been cowed by her and stayed out of it. Dad told me that she once explained to him that the beatings came from her "certain knowledge of what kind of thoughts are in the minds of young boys."

In reaction to this abuse and throughout his life, my father was dependably, obsessively, uncritically dutiful to his children, in all things short of an emotional support he didn't have to give. He never demanded that we share chores, never insisted on homework, never wanted to know why we had stayed out late. We wanted for nothing he could provide, but we certainly needed much that he couldn't. At times he was gentle, intimate, interested, but more often, harsh, angry, and verbally abusive. I didn't realize then what I came to understand years later, that his explosions were always matters of a passing emotion, his gentleness always deliberate.

On one occasion he explained to me with care and sensitivity that he was going to have to destroy my dog who had begun to kill lambs, and that the dog would be gone when I returned from school the next day. On another he angrily stormed into the house, got one of his guns, and in my presence, with no words, shot another of my dogs whom he had seen chasing geese and turkeys. After he had buried it and his emotion had passed, he gently, almost penitently, explained to me why he had shot the dog.

There were special moments of intimacy between us that surprised me into tears at his funeral in 1980. I remembered, for example, the day when I was very small and he was preparing to fill a tractor with fuel. He winked at me as he said that before two minutes had passed I would use the word *oh*. I asked why he said that, but he only repeated his statement. I set my teeth and announced I wouldn't say oh "no matter what." He began turning the pump handle on the fuel barrel and out poured a grade of fuel that refineries had just begun to color code a brilliant blue that became liquid sapphire in the morning sun. "Oh, Pop! Look at that color!" He laughed his best laugh that made me feel good in ways I seldom did.

And then there was the day some years later—same fuel pump, same tractor—when he shouted an uninterrupted flow of invectives at me because I had not topped off the tractor's tank before starting it.

I saw my father as dangerous. There was no way I could have known then that he would never once, in fact, hit me. After his death, my stepmother said he once told her he had promised himself he would never strike any of his children. He never did.

Before I began to go to school he often took me along on

Saturday afternoons when he would "go to Johnny's," the family's tag for his weekly ritual of visiting Johnny Stone's Tavern in town. There he and his friends would gather at an old-fashioned bar complete with brass rail and spittoons that I thought had to be the shiniest brass objects in the whole world. I used to marvel at the way some of Johnny's patrons could aim for those glittering targets from what seemed miraculous distances and never miss. I would shudder at the thought that sooner or later someone, somehow would have to clean them out. I once asked my father how they were cleaned, and he said he didn't want to think about it.

Each week I would have a bottle of pop, usually while seated on the bar, at the same time dad and his friends had their beer. There were many colors of pop in clear glass bottles in those days, and it became an expected part of the Saturday afternoon ritual at Johnny's for everyone at the bar to help me deliberate over what color to select.

An awful day came when, as my father said, I embarrassed him in front of his friends. I had grown accustomed to the bar and slowly began to see myself as a budding peer in the genuine camaraderie that prevailed there. I became more and more determined to be heard in this weekly rite of male bonding. On the fateful day of dishonor, one of dad's friends offered to buy me a second bottle of pop. It had happened before and I usually somewhat reluctantly turned them down, but this time I was prepared. "No, thank you, sir . . . but I'd be glad to accept the dime instead." The bar exploded in laughter, although my antenna immediately told me dad's laughter was not wholly spontaneous. On the way home he repeated several times, "A man never, never, never does a thing like that!" I was totally mystified by his statement, which he said didn't need explanation. For a long time afterward I was confused, for what I had said seemed eminently fair to me. Mr. Mills had been planning to get rid of the dime in my behalf anyway, so why not? Nevertheless, the earnestness of my father's counsel somehow impressed me, and I resolved never to repeat the blunder. I thought of asking my stepmother to explain the matter to me, but why embarrass myself in front of her as badly as I had done in front of my father? I took it on faith that dad had taught me a major, if mysterious, lesson about the rules of being a man among men.

There were good times, but the bad ones far outnumbered them. My brother, sisters, and I were never physically abused, but neither did we escape sharing the brunt of our father's own abusive childhood.

The trauma of his young years was hugely compounded early in his marriage to my mother. Less than two years after my own birth, her third child died in early infancy, and she swore she would never bear another baby. Three abortions followed in less than three years, and during the night following the last one she bled to death. She was twenty-three. Bernice was six and I was just past my fourth birthday.

When our mother did not awaken as dad returned from morning chores on the ranch, my sister and I remember seeing him seat himself beside her body on their bed and gently hold her hands. We stood across the room leaning against a piano, crying and completely confused by what was happening. Why did he keep trying to open her hands? Unknown to him, she had died during the night and her body was already clamped in rigor mortis.

Bernice remembers him crying. I don't. But I do remember that from that moment he withdrew into what years later, when he visited my wife and me in San Francisco, he referred to as his unforgivable guilt. One morning over breakfast coffee during that visit he forever carved into my mind and heart a stark sentence that made me realize something of the agony of his lifetime: "I thought I smelled alcohol on that damn doctor's breath when we walked into his office, and I knew damn well I should take your mother out of there and not let him get close to her."

From the time of our mother's death, for which he blamed himself, he never physically touched my sister or me again, either in discipline or affection. He seemed unwilling, or unable, to touch us. The most he could ever manage was a handshake, and then only on the most special occasions.

Two photos of me have survived from that era, one taken four months before my mother's death and the other, coincidentally, four months after. The first shows a bright-faced, tousled boy of four looking mischievously out on what, evidently, was a secure world. The second is of a confused young face with tight brows and eyes staring into nowhere. I only vaguely remember the pain of those days, but I do remember that it was my father whom I was missing, not my mother.

Mother's death was the continental divide in my sister's and my early home life. Before it, things were well. After it, hell arrived. It became as if we were someone else's children. When neighbors offered to adopt either of us, our father was indignant and years later had not forgiven them for asking. He angrily announced he intended to keep us and promptly set about hiring a succession of housekeepers. We became the responsibility of the current house-keeper. Beyond providing for our material support, Dad was far too occupied taking care of his own agony to have space for us.

Two years and several housekeepers later, the most pleasant of them stayed on longer than the others, and after a brief return to her home in Idaho—when we thought she, too, was gone for-ever—she returned to marry our father. Overnight, my sister and I had a new mother. Even as a housekeeper, she had been excep-tionally warm and generous, and she told me years later that almost immediately after her arrival I began telling her she was a "cuddly" person. She filled my sister's and my needs admirably, willing to give us the hugs and attention we had sorely missed. An aunt told me years later that since everyone saw me as an unusually sensi-tive child, I had surprised them all by not seeming to miss my first mother in the weeks after she died. I wonder what that says about how "cuddly" she was.

Pearl, the remarkable cook all the neighbors were soon talking about, made an immediate difference in our home. She played the piano that had, until then, sat brooding, untouched and untuned, in the corner of our living room. She wallpapered the bedrooms, refurbished the kitchen, removed a wall to enlarge the living room dramatically. Most significant of all, to me at least, she brought information about God into our family. Dad told me once that he and my first mother had never been in a church except for a wedding or funeral. My new mother, in contrast, was deeply, light-heartedly religious, and she made the God I had forever wondered about a bit understandable and even somewhat likable. Years later, shortly before her death, she told me that as a child I pestered her constantly with questions about God. With a verbal nod to the years of theology she knew I had by that time studied, she almost apologized as she told me, "I didn't know how to answer your questions very well, but I just did the best I could and told you what seemed the right thing to say." As she said this, I saw again the little boy hooking himself under her arm and leaning tightly against her as she read the Bible to her children. She had theology where it counts: in her heart.

When I was in junior high school and was frequently in some crisis or other with my father, she was always there to listen. One of her favorite strategies was to pursue me around the ranch house, catch me, and not stop tickling me until I'd start laughing. "See how much better you feel when you drop that silly attitude?" she'd ask. Many times she told me I didn't have to help her do dinner dishes, dust the furniture, or make the beds, but while she saw me as being generous, the fact was that I simply enjoyed being with her. When I wanted to take violin lessons, she supported me and furnished me her own "copy of a Stradivarius" that she had played for years. When I needed a new jacket for a prom, and dad hesitated, she convinced him I should have it.

On her deathbed in 1990, two of my three sisters attending her asked her to be more serious because she was dying and should be singing hymns, not Broadway tunes. She laughed in amusement, said she would sing what she wished, and then continued, almost uninterruptedly, to sing her favorite tunes for the last eighteen hours of her life. My sisters and brother each spoke at her funeral, but I felt both unwilling and unable to share what had passed between us. How do you adequately tell people that for a lot of years the person whose body lies there in the casket was the only raft on your rampaging river?

The home we knew, even with this new woman's healing presence, was only seldom, and then precariously, peaceful. I had a tender and dependable relationship with her and for one special year with a memorable hired hand, Alan Lawson, who seemed only too willing to play surrogate father to a frightened little boy. From the time the school bus dropped us off until it picked us up the next morning, however, I had no other close relationships during all of my childhood. Unfortunately, by the time our new mother brought her own young daughter, Alain, to become a permanent part of ranch life, my older sister and I had gone a long way down a wrong path. We were perpetually arguing as we played out our trauma and insecurity.

A thousand anecdotes could illustrate the destructive behavior of our family. There was the time Bernice tried—and could easily have succeeded except that Mother and Dad returned home earlier than expected—to hang her hated "model" brother in the root cellar. There was the time I sliced her hand with a thrown butcher knife. The wild West rode again in our house, and there was no hangin' judge around to temper it.

Grandfather lived on the ranch with us and, after some years of my and Bernice's apparently unexpected survival, is reported to have remarked to a visiting aunt, "Well, Ruth, it looks as if these two children might make it to adult life after all." And my sister and I did prove to be survivors.

After hellish school years, two carefully loved children, and a divorce, Bernice sought an education and has since become a lecturer and published author of both prose and poetry. Her children demonstrate today just how successful a single-parent family can be. Several times during the years I was an active Catholic priest, I riled fellow priests by remarking that a divorce is better than an unhappy marriage and disturbed home; Bernice and other loving single parents were the models I had in mind when saying this.

None of her achievements surprise me, for even in my childhood, when I was certain she was the Devil incarnate, I secretly envied her rebellion and wonderfully original, sometimes destructive, often dangerous survivalist creativity. She was the hellion, I the "sweet child" who—unfortunately for my safety—was forever being held up to her as a model of behavior. I secretly admired her independence even when she was being disciplined for its excesses.

It is no surprise that adults found me easier to live with than they found Bernice. I learned to survive in a way exactly opposite to how she did. Mine was far less effective, one in which, if I was visible to adults at all, it was as a piece of furniture for them to place wherever they chose. I was an inert exhibit that reassured them that everything they believed about and expected of children was exactly correct. I used a prescription all my own, the best I could come up with at the time. It read like this: satisfy everybody; get everyone's approval at whatever cost to yourself; and pretend involvement and ease even when you're hurting, crying, or tired inside.

Yes, I was far easier for others to live with, but inside, where it counts most, Bernice found herself vastly easier to live with. She was at odds with those around her, but I was at odds with myself.

Our gentle and not-so-wounded stepsister Alain spent her first years on the ranch jockeying loyalty between her new sister and her new brother. Bernice and I were so alienated from each other that we never once, as I recall, joined forces against her. We used toys to bribe her to join one of us against the other, but if she was confused, she didn't show it then and doesn't show any signs of it today. Slightly more than two years my junior, she was a sweet note in our home, something of a constant surprise in my life. Once, for example, when I had written and wanted to stage a play, she so willingly let me make her up with Mother's cosmetics and dress her in a succession of outlandish costumes that I wondered if she was perhaps frightened of me. When I stopped to reassure her, she didn't understand what I was talking about and instead remarked on how much fun we were having. It would be years later in the monastery when reminiscing about our ranch life before I finally realized what a jewel she had been as a sister. She is a happy memory from the first day I saw her, age three with long, beautiful ringlets, in the arms of her mother.

Through this mix of love and hate moved our compulsively overworking father. He was forever lost in the labors of saving a ranch during the country's Depression and himself from a still more destructive depression inside. It's not surprising that when I was fourteen and the opportunity presented itself for a corner-drugstore job in nearby Conrad, I jumped at it. Dad reluctantly let me move to town to live, initially with a newly widowed Aunt Myra and my two favorite cousins. I departed with uncamouflaged excitement, oblivious to how deeply this must have hurt my father. He was too unsure in his fathering to forbid me to go, too emotionally constipated to know how to share his hurt with me. I was too young, too self-absorbed to be aware of more than the desire to get away from home. My leaving probably just confirmed for him his sense of failure, much as, far more painfully, my leaving for monastic life would do all over again some years later.

I was a sophomore in high school when I left the ranch. While moving into Conrad did get me away from a distressed home, it left me yet more alone and locked up in a body I despised. In high school photos of the time I'm a not unattractive, clear-eyed, intelligent young man, but I couldn't have managed such a positive assessment of my resources at the time. I was a superior student as far as grades go, but inferior in every other area of my life in my own judgment. I cleverly managed to avoid all sports and physical education classes where obsession with my unacceptable body might have had any chance of being confronted and healed.

Efforts at pretending to be okay and to please, and my growing feelings of self-alienation, became more and more automatic. By my senior year I had gained several distinctions: costar in the junior play, chairman of the junior prom, editor of the school newspaper, recognition as the best dancer in school, winner of a local Heisey Award for student excellence. I was always on the honor roll. These achievements, however, fell on deaf ears within me, for I saw them only as more evidence of my success in pretending. When the junior class chose me to design the theme and decorations for the prom and they were accepted enthusiastically, I nervously made my way through the school hallways lest anyone realize I really didn't have that much talent after all. I accepted praise gladly, but only as evidence of my continuing success at the pretense needed to make it through another day. I saw congratulations as proof of my deception and turned them into reasons for guilt.

A paper I wrote for senior English has survived in a family trunk, and in it I hear myself asking "Isn't there something more?" My unforgettable Vassar-graduate teacher of that class, Ruth Robinson, heard the plea and tried to reach out to me, but I only knew my need and not yet how to open up to anyone about it. Another alert teacher, Frances Kipp, class adviser in my junior year, also tried to reach me through special attention and encouragement, but I saw her as just more than ordinarily friendly, and so missed a second chance. I've often thought of these two women with warmth and gratitude for the help they tried to give me. I wasn't at home with myself when they came calling, so I couldn't respond to their concerned knock.

Of the relatives and adult acquaintances who often congratulated me for my grades, not one knew of the pain I felt back in my room. None knew how long my nights lasted. Even the good feelings that buddies in school reported they found in "beating off" were denied me. Masturbation started out as a new kind of delight in my life, but it was soon overlaid with guilt and fear by my father's counsel, backed up by a little book he gave me that warned of blindness and impotence. Within weeks my new pleasure turned on me and became a source of still-deeper self-rejection.

The first girl I ever chanced going all the way with in the back seat of a cousin's car asked me afterward, "What was wrong?" I had been so convinced beforehand that I would fail her that I effectively made sure I did. Her words cut me as deeply as any ever had. I had no idea how to answer her question, or how to quit repeating it over and over in my head for months afterward.

Datus was the messenger of light who finally broke through my hardening shell of frantically driven pretense to give me a first-ever feeling that I was okay.

5

First Lessons

Datus sat waiting for his answer. He'd asked me to tell him something about myself, and I couldn't think of anything to say. At least not anything I wanted to say. I didn't like to repeat most things I felt about myself even in my own thoughts, much less to anyone else. Anything good I could tell him about myself would be untruthful, and I already vaguely sensed this new friendship had to be honest all the way.

I sat in silence, my eyes nervously bouncing between him and the objects in the room. His question had come slowly, and it disarmed any fear. My confusion at that moment was of a safe sort. The gentleness and sincerity of his interest were palpable—no patronizing, no pushing. But I continued in silence simply because I didn't know what to say.

Never in my life had parent, sibling, uncle, aunt, teacher, or firehouse lover spoken to me the way Datus just had. No one had ever openly and explicitly expressed so much interest. Or, if they had, I hadn't heard them. No one had ever reached out to me the way Datus had. My father's love was undoubtedly genuine and certainly faithful. But it was snowed under by the habits of home. My stepmother was warm and loving and had drawn closer to me than any other person, but even she had never talked with me as Datus was now doing.

It was clear Datus could outwait me, and that he was not going to settle for silence as an answer. I remember embarrassment as I finally stumbled out a beginning, "Well . . . what do you want to know about me?"

He broke out laughing, and then, as if that wasn't disconcerting enough, compounded my confusion by putting his arm around my shoulders and giving me a hug. He left his arm there and continued waiting in silence. He was comfortable; I was not. He obviously came from a family that touched; I obviously did not. Sometimes as a younger child in bed I would imagine one of my hands was that of someone else, and would let it explore my face and arms and the rest of my body, trying to feel what it would be like to be touched so gently by another.

As a grammar school student and young man, my body not only embarrassed me, but also astonished me. I disliked its whiteness, its red hair, its lack of clearly defined muscles, but I was equally obsessed by its dexterity, its movements, its ability to assume almost any position. I was amazed at the way I had to struggle to play a scale on the piano one week and then two weeks later could do it accurately and with ease. I sometimes lost my place in a music score through being distracted as I watched my fingers move over violin strings or working the valves of the baritone I played in high school. When a fellow student in the fifth grade detailed for me how to masturbate as he had learned the night before from his older brother, I found a new reason to wonder at the functioning of my body. I was surprised and remember feeling disappointed whenever we spoke of masturbation during recesses—as we often did with a strange mixture of sniggers and pride—that none of my classmates seemed to share my curiosity about how the body managed the whole ejaculatory process.

I've never understood either my dislike of my body or my great fascination with its functioning. A psychologist once suggested that perhaps I was sexually abused as a child. No, I was not. A gay friend said all gays are similarly obsessed by their bodies, and that, by the way, therefore, I was gay. No, they are not and I am not. A psychic volunteered that I brought my body hatred into this lifetime from a previous one. I have no data with which to judge her statement, and for that reason find in it no satisfactory clarification. All I really know is that when I met Datus, for whatever reason, I had always disliked the form my body took and every bit as much had appreciated its suppleness.

For an instant, Datus's laugh made me wonder if he was, after all, having fun at my expense. By survival instinct—or flaming neuroticism—I searched his eyes a final time for any sign of deception or mocking. There was neither. I tried to begin again, but once more floundered in the unfamiliarity of it, honestly not knowing how to play the part now expected of me.

Eventually he stepped in to get me off the hook. "I've got a feeling you don't have much good to say about yourself, George. You could share that for starters."

Damn! He'd pegged me. Or was it much more likely that I was glad we were starting out with him knowing the bottom line?

In that instant a conscious choice became clear, one that can still make me shudder when I think of what incarnations of consequences may have hung in the balance. It was the first of similar crossroads I would recognize later in life, moments when I would be consciously aware that I had the choice of facing up to a challenge or of slithering off to the side in fear. Fortunately, on this occasion, as I would characteristically do in later ones, I confronted the challenge and answered honestly.

"You're right, I guess I don't."

Long silence, which Datus respected.

"There's really not much I can like, I guess."

More silence.

Then, defensively: "Well, I get invited to all the parties, and I guess most people like me, but, well . . ." What in hell was I supposed to say?

"But *you* don't," he volunteered.

"Yeah. Exactly."

And now the longest pause of all. He let me take my time. He was running his hand back and forth across my back as if to signal participation in my inner drama. I was searching for words, but for more than words: I was looking for an understanding of the problem I wanted to put into those words.

"Look at me compared to you," I finally blurted out, "and this is the sort of thing I've had to live with all my life. You're one of the best-looking guys, best-built guys I've ever seen. You were probably varsity in every sport you ever went out for. And everybody likes you, everybody in town takes a second look at you, everybody. . . ."

For the first time calling me the name he would use throughout our friendship, he interrupted: "Two mistakes so far, Little Brother. First of all, I did *not* go out for sports in school, simply because I think it's like being on display, and I'd rather get my exercise swimming or biking out in the hills. And, second, a big difference between you and me is that build and looks aren't as important to me as they seem to be to you."

He loosened his hold and shifted his pillows as he swung around so he was facing me. After a long swig of his remaining cocoa, he continued with a thoughtfulness that was as easy as it was intense. No compulsive talk in this guy.

"I've got older twin brothers, always our school's top stars in sports. Good-looking guys with great builds, popular with all the girls and all that. I've spent most of my life watching them lifting weights and preening in front of the mirror in our bedroom. I've heard them brag to each other about their conquests in the back seats of cars and listened to them argue about who looked best when they got dressed up. I've seen them come home bragging about fights at school dances. They're good guys at heart, but I've never been impressed by most of what I see in them, most of what they stand for. And the older I get, the less I'm impressed. They're both married now, but still spend a lot of time with old school buddies guzzling beer at the same pool-hall hangout they almost lived in during high school. That's not how I want to live.

"I began to realize I wanted to be different when I was in junior high and they were in high school. That's when I started wanting to find a friend who'd see their game as I do. But I never found one"—he tilted his head and gave me one of his twinkles—"maybe until tonight."

Again his hand came out, this time to rest on my shoulder close to my neck. "What I want for myself in a friend isn't some impressive jock. I've had enough of that. I want somebody who's interested in more than football and beer and ready girls. I want to be around people with sensitivity and gentleness—around *humanness.* Horses have great muscles. A lot of animals are beautiful. I want more. I want to be *human!*"

It all came easily and naturally, and I didn't believe a bit of it. He was just trying to make me feel good. A prince sitting down at the table of a pauper. Nobody could really think great builds and good looks aren't important. He couldn't really mean any of this.

It was only a couple weeks later that I finally no longer doubted that Datus actually did mean every word he told me that first night. Only then did it hit me that his attitude about physical build and beauty could lead to a total reversal of thoughts I'd taken for granted all my life.

If after all these years the words I've used to reconstruct what he told me that first evening are not historically precise—and I make no claim that they are—his ideas and attitudes became so familiar to me in the months that followed that I know what I've written is substantially what he said. One thing I do remember, distinctly, is that I first heard these ideas that night, and I remember remarking to myself at the time that what I was hearing was exactly opposite to what I'd believed and felt all my life.

"Ever since high school," he continued, "I've wanted to have some guy as a friend who I could share my books and thoughts with, somebody who would look for more in friendship than beer busts and getting it off in a car or haystack. I've made out with girls, yeah, and that's great, but I have this thing in me that wants more. Do you know what I mean?"

I didn't answer. I didn't know how, and it was a rhetorical question anyway. He left no opening for an answer even had I had one.

"You don't seem to realize what you've got going for you, Little Brother. You were really paying attention to Mrs. Maclean in the restaurant tonight, and that's what first got my attention. It made me begin to see you for who you are. I know you can't care that much about her husband's truck problems, but she was all worked up about them, and you listened, really listened, because you didn't want to hurt her feelings. That's sensitivity. That's kindness. I like those qualities in a guy much more than muscles and looks.

"Then in the movie. You tried to hide it, but I saw you tear up several times. So did I. It felt good being with you. We both got sentimental and showed it. You don't have to hide your tears when you're with me, you know. In fact, I'd feel better if you make a point not to. I don't try to hide my tears any more. They're more important to me than the body I've been hearing about all my life."

I was trying to follow, to *believe,* what he was saying as I sat watching him in silence. I remember he suddenly seemed surprised at something: "I just realized this minute for the first time that no one has ever congratulated me on my tears. They should have! They're a lot more important part of me, of who I am, than my body. I don't think my brothers even have any tears. I don't ever want to be like that."

He went on to say something he would repeat several times during our future weeks together. "Who could have guessed that I'd have to come to the little town of Conrad to find the friend I've always wanted. Don't ruin it all by being too impressed with my body—don't get stopped there as most people seem to do. There's more to me—just like there's more to you—than body. Let's not be friends for how we look."

Datus had certainly gotten through to my heart, but he was reaching my mind with difficulty. I couldn't comprehend what he was saying, but the hope that it might be true had my complete attention. Even the possibility that he might be right was loaded with emotion for me. I felt tears begin to form in my eyes and, despite my best efforts, one made its way down my cheek as I tried to act as if it wasn't there. Datus reached out and with the gentleness of a lover rubbed it away with the back of his hand. He sensed my embarrassment, but was determined, as he told me later, to break through all the games.

He had saved his biggest salvo for my weakest moment: "I like what I see in you."

That did it. Where there had been one tear, there was now a face full of them. I remained silent, looking at the floor, not now so much in embarrassment for my tears as weighed down by unaccustomed intimacy.

He let me be with myself for a moment and then slid closer as he said, "Come here." He pulled me to him in the first real hug I'd known since my father drew back after my mother's death. He held me strongly, long. My father's frequent reminder that men don't cry was still putting up a fight within me—but its battle this night was forfeited from the beginning.

The hug lasted long enough for my surprise and uneasiness to give way to honest pleasure. I began to relax and then to return his embrace. It was an important moment, and I remember it precisely. It was as if I had just become aware that I had emerged from a gauntlet where I'd had to guard my every side and watch my every step, and was now suddenly secure and being embraced, not beaten, from all sides.

It's fair to say that I learned to hug that winter evening in Montana. But something even more significant happened as well. Doubts and confusion remained, but in those moments of unaccustomed intimacy, I took my first step on the path to self-recognition. I have remembered that evening so warmly through the years because I have always known that it was *the* major turning point of my life. It didn't immediately or permanently solve all of my problems, but I could never again doubt, as I had, that solutions and love were to be had out there somewhere. This realization is, perhaps, the greatest gift in anybody's life.

When we relaxed back onto our pillows, still facing each other, I could speak at last. I was flushed, I knew, and my face was wet with tears, but I no longer cared. "You're quite a guy, Datus. That was a first."

I remember his smile as he quietly answered. "I've hugged and been hugged lots, but ... well ... we're going to be special friends."

I shook my head, not in denial, but in dismay. I'd never known anything like this. "Datus," I said, "I've never really had a friend—lots of 'friends,' but no real friend. Never anybody close to me. Maybe I've never even imagined this kind of closeness—especially with a guy. Maybe I still wonder how someone like you can feel as you say you do about someone like me and if—"

Datus reached up as if to put his hand on my face and thumb across my lips once again, but his hand stopped in mid-air, this time almost as a gesture of impatience. "You're still judging us both by appearances, Little Brother. Trust me. I don't see us as you do. Don't let girls or coaches or the movies tell you what makes you okay."

Despite lingering confusion, I felt good—incredibly good. "That makes sense" was the closest imitation of an intelligent response I could manage.

Did I wonder if Datus was coming on to me sexually as he ran his hand across my back, touched my face, and several times hugged me? I would learn later that he was not homosexual, but on that first evening I didn't yet know this. I didn't know it about myself either. What I must conclude is that if I had thought then that he was trying to seduce me, I am sure I would remember it. This is not necessarily to say that I would have been frightened off—although I think I would have. It is simply to say that such a play on his part would have been so remarkable an experience in my life that I would at least have recalled it as vividly as I remember what did transpire between us: the beginning of a loving friendship.

Our conversation became practical and specific as I began to question what I could do to change my thoughts about myself. "It's easy for us to talk about what we think and don't think about ourselves," he said, "but changing how we *feel* is what counts. I've had to work hard on that. Until I was in high school, the only reason I was ever given for feeling good was that I was a good-looking kid. I had to work hard to realize there was more about me than looks. My dad was so hung up on how good looking and strong my two brothers were that the only thing he seemed to want for me was to look and act like them. He and my brothers will probably never know how much they helped me get over any hang-up on my body I might have had but for them. But it still took a lot of effort to find my own reasons to feel okay. I always knew I didn't want to be like my brothers, but I had to work to figure out what it was I did want to be like—and what would make me feel good about myself."

I started to protest something or other about his one-time self-doubt, then stopped.

"But it can be done," he went on with his own line of thought. "What we need are feelings that match what we think. If you've felt bad about yourself, you were just matching the thoughts you had about yourself. Now you need to go after new feelings—good feelings this time—and that means changed thoughts about yourself."

"How do I do that?"

"Well, that's what those books are about," he said, nodding sideways to his apple-box library, "getting a new experience of oneself by getting rid of put-down ideas and developing new ones.

"I got into all this through a friend of my mother." I would learn that Datus never looked more gentle, more loving than when he talked about the woman to whom he was about to introduce me. "When I was in the seventh grade I'd go over and she'd read to me from her books. She used to say that she was lonely and I looked lonely, so we made a good couple. She always had cookies or muffins, and we'd have long talks while we ate. I felt proud that she let me drink tea at her house. She had no one else to talk to, and I liked to listen to her. She'd tell me stories about holy people and authors she'd read, and she'd read spiritual books to me. By the time I was halfway through high school I must have had half of her books in my room. I spent lots of time with her, three or four times a week, and even more time reading and thinking. That's how I got started meditating.

"You can borrow any books you want, or we can go through them together, just like Mrs. Greytak and I used to do."

I started to tell him I'd like that, but he was on a roll.

"I promise you, Little Brother," he said, his hand on my shoulder again, and with that name, "it'll make a difference. You'll see as I do that you're more than a body and with a lot more going for you than if you'd been some sort of knockout jock."

Eventually, our conversation lightened up. I told him about the ranch and my family, and he told me about his home and family. In the wee hours of the morning we had what must have been our fourth cup of cocoa. Datus turned out to be actually very funny, and I found myself laughing a lot with him. It was new and felt unbelievably good when I found myself laughing without being— or feeling—either contrived or compulsive. With him I was more honest than I'd ever been in my life. I *felt* honest and unpretending around him.

I remember asking Datus about the name he called me, Little Brother. I wasn't sure I liked it. It was warm and friendly, almost intimate, but it could also sound patronizing, condescending. His answer was quick: "Because I've never had a kid brother, and tonight I think I've found one." He made no apology, said no more, and never once asked if I cared if he continued to call me that. That was typical of him. I never winced at the name again, and he used it regularly for as long as our time together lasted.

When I left his place to walk home to the fire station, I knew I, too, had found a brother and friend. He exceeded what I'd ever thought possible or, certainly, likely.

Today I'm certain that our friendship, like his with Mrs. Greytak, had been born in eternity and fostered by previous lives in whatever dimensions. Ours was a friendship, a love, that would last forever because it undoubtedly had already done so.

If my understanding of all this was still off in the future, appropriate feelings for such a realization were suddenly in place. My young life had begun to turn away from pain.

6

Setting the Pace

It was two or three A.M. when I finally left Datus's cabin. Hope walked beside me and kept promising wonderful things as I made my way home through the snow-crunching streets of early-morning Conrad. For the first time I noticed that the snowflakes in my boring little hometown were jewels riding their sleds out of the sky and playing in the light of the street lamps as they fell. The street was a white-water river of light. Frost-covered trees were upside-down crystal chandeliers. I fairly danced as I walked, more awake than I'd ever been in my life. My steps returning from his cabin were as different from those going as the blooms of spring are different from the autumn of a failed harvest.

I had found a friend. I'd risked telling him everything, and he had not drawn back. He'd even said he liked what he saw. The mystery of his sudden appearance in my life astounds me today as much as it did then. Masters appear right on schedule. The universe has its timely gifts for us. Datus was—simply, overwhelmingly—a gift.

As prearranged, I met him for breakfast about nine the next morning at the Conrad Hotel, the only place with a restaurant open for meals Sunday mornings. The magic was still there when I got to the table where Datus was already seated.

I felt a new fondness for the familiar restaurant as we gave our order to Old Gib, freshly starched, immaculate, and stiff, a waitress of renowned bitchiness who had ruled the place with imperial efficiency for years. She knew me well and shot me a glance of danger as I said good morning with what, fortunately, she must have judged was the barest tolerable degree of warmth. More than once I had been the brunt of the loud sarcasm with which she ruled her kingdom, probably the only place of adequacy and power she'd ever known.

It says something for all three of us that before Datus and I finished breakfast, Gib, in a gesture common in small town restaurants, came over with her cup of coffee to sit with us for a few moments. Angular, regally distant, she seemed to be biting her tongue in every other sentence. I remarked to myself that I'd never noticed this in her before. Did she pick up something special between Datus and me? I've always suspected she did.

From the hotel we made our way back to Datus's cabin, where we spent the day until early supper back at the hotel. He had snacks at hand and, most of all, his books. And we had our new friendship. He turned up the heat and we settled in for some serious living.

This was the first of many days and evenings we spent together. Our alternating crescendos of heady talk and outrageous humor were freewheeling and no more predictable than our runs and hikes on the surrounding Montana prairie, weather permitting or not. We moved as our hearts urged us and with virtually no other constraint. It was the best of times and in no way whatsoever the worst of times. I found myself looking forward to every minute we would spend together, almost reluctant any longer to be with my accustomed high-school friends.

After a few weeks of increasing and unexplained unavailability, the girl I'd been dating for two years, Peggy, asked me what was wrong. As I look back on it today, it was harsh, even cruel, that I felt no need to tell her (or anyone else) about my new friend, but at the time I didn't see it that way and gave no explanation to her at all. What I did see was that my frantic habit of seeking approval and reassurance by compulsively sharing everything with everybody was beginning to lose its grip on me. Somebody, at last, was clearly and singularly approving me; the need to seek reassurance elsewhere no longer seemed necessary.

I soon learned that Datus dated infrequently, and I envied him his freedom. Having a girlfriend was something all my peers in high school did, and I always felt compelled to do likewise. In that matter, at least, I knew I was lucky; I'd had Peggy as a full-time girlfriend since early in my junior year. Straight A's, a wonderful dancer, good looking, she was one of the liveliest and best-liked girls in school. I often wondered and sometimes asked her why she was interested in a person like me, and, faithfully, she always said she didn't understand my question and then changed the subject. Unless she reads this book, she will never know what it was that cooled off and eventually put such a heartless ending to a relationship that she and I, most of our teachers, and our parents expected to end in marriage.

From the beginning of our relationship, Peggy and I managed to party with our friends two or three times a week. After Datus came into the picture, and when his work took him to Valier, Shelby, and other nearby towns, I continued to join them as usual, for I was far too driven to sit in the fire station alone. But when Datus was available, I hardly ever spent time with anyone else.

A question that I have often asked myself about those days is whether there was even the beginning of genuine love in my relationship for Peggy. I was so profoundly self-alienated and self-doubting that I suspect Peggy and my other friends, maybe even Datus, were simply props I used and occasionally hid behind on the stage of my life. I remember feelings of what I took to be great love for Peggy, but they were usually easily set aside when someone who met my needs more effectively came along. I also had what I thought were feelings of love for Datus, although I suspect even he would have fallen by the wayside had a still better support ar-

rived. I realized none of this at the time, of course, and I continued, in effect, stringing Peggy along until later when Catholicism
presented me with an escape, the celibate priesthood. I didn't realize what I was doing to her, but I remember well how all the
small intimacies we shared—including the Evening in Paris per-
fume that she always wore because she knew I liked it so much—
seemed to make it impossible to think of going on without her,
even on the now-curtailed schedule Datus had occasioned. I'm
surprised she was satisfied with that.

Many times I dallied with other girls, but I always thought of
Peggy as above being used, and she never once came to my
firehouse at night. She has remained a bright spot in my memory,
if a painful one.

The days of my senior year stretched into spring, and by the time
the weather was warm enough for us to do our hiking in T-shirts,
Datus's and my friendship was probably as close as friendships can
get.

Mrs. Maclean—blessing us with her mischievous smile as she
forever talked about us to others—soon began calling us her
Bobbsey Twins. She brightened visibly whenever we showed up
together for breakfast or supper, as we usually did, especially when
duties permitted her to take a few minutes to sit with us. We easily took her into our love. She sensed something special between
us, drawing close to share it, and was visibly pleased when we told
her she was our mother away from home.

By spring she was openly announcing she didn't know how she
had managed to carry on her twelve-hour-a-day, six-day-a-week
schedule before her twins came onto the scene. We no longer ordered from the menu; she knew what we each liked and served us
her own selection of our favorites whenever we came in. If a milk
glass was partly empty, she'd refill it until we made her stop. Had
we not been young and active, we would each have weighed two
hundred pounds by the time I graduated from high school and
Datus finished his job in Conrad.

Apart from when Datus went home for four days at Christmas, days I spent with my family out on the ranch, not many days or evenings went by between mid-December 1945 and early June 1946 that we did not see each other. People joked about how inseparable we seemed, and my father questioned me once about Datus. I can't remember how I answered him, but my reply must have been satisfactory because he never questioned me again about our constant togetherness. The fact that we both ate all our meals at Mrs. Maclean's and studied together seemed to be explanation enough for everybody, including Dad.

Had my father known the kinds of ideas we were studying, he would have condemned them as loudly as he did the fact that I was studying extracurricular German with Ruth Robinson. His exact words: "Why in hell do you want to learn that goddamned Nazi lingo?" Miss Robinson was the most inspiring teacher I had yet had, and she made a huge impact on my senior year. After Vassar College, she had done graduate work at Heidelberg University in Germany, and her fluent German added greatly to the mystique of her astonishingly big world. She became a major chink in the small-town wall surrounding me. When I expressed an interest in learning German, she said she would be glad to tutor me. Somehow, being with this cosmopolitan woman and learning the language being spoken in the Nazi Germany of the time seemed to move me out of Conrad and into a world that had until then been real for me only in the movies. Datus thought my weekly German lesson was a great idea. He had studied German in college and helped me read through a small beginner's book Miss Robinson gave me at Christmas, something about *Eric und Berlin*.

Whether I spent time at Datus's cabin or he at my firehouse, everyone was exactly accurate in concluding we were together for the sake of studies. We *were* studying—albeit spirituality, Mme. Blavatsky, Mrs. Eddy, oriental religion, and the launching of my selfhood.

The fact that a universally liked, bright young man from out of town was helping a bright student from the local high school with college preparation only added to the general approval we met on all sides. Mrs. Maclean used to ask us, "Aren't you two ever going to stop studying?" We hoped not.

Adeodatus Nikos's quiet ways and winning smile held almost everyone we met spellbound. My own scholastic achievements often seemed to have the same effect, although I do remember feeling hurt several times when others would patronize me about my grades and then, with a totally altered affect, fairly grovel to the handsome young man beside me. Older people rarely made that distinction in greeting us, and this was not lost on me. In fact, a few times the tables were turned and some of them were almost cool to Datus as they congratulated me on seeing my name on the honor roll, which the local weekly newspaper always published. That shift wasn't lost on me either, and I was irritated by their coolness to my friend. I'd become equally defensive for both of us.

The bottom line and genuinely warmhearted response in the small community in which we lived seemed to be that if this wonderful college graduate from out of town was willing to spend so much time with this wonderful student getting him wonderfully prepared for some wonderful college he would go to, then wasn't everything wonderful!

All this time much more was happening to me than learning new ideas. Datus's words that first evening in December, about me being more than my body—words he had to explain again and again in the succeeding weeks—became the chief lesson of my senior year. Slowly, but undeniably, his message moved into my deeper awareness. I began to stand taller. My talk grew dramatically more considered, less compulsive. Miss Kipp noticed this at school and asked me what was going on. For a brief instant I considered telling her about my friend, but, perhaps unfairly to her, I chose not to. She, like everyone else, probably chalked up the changes in me simply to growing up, implying perhaps that I had been late getting started. I would not have denied the implication.

My partying friends noticed the change in me in our last months of high school, and particularly during the brief time we were together once school was out, after Datus had left and before we all went our separate ways into life. During these weeks I was, indeed, more than ordinarily quiet. Several remarked on this, but the explanation for the change had to pass for something other than what it was, for I never told any of them about the real nature of Datus's and my friendship.

Why the separateness? Why the secrecy about Datus? In small part, I suppose, though I don't recall this was a big concern, lest our relationship be thought of as "queer." Much more, I think, because I feared he might get pulled into the party scene and my new well would run dry. He was showing no interest whatsoever in an expanded and rowdy social life, but I was taking no chances. My distrust of his stated disinterest in partying probably came from my own great dedication to it, vested in it as I was for whatever bit of a sense of social adequacy I might gain from it.

The misery I'd felt in the first three years of high school was almost totally gone by graduation in May. My sense of well-being had become conscious and began showing up in my daily habits within a few weeks after meeting Datus. I would rise each morning, wrap myself in a blanket, and try to meditate (what I actually did, I realize today, was "try to concentrate"). Then I'd shower, shave, and dress, all with a realization of being a bit more valid, more authentic, more real as a person. I remember smiling one day when I caught myself whistling as I locked the fire station before walking next door to Mrs. Maclean's place where Datus usually met me for breakfast. *Me,* spontaneously whistling? It was one of those heady moments we are rarely given when we can glance back down a ladder and see how many rungs we've climbed.

It was not the love I felt for and from Datus that birthed these new feelings in me. What made the difference was what that love had uncovered in me: a sense of being me, a feeling of a "self." Anyone who's never lacked this basic sense of being valid and real can never understand what it feels like to know it for the first time.

I found myself rolling up my shirt sleeves at school when the warm days of spring arrived. A small indicator, perhaps, but a dramatic change for a guy who was always so ashamed of his white arms that he had never owned a short-sleeved shirt.

There was a large mirror in my bathroom, and I began watching as I stepped out of the shower and dried my body. A few times late at night I watched as I masturbated, and I particularly remember the first time the experience left me feeling good and not guilty. I had experienced at last the upbeat feelings that "jerking off" had apparently been giving my high-school buddies since grammar school.

The next day, to celebrate my high, and for the first time in my life, I played hooky with some other students and we shared a keg of beer on the banks of the Marias River. All of us were later given detention after school as punishment, but I was called to the superintendent's office, where he politely invited me to sit in a chair beside his desk and then confidentially asked, "What in the world is happening to you, George? You've always been such a fine student." Later the same day a favorite teacher told me, with studied pain on his face, that he was "astonished and deeply disappointed at my slippage." Through it all I was polite but completely unrepentant. At last I had begun to hear George's voice somewhere in the huddle.

Slowly it began to dawn on me how unfair my prior assessment of my body had been. I wasn't tanned, didn't have strongly defined muscles, still had red, not black, hair, yes. But—*damn it!*—my shoulders were broader than my hips, my waist substantially smaller than my chest, my limbs and digits all with me, and I had no sores, had never even had adolescent acne. Curious inventory for a seventeen-year old, but it was new and exhilarating as I made it.

During one of our long Sunday walks I shared the excitement of this inventory with Datus. He gave me one of his twinkles and leaned over to whisper, "Right! . . . but not as if you'd not be real if you were missing a leg or two, Little Brother."

Datus had never had to learn to like his body, but he seemed to understand me as I began learning to like mine. I wanted to share the feelings I was at last finding in solitary sex, but I doubt if I ever mentioned them to him. There was a reason for this. I kept telling myself that what I was enjoying most was not the orgasm, but the sense of what today we'd call individuation, the same sense that my friends said they gained from masturbation. I felt that not even Datus might understand this tight—and totally airy—distinction. But it was extremely important to me, for it was my unrecognized final salute to the necessary guilt for genital pleasure that I'd been taught.

But I did tell him about a related experience. It must have been about March, so we'd been together for about three months at the time. One morning as I was urinating and with no previous related thought whatsoever, I was hit with the realization that my penis was attached to my body, that it was a part of me. It's not that I'd ever precisely thought of it as unattached. It was instead something clinging, pasted on, an alien contraption, an instrument of temptation, a tool for future family purposes at best. And now suddenly it was a part of *me,* of *my* body! Datus laughed when I told him and his response was typical: "Well, where did you think it was? In your hip pocket?" Today I could write a paper about that breakthrough, but all I could do then was live it and luxuriate in an experience I understood not at all. And all Datus could do was watch as his friend started to wake up.

This incident has another side to it that was disturbing and confusing to me. I wouldn't understand it for years to come. When I began to experience my penis as part of *me,* for the first time in our relationship I began thinking about *his* penis. I didn't want to touch it, even to see it. I simply obsessed on it for days, maybe even weeks. This terrific friend whom I'd drawn close to and often sat near had all this time been walking around with a penis! I wondered if I was a homosexual after all. I'd reassure myself that I was "still okay" because I had no desire to do more than think about it, but I worried at this new turn of events all the same.

Eventually, the first flush of experiencing my own penis in this way faded, and with it went preoccupation with his. It's clear to me today what happened. Lacking any well-established sense of my own validity, authenticity, realness, I had been mesmerized since childhood by what I identified as symbols of these qualities in others: good looks, clearly defined muscles, black hair, chest hair, athletic prowess. Now, overnight, suddenly, and for exactly the same reason, *penis* came to join this list of powerfully felt symbols of personal validation as a man. When I realized that I, too, had this distinctly male symbol, it's not surprising that I was obsessed by the fact—in joy and relief. Simultaneously, I realized that Datus, too, possessed this symbol. Since he was someone I looked up to, the reality of a penis on him underscored how accurate and meaningful a symbol the same thing was on me. Preoccupation with penises, his and mine, temporarily overwhelmed me.

A similar obsession would return within a couple years, halfway around the world. At that time I would be far more prepared, and far less constrained.

Here, still in my senior year, I kept Datus a secret, but in some ways I wanted to tell everybody what was happening to me as a result of my friendship with him. I wanted to tell them what he was like, what I was beginning to feel I was like as a result of being with him. I resented the silence I felt constrained to maintain. And this much was certain: I wanted to *tell* them, not to ask for their approval. For the time being, at least, I no longer felt a need to ask anyone's approval for what I was learning or the way I was learning it.

Many years later, in the early 1970s, in an encounter group, I finally talked about Datus and our special friendship. For more than twenty-five years he had remained a secret memory probably for no more adequate reason than that I carried him like a sacred fire of magic warmth in my heart. Too sacred to treat lightly, too special to bring out except where appreciation could be presumed, too multifaceted to talk about without the occasion to do so adequately. I had told my future wife, Lori, and no one else about him. At the end of my telling the encounter group about him, one of those present spoke in response, and the sense was that he spoke for everyone present: "I can only envy you for having had even one such friend."

Some of those whom I have told about Datus in subsequent years have said that he sounds too good to be true. I smile each time I hear that because I often told myself the same thing while he and I were together .

Today I am convinced that "too good to be true" seems equally characteristic of every gift the universe has for us.

7

Off the Ceiling

Datus and I were never unaware that our time together was to end in the spring. It was vaguely okay to each of us. We didn't dwell on the painful day to come, but we didn't refuse to talk about it either. We had moist eyes more than once in the last couple of weeks and talked a few times about how fast the clock was ticking. Somehow, though, the future never reached back to cloud the present. Maybe that present was so good and we were so young that we never actually thought much about the future, but I think there was more to it. We had never demanded a clear understanding of all that was happening in our lives and we didn't do so now. Intuition outweighed conscious understanding, and we built our peace on that. A bit of eternal wisdom seemed to be whispering, "All is well and all will always be well. Trust. Move on."

The day of separation did finally come. It was the second week of June 1946. I had graduated from high school a couple of weeks before, and my father had already paid my first quarter's tuition at Cornell College in Iowa, where I was headed in the fall. The college had even provided the name and address of my future roommate who, day after day, I promised my parents I'd write to, but never did. I wondered what kind of friend he'd turn out to be and how he'd compare with Datus. My whole world seemed to be oriented to the fall. And then there would be winter.

Datus was directed to be back at his home office by mid-June. His company told him he would have two weeks at home and would then be sent for six to nine months on state work to another small town somewhere in Big Sky Country.

We stayed together with scarcely any sleep during his last forty-eight hours in Conrad. The evening before he left I helped him load books into his car. This was difficult for me and I was more than ordinarily quiet. No compulsive chatter this time. I was intact to a degree that surprised me. I had expected that kind of emotional stability in him, but I was surprised to find it in me. It would never have occurred to me that I would one day be walking tall through so much pain.

As would happen over and over throughout my life in times of crisis, I felt as if after a certain point of stress an automatic pilot kicked in and habits of fear and weakness were set aside. Many times in life I've cried out over some pain, but I've survived them all with a degree of peace that has probably surprised me more even than others. The first of these survival episodes came as I helped my friend pack to leave. I have come to realize that a mother lode of strength lies waiting in all of us, unmined gold yearning to gleam in the sunlight. Sometimes it takes a crisis to bring it to the surface.

We spent our last hours sitting semilotus on his pillows (the last items to get put in his car) sipping cocoa, by now a sacrament of our intimacy, and wandering in the countryside. My mind, far more distressed than my emotions, kept replaying the givens and demanding answers. Life had been so good, and now it was going to be so bad. How come? What was going on? I found no answers. I remained confused, and yet okay.

We talked about what had changed for us in the past five months. Datus told me several times how much he'd gained from our friendship, and that my enthusiasm for what he felt most enthusiastic about was the greatest gift he'd ever received. He said he knew he'd helped me start meditating and change some ideas that needed changing, but that his own best and deepest experiences in meditation had come while we were seated together on his pillows as we had done for countless hours. Most of all, he said he felt he'd found the friend he'd always wanted.

I was aware that almost none of the physical traits that had so recently spelled adequacy for me seemed now to mean much. I no longer hid my lessened sense of poverty behind a barrage of words. I spoke less, more softly, and—Datus pointed it out first—from deeper in my chest. My voice was changing a second time. I was beginning to be present in my words. I seldom masturbated, and when I did it was, just perhaps, as Datus had described it months before, an act of love for myself. I'd quit being the class clown, and this worried some of my friends—"Are you down?"—but felt good to me.

Datus's books had given me at least a nodding acquaintance with Hindus, Buddhists, Sufis, and Taoists. I suspected then, and know now, that I comprehended very little of what we talked about, but I was honestly interested and completely intrigued. He had a book on Western mystics that struck us both as being too Catholic, and some writings of Emerson that we both particularly loved—although I remember we sometimes laughed at Emerson's stuffiness. We read several books together, and while the spiritual masters I was meeting were not yet my close friends, I would encounter them all more intimately years later, and I could never forget it was Datus who had introduced us.

I didn't know it yet, but during that winter and spring I was forever emancipated from being able, ultimately, to accept Christianity's claim to uniqueness. This insight was about to go into hibernation for a lot of cold winters, but eventually it would emerge from its cave and yawn awake in the springtime of a much broader consciousness. Within sixteen months of Datus's and my separation, I would embark upon a long project that seemed to forfeit any likelihood of ever emerging from that cave. Fortunately, however, I now had an insurance package built into my life: meditation. The floundering meditation I faithfully clung to from this period of my life onward was what, in the end, would bring on my springtime, no matter how deep or long my winters.

In my beginner-level, stumbling meditation with Datus, I already contacted something deeper than the kind of dogged preoccupation with church doctrines that I saw in the churchpersons I knew. There is much more about meditation later in this book, for it has been central in my life, but at this point it's sufficient to say that the reason meditation would be my safe passage is that from the start it gave me an *experience* of my life within, of my essential self that lay beyond appearances. Meditation provides an experience that nothing else whatsoever can do equally.

How did Datus handle our leave-taking? I honestly don't know. On the outside he appeared strong and stable to the last. His eyes were moist as often as my own, but neither of us broke down. Something was happening inside of him that I'd not witnessed before. I've never known if I read more into it in the months that followed, or if I felt at the time that his mood seemed more than just sadness at our impending separation.

The clock means nothing to youth, and dawn was piling up in the east after our last night together when Datus said something he admitted he himself didn't much understand: "I won't miss you, because I plan to stay close to you." We were walking along a small creek that meandered across our part of the Montana prairies a few miles out of town, and I didn't know how to reply. After some minutes he added, "I feel complete. I've shared with you what I've had for you as much as I've had it for me, and you've given me what you had for me. I know what true friendship is now. I have this strange feeling that I'll always be close to you."

Then he added something he'd never said before, something I've recalled countless times over the years: "We have been brothers before."

I asked myself over and over in the next few months if he was sensing the nearness of his death. The words I just put in his mouth are substantially accurate, but although they've stayed with me, I

still don't know their full meaning. I do remember that as I listened
to him in these last hours I realized that I, too, felt a vague assurance that we would remain close and would always be friends in
a special way. His words cut deep, but I felt a peace at odds with
everything I thought I should be feeling. In the months to come,
my feeling of loss often overtook me in bed at night, and I returned again and again to a mysterious state of deepest, saddest
loneliness . . . and soaring, happiest peace.

It was with that sort of ambiguity—hope and eternal loneliness
coupled with a despairing okayness—that I watched him drive
away from his Conrad cabin, *our* Conrad cabin, just before noon
on that June day.

Two days later, before we had an opportunity to exchange even the
first of the frequent letters we'd pledged, a highway patrolman who
knew us came to awaken me at the fire station. With uncharac-
teristic soft-spokenness he told me that on the previous afternoon
a large truck had crossed lanes as it came around a curve on a
canyon road and had gone over much of the top of my friend's
small car. Datus had undoubtedly died instantly.

Within the hour, I was out at the ranch walking with my dog
Mitz across prairies that even in my childhood had seemed a
melancholy landscape. Silent tears flowed nonstop from a waste-
land inside of me that was vastly more barren than anything the
endless expanse of Montana could represent.

Had my grandfather walked these same hills when his first son
died in 1898, and when his wife came to resent him early in their
marriage? Had my father walked here when his young wife died
suddenly in 1933? Had the native Sioux that lived here before us
walked their own sorrows through them? Was this place designed—barren, treeless, endlessly flat—to symbolize and comfort human grieving? Is that why, to model the miracle of healed
memory, it faithfully renews itself in the dew and attending stars
of each overarching night?

I found myself mulling over such thoughts, but more often there was only a wordless, noiseless pain that left my mind numb. And always there were silent, unstoppable tears.

Dad and my stepmother—who, eight months into her marriage to her first husband and already pregnant, had lost him within six hours to a sudden onslaught of meningitis—tried to respect my grief, but they clearly felt it was disproportionate. How could they have felt otherwise? How could they have possibly understood? They knew nothing of what had been going on in my life. Men were only supposed to love women the way I loved Datus, so even had I wanted to, how could I have shared with them the extent of my loss? They didn't express it openly, but they were doubly exasperated when I quit my drugstore job and for almost two weeks chose silence, my dog, and the prairie as my only friends. I don't recall appearing even once for a meal; I stopped by the kitchen, instead, when no one was there.

In the months to come I would wonder if I did, as my parents thought, exaggerate my grieving. Was prolonged grieving what precipitated the years of relapse into self-rejection that came rushing back upon me? Or was that backsliding just a normal pattern in a life process into which Datus was meant to bring nothing more than a vision of, a hope of, a first brief experience of wholeness?

Whatever the answer, when he died I soon discovered that I had not yet learned my lesson well. He had been an oasis in a desert I had only begun to cross. I had far lower depths of self-rejection and self-contempt to plumb before I would finally learn what there was for me to learn, before, that is, I would ever learn to dance.

I didn't know it then, but I had just bounced off the ceiling. And when you do that, the only direction to go is down.

8

The World a First Time

In 1946, the year after World War II ended and the year of my high-school graduation, military service still had for young men of my age most of the glamour it had gained during the war years. It meant foreign places—castles along the Rhine front, palm trees along Pacific island beachheads, great ships dodging subs in the Atlantic, and kamikazes in the Pacific. Most of all, it meant uniforms! My generation of war fodder had romanticized life in uniform so fully that probably only a few of them lost that conviction later along with the rest of the nation in the Vietnam era. During the summer before my senior year, I pleaded with my father to let me lie about my age and enlist as one of my friends had done, but he was immovable. "Graduate first, and then I'll let you go." Whatever dad's problems at emotional control, he never failed his kids when the chips were down and there was time for reasoned consideration. In telling my story I must often paint him as difficult, explosive, emotionally unstable, but, equally, I must never suggest that his heart was wrong or that he didn't have the welfare of his family foremost in his good intentions. My stepmother also listened to my repeated requests to leave school and enlist, and each time shook her head as she looked at me in disbelief. Uniforms and wars never made sense to her.

Despite the stars in my eyes for the navy, I doubt if I would ever have actually enlisted had it not been for an incident that happened when Mitz and I had already been grieving Datus's death too many days out on the prairie. A high-school buddy, Willy Schmidt, left a message with my stepmother that he and two other former classmates were going to have a party and would I come. To my parents' relief, I decided to go.

It was stag, and by the time we made our way home about 3:00 A.M. all four of us were unbelievably drunk. Somewhere during the hours of our stupor we swore to each other that we would do what we'd been talking about for months: enlist. And that we did. As unbelieving parents stood by two days later, we boarded the bus for the nearest recruiting station in Great Falls and signed up, two for the navy, two for the army.

When we brought the papers home for our parents to sign (I was seventeen, my three friends eighteen), they seemed so eager that all four of us were a bit hurt. But I knew they were right. I didn't know about the other three, but I knew I needed to shift gears, and fast. A couple of days later we all climbed aboard a bus once again and headed south on the same highway Datus had taken three weeks before.

I knew I had to leave Conrad because I wasn't doing a good job of handling the loss of my friend. I was tired of talking to my dog, and I sensed that she, too, was getting depressed, or at least bored with the daily prairie routine. Escape was clearly my best move. Two years in the military and as far from Conrad as possible sounded as painless as anything could be. Besides, I wanted to try out my new feeling of okayness on companions who would know nothing about the guy I'd always been. Where better to do this than as a sailor on a ship at sea or in some foreign port?

I also knew I had to get away from alcohol. Getting drunk with friends may seem a strange antic for someone in deep grief, but it was as much a part of my search as was walking the prairies. I had been in exactly this kind of double-barreled search, in fact, all the time Datus and I were together. I was at my best and most sober with him, and then in the same week could be found raising holy hell with classmates. Datus didn't drink alcohol at all, and although I honestly wanted to be like him in that, my own drinking remained out of control.

The only consistency in my youthful life, so filled with contradictions, was my frantic search for okayness, and this search was ongoing whether I was abusing alcohol or trying to meditate.

There was another reason it made sense to enlist. Although my father had never complained, I knew the costs of a private college would be a major strain on family funds. I had dodged the thought all through my senior year, but as more and more of my friends couldn't understand why I wasn't going to the University of Montana with them, where costs would be a fraction of those in Iowa, I started to pay attention. When a classmate, Herb Robinson, told me that if we put two years in the military the GI Bill would pay for our first four years of college, I found out he was right.

When I finally arrived at the naval training station in San Diego, the navy turned out to be more of a challenge than I'd bargained for. It's still not clear where the wildly arbitrary, often blatantly unjust, frequently whimsical, and always absolute power wielded by enlisted company commanders in those days came from. Was it deliberate navy policy to train recruits in as short a time as possible in the fine skill of instant obedience, or was it the result of a neurotic exhilaration in chief petty officers permitted for a brief day in their careers to be addressed as "sir"? I was now strong enough to take it all in stride, but I remember shuddering many times when I considered how things might have been for me in San Diego had I never had my time with Datus.

Sitting alone outside the barracks in what little bit of evening they sometimes allowed us, I was more than once told by fellow recruits that I looked sad, and I no longer cared that sometimes there were tears in my eyes. From a quiet explanation to a fellow recruit one evening, word got around that I had just lost a brother—how right that was—and my preference for being alone was respected. I took part in all the prescribed activities and sports, but most of my free time was spent alone. A picture of me has survived—bleary-eyed with alcohol once again—seated with three other recruits in a San Diego bar, the single occasion of escape I found during my eight weeks of boot camp.

At least in the early weeks, I didn't panic or become really depressed. Countless times every day I thought of Datus. For those first few weeks I was too busy flexing my new mental muscles, in an almost masochistic manner enjoying whatever the navy dished out to me.

Recruit training in those days seemed aimed at reducing newcomers to confused, self-denying, panicked automatons. I didn't panic as some did. For a time I was untouchable in my feeling of equality with my companions. I saw the harangues of our admirals-for-a-day as a personal challenge to see how well I could exercise and *enjoy* my new equilibrium and self-awareness. I remember laughing once when the thought came of seeing my blustering, five-foot-seven-inch chief-petty-officer company commander, an indelibly imprinted Chief Sterling, as the lordly Ruler of the Queen's Naivee in *HMS Pinafore*. Sterling was humorous and likable, but a complete caricature of strength—a stereotypical small-pond carp fueled by bravado and bluster as he moved back and forth through his school of minnows.

My too-studied cool clearly needled him in a way he found intolerable. I took perverted joy in being precisely exact about every one of his petty rules and slipped only once to give him his longed for and elaborately enjoyed "gotcha!"

The weeks marched past more slowly than any in my life. I learned what I had to learn, and tried much too hard to keep myself intact. Sometimes when things got tight, as they often did, I remembered Datus's promise to be with me always. I tried to imagine how he would handle this or that incident as each came along. More than one interminable parade was walked with him beside me, and I was standing straight all the time. There was a new firmness in my body and, for a while, a suppleness in my mind and spirit.

My togetherness was as brittle as it was deliberate, though, and if truth be known, I stood *too* straight in those parades. Inevitably, the act began to give way. Whatever victories I achieved over Chief Sterling were won by compulsive control, not strength. I knew it, and maybe what needled him about me was that he knew it, too.

I kept repeating Datus's words, kept telling myself I was valid, but his modeling and the sound of his voice had faded. His words no longer carried any power, his influence was leaving me. My new freedom slowly succumbed to a boot-camp training running roughshod over me and my fellow recruits, a training upon which the navy itself realized some years later it had to impose substantial restraints.

By the end of eight weeks in San Diego, my recently acquired self-image had almost completely crashed. I caught the long train home to Montana not sure what was ahead either there or when I returned after a ten-day leave for transfer to a submarine base in the Philippine Islands.

My short stay in Conrad passed with a merciful quickness. Leave was a dream, a bad dream. Dad's outspoken pride in a son who, by joining the submarine service, was at last doing something he could understand, was extravagant and foolish. An officer at the recruiting station in Great Falls had written to tell my parents that their son had achieved the highest score on entrance tests of any recruit who had ever gone through their office, and Dad was determined that all his friends should hear about this as he took me everywhere to show me off in my uniform. His hang-up on uniforms turned out to be even greater than mine. At his insistence I accompanied him once again to Johnny Stone's Tavern, but when we finally left I swore to myself I'd never go there again. The fact that I could now have a beer and stand leaning against the same bar I used to sit on as a small boy, my foot reaching down to the brass rail at last, made no difference whatsoever. Dad embarrassed me far worse than long ago I had embarrassed him over a dime for a pop in the same tavern.

I did my duty, smiled, visited relatives and friends (mostly Dad's), and again walked the prairies with Mitz, who shadowed me every minute I was at the ranch almost as if she feared I might disappear on her once again. I tried, but it was difficult to camouflage my eagerness as I finally boarded the train and headed back to San Diego. Maybe being out in the fleet would help me recover what I had lost in the charade of boot camp.

The rest of my two years as a sailor can be summed up by saying I was a military tourist. My generation of servicemen was meant solely to fill billets so those who had done the fighting could go home. The war in the ocean I was crossing had been over for only a year. Everywhere we went there were signs of battle. Manila was totally destroyed, its harbor a forest of protruding masts, and some of the jungles of Luzon were full of Japan's rusting tanks lost as MacArthur retook the islands. Pearl Harbor had not yet been emptied of all the leftover tragedies of a Sunday morning nearly five years old. The USS *General Butner* carried five thousand of us past the hastily gathered fleet of surplus ships that had recently been subjected to an atomic blast at Eniwetok. We were a bunch of wide-eyed kids sent to help dismantle a huge war machine. We took ourselves very seriously, even when the old salts around us did not.

I spent my two years as a yeoman and standing an occasional sonar watch. I saw a good bit of the west Pacific, stopped at a number of islands in the mid- and South Pacific, and spent about ten months each in the Philippines and Hawaii. The best my recruit buddies and I would ever know, even though we were now bona fide sailors, was a glory reflected from sailors who had mostly now returned home from the war just over. Adventure we still had, though, and we loved it. If a young person of seventeen has never slept out under the South Pacific stars aboard a troop ship plowing its way through what until recently had been "enemy waters," he or she will never know what we felt as we lay sensing the throb of the great ship beneath us, almost refusing to waste time sleeping. We swapped purloined war stories into the early hours of every tropical dawn of the thirty days of island hopping it took us to reach Manila.

On the outside, my life seemed exciting and valid at last.

Inside, though, my stint in the navy did not feel nearly so romantic. It was not new to me that balance and okayness on the outside could coexist with the daily agonies of inner self-belittlement and doubt. I had become an expert at that duplicity through most of my previous life. By the time I was ensconced on the submarine base at Subic Bay, six weeks after I returned from leave, my sense of self and authenticity were back where they'd been before I met Datus. All that remained for me now of our honeymoon together was a memory—a fading one—of how much better things could be. I desperately tried to rise again, but I was not clear what to grab for. I carried on as though nothing were wrong, but a glance inside showed that just about everything was wrong there . . . again.

My old embarrassment about my body returned with a vengeance as I saw awesome, tanned physiques, usually naked, parade through our steaming tropical barracks or swim alongside my whiteness in our jungle swimming pool. There were, of course, other slightly built and pale-fleshed sailors. But I secretly despised them even more than myself when I saw what I took to be their pretense as they interacted self-confidently and easily with everyone around them, apparently indifferent to the discrepancy between their bodies and those of the "real men" around them.

Meanwhile, my job as the commanding officer's yeoman at the sub base was going well, singularly well. I was hardworking, and the skipper, Captain George Browne, who would later retire as an admiral, openly showed his appreciation. I successively competed for two promotions and easily got them. His second in command, the executive officer, often came into my office to sit on the edge of my desk and talk about Montana, the sea, and—always—native girls. His wife had accompanied him to the Philippines, and he seemed to be immensely curious about the escapades of a young man like me, *sans* wife, amid the abundant supply of unmarried women in the local villages. He never did, I think, believe me when I told him I was not visiting the female population. Whether our conversation started with navy business, Montana, native foods, or the latest typhoon, he always brought it back to what he was certain must be my latest exploit with native girls. I had for a time lived vicariously through Datus, and now this jovial man, who seemed to see himself as caged, was trying to live through me. I overheard him describing me one day to a visiting submarine skipper as "our bright young yeoman from Montana."

When Captain Frederick Russell replaced Captain Browne as the sub base skipper, the new CO retained me as his yeoman, and we developed a friendly relationship. This astonished me as much as had my successful association with the departing captain, whom most of the base personnel seemed to fear. The new CO and his wife occasionally invited me to share a meal with them, and he sometimes asked me to drive her across Subic Bay on shopping trips to the nearby and much larger naval operating base. Once he invited me to accompany him on a trip to Manila. Buddies in the barracks would ask me what sort of intimacies I was providing either the CO or his pretty wife for all these attentions, but it was said in good humor.

The friendships I was experiencing with both the officers at work and enlisted men in the barracks could have provided an ideal situation in which to relax and recover the selfhood I'd so recently lost, but I didn't let it. Sundays, in particular, during what we called our bullshit sessions, the time between late-morning chow and early supper when everyone in the barracks shared letters and goodies from home, were custom-made for a young man in need of healing. I seemed to be respected by everyone but myself. There was never a single occasion when I felt I was not as accepted as any other man present. It was not they who were giving me a bad time, but myself.

Why had I taken this nosedive so quickly after my experience of wholeness with Datus? Evidently, my budding self-affirmation was not ready to be weaned as suddenly as it had been from the kind of daily, personal support and modeling Datus provided me. When he disappeared, his nourishment disappeared with him, and my self-realization was too newborn to live.

It's easier now for me to understand that his role in my life was not to provide a quick and too-easy fix. It was only a point of reference to which I could look back and forever know that wholeness is possible no matter what growth is still required to achieve it. Had it come easily, I might have stopped halfway.

My time in the navy was not completely without lasting significance. Two events in the Philippines would influence the rest of my life.

One was a venture into a homosexual relationship, my first. It made me realize for the first time that had Datus been so disposed, his and my relationship could have, almost certainly would have, become overtly sexual. But he was not and it was not. With Mike in the Philippines all that changed.

Mike worked at the base dispensary. I remember the evening we met when, apparently by chance, but actually deliberately, as he later confided, he seated himself across the table from me in the mess hall. It was only a few weeks after I'd arrived. Instantly, as it had been with Datus, despising virtually everything about my own body, I liked virtually everything about his. Perfect teeth, dimpled smile, dark eyes that seemed lit from inside, he was a young, tightly muscled five-foot-ten-inch gypsy of a man of black-Irish blood. He was also bright, outgoing, verbal, easy to talk to, warmly friendly. As I got to know him, I found out something still more important to me: he was one of the few sailors on the base who was not obsessed with native women or the imported Australian Bulimba beer that, at five cents a can, flowed in great abundance seven evenings a week, and that I had quickly learned to love and abuse. I was still free enough to long to feel okay without compulsive recourse to either sex or alcohol, and I still liked reading as much as I had in high school. Mike, with apparently identical priorities, struck me as an ideal friend.

Because we were isolated on three sides by a jungle filled with snakes and wild boars and on the fourth by a bay full of sharks and barracudas, the navy provided us not only all the beer we wanted, but also a different first-run movie every night of the week. Mike and I started out going to the movies together, and went a few times to the "beer Quonset" for some Bulimbas, but we were soon more usually going directly from evening chow to the base library.

We were the only two sailors of about two hundred who regularly used this remarkably large facility left over from when, as a major submarine resupply base, there were more than ten times that many submariners stationed there during the last year of the war. We found ourselves alone amid the books almost every evening.

Right from the beginning, we did far more talking than reading. But the talk was wide-ranging and general, never the analytical stuff about the how and why of self-acceptance, as Datus and I had done. Mike showed a lightness of spirit that proved he had no need to talk about self-acceptance. Nor, unlike Datus, did he seem interested in helping me on the topic.

He loved to read Shakespeare out loud, and while I had not had the least interest in the few plays we studied in high school, my love for his plays and, especially, his sonnets blossomed in the Philippines. Sometimes we selected roles and read plays together, as often as not hamming the meaning beyond recognition. We talked and laughed and dodged the huge spiders that inhabited all the stacks and would sometimes drop onto us from the rafters as if to check out which of their books we were presuming to tamper with.

During my days in the CO's office, I found myself distracted by thoughts of the coming evening. Inevitably I began to expect from

Mike what I had received from Datus. Maybe he would provide the chance for me to recover and stabilize what Datus had helped me find and launch.

After a couple of weeks, I got more than I was looking for. It began to be clear that Mike didn't envision our developing friendship as something Platonic or just a matter of shared bookishness. I was not at all reluctant—I was openly pleased, in fact—when he started standing close with his arm on my shoulder. It reminded me still more of being with Datus. But it did come as a complete surprise when he came up behind me one evening and, after massaging my shoulders for a moment, let his arms reach around me to rest low on my waist and then slip down to my groin. I extracted myself like a horrified nun, but almost immediately wondered if I should have—and just as quickly was sorry that I had.

The ease with which I followed Mike's lead from that point on says a lot more than the fact that I was so lonely. But it's too easy to conclude that it says I was a homosexual waiting to happen. As later life would show, about the only thing it indicated was an openness to possibilities, a little daring, a general willingness to experiment.

I would spend years after this relationship, however, worrying if it had, in fact, given indication that I was a homosexual. The possibility was full of fears and imagined horrors as long as I was a Catholic, but even after I started doing my own thinking and had met countless gay men and lesbian women and was no longer loading their lifestyle with negative judgments, I still had to question why I had followed Mike's lead so readily.

It was, in fact, without a trace of hesitation—after the first knee-jerk reaction—and with mounting enthusiasm that in the days after Mike's first move I followed him into quickly evolving physical expressions of our friendship. I was not yet sure just what I needed or wanted or what I was expecting out of life—or from this relationship in particular. At the very least, it was easy to fantasize that this "experiment" held the possibility of getting me off the dime of stagnation in self-rejection.

Mike was a prince. He knew what he wanted and went strongly—and gently—about getting it. He had only finished one year of college when, as with my Conrad friends and me, the lure of the GI Bill had drawn him into the military. He was mature enough, enough his own man, that he knew how to ensure that this two-year hiatus in his education would not be an interruption in the rest of his living as well.

But if I was quickly daring, I was almost as quickly disappointed. While I was fascinated with his body and excited by the chance to be close to it, to explore it at whim, his biceps interested me more than his genitals. The hair on his chest was more mesmerizing than the hair in his groin. The hardness of his deltoids more impressive than that of his penis. I found little satisfaction in genital exchange with him and found it less than what I remembered about sex with girls. I couldn't seem to surmount my disgust with anal sex in any configuration, and oral sex was uncomfortable for me to provide and disappointingly unsatisfactory to receive. Mike was confused by this and was forever guiding me to "get on with it" as I explored his chest or back or tightly muscled legs. He knew no such hesitation himself and clearly got great satisfaction out of anything remotely genital, active or passive.

Still more telling, after a few weeks I began to understand something else. With Datus it had been love without sex; with Mike it was sex without love. For him this kind of intimacy was a recreation, a fling of good fellowship, nothing more. He had never promised or intimated it would be anything more, never gave any indication he wanted anything more. It was I who had laid higher expectations on it.

As my reluctance and different interest in closeness began to become more evident to both of us, we spent many confused, though sometimes still passionate, evenings talking about what was going on between us. In the end, both of us knew and, with equal reluctance, faced the fact that we had different purposes. We were both hurt, but could not help but remain friends and still frequently ate meals together. After a few weeks Mike found a newcomer who was, as he told me without a trace of recrimination, more clear about his sexual orientation than I was. Mike later told me he missed doing Shakespeare with me, a pastime Jerry wouldn't tolerate. Now there were three of us eating together. They knew their secret was safe with me.

I ended up more deeply confused than ever. Mike had everything I envied in a man, and I certainly remained strongly attracted to him. But sex with him had proved to be not what I was looking for. Even exploring his body had ultimately paled. I was still as fascinated as ever at his and other men's muscular bodies, but now I understood even less why they fascinated me.

The only consolation I carried away from my time with Mike was that I didn't feel any guilt for what we had done. I remember being particularly surprised by that. Guilt had always been an expected and painful part of the morning after—the morning after almost anything that I figured would not be approved by the authority figures in my life. I had experimented with Mike in good faith, had miscalculated, and now walked away with no recriminations, no regrets, and, for some reason, no guilt. The Mike incident, as it turned out, forever freed me from feeling guilty about whatever I undertake honestly and without harm to others while searching for adequate answers. That was lucky for me, because experimenting was going to be a big part of my life.

Another lesson I learned with Mike had to do with love itself. It was not clearly formulated in my mind yet, but a conviction was forming that the intimate sharing of bodies, by itself—however high the moment—carries with it no healing or wholeness. I should have learned that in high school, but I was far too driven, too compulsive, too involved in the superficialities of "going all the way" for any high-school experience to teach me anything significant. Girls, I recognize now with much sorrow, were then only objects to me, like shoulder pads or straight-pipe cars, to prove one's burgeoning manhood. I now began to see that if sexual exchange is to help heal, more than physical appetites must be engaged. Instead of learning that lesson from girls in Montana, I found myself learning it from a man on the opposite side of the Pacific Ocean. I didn't know then that there would be more training on the same topic years later.

The second significant event in my navy days had more far-reaching consequences.

9

Mother Number Three

For a few weeks after Mike and I called off our nightly liaison in the library, I began doing a left face along with everybody else who was leaving the mess hall after evening chow. That put us on the path to the Quonset-hut beer hall. I was immediately back into heavy drinking, a habit I had briefly jettisoned after meeting Mike. I was, again, as the saying went, "one of the last dogs to die"— among the last to make it back to the barracks before lights out at ten. One evening when Mike and Jerry invited me to go to the movies with them, I declined and also skipped the beer hall and went instead to the library, alone this time with the spiders. I had missed the place.

I was as lonely as I'd ever been in my life and shuffled about aimlessly, almost feeling gratitude for the spiders as they appeared. After some random reading, I surprised myself by beginning to pray. Until the last few months, when a growing despondency and then the excitement of Mike's friendship distracted me, prayer had always been a part of my daily routine. Not a very sophisticated level of praying, I now know, but regular, reassuring, and honest nonetheless. My stepmother had made bedtime prayers a routine in Montana, and the habit continued with me throughout high school and into navy days.

Through the paneless windows of the library I could hear bits of the movie playing at the base's open-air theater some distance back in a jungle clearing. From another direction came the loud laughter of the beer Quonset. I felt painfully alone, abandoned, as I began to pray. I remember speaking to God with an earnestness, almost a fierceness that surprised me and that I feared might be irreverent enough to verge on blasphemy. Frankly, I didn't give a damn if it did. At this stage, any prayer I might say was not so much a petition as it was a demand. The substance of what I prayed that night is as clear in my memory today as it was when I spoke it. Later, in the monastery, I referred in my journaling to the prayer of that night as "my Philippine prayer." I came to appreciate it as a major turning point in my life. From that night on, things got better. "If you ever listen to anybody, God, listen to me now," I insisted. "Show me a better way to live my life. If your concern for us is anything more than theory, show me something better than what I'm now doing with my life. There has to be a better way to live than the way I'm living."

From what followed in quick succession, I have to conclude that I was heard. Within two weeks a new friend and some of his books started me on the road to something I never in my wildest imaginations would have thought likely.

I became a Catholic.

Exhibiting the same curiosity that had driven me to question my stepmother incessantly on religion, in my high-school years I visited almost every church in town. Never once, however, did I consider attending Mass at the town's only Catholic church. Everybody knew that Catholics were too strange to take seriously. A venerable old farmer's remark to my father, which I had overheard as a small child, summed Catholics up for me: "Even their graveyard out west of town is fenced off from the graveyard of us normal folk."

The chain of events that led to my conversion to Catholicism happened rapidly. It all started because the new sub base com-

mander wasn't as patient as his predecessor had been about the
delay in radio dispatches being delivered to his office. These were
still the days when military communication took advantage of high
places for antennas, and the radio shack was partway up a mountain behind the base. The normal procedure had been that when
a dispatch came in, the sole radioman would notify the motor pool
and then had to depend on someone there to come get the document and take it to the CO. There were delays and frequent failures to appreciate the skipper's sense of urgency. The new CO
decided to solve the issue once and for all by having a jeep issued
to me. It became my new duty as his yeoman to pick up dispatches
the moment they arrived. It was in this way that I came to meet
Radioman First Class Edwin Kiefer. And his Catholic church.

Kiefer (we routinely called each other by last names) and I
quickly became fast friends. His Filipina lover worked on the
base and each morning brought him freshly baked rolls from her
home town across the bay. Almost every evening Kiefer and I
would lift ice from the officers' mess and make ice cream to go
with his girlfriend's rolls, which we loaded with thick slices of
canned Australian cheese. We often talked late into the night
over this feast in his radio shack. It certainly beat the daily boiled
rice in the chow hall.

Kiefer was a recent convert to Catholicism and was deeply passionate about his new religion, as converts typically are, a thing I
would witness over and over in the years to come. He'd been
aboard the submarine that entered Tokyo Bay in 1942, to gather
weather data for Doolittle's first air raid on that city, and had found
religion during the scary process of leaving the bay. Now, safe
ashore again and for hours on end, he shared his new church with
me in his soft-spoken, Bohemian manner.

One night during our talks and in a context I've forgotten, he
said to me, "Fowler, you show the most remarkable ignorance of
the Bible and of history!" His remark hit hard. It was too honest. It
was another of those incidents—like the one when Datus asked me
his first question about my self-estimate—in which I was faced

with the choice of turning aside in embarrassment and fear, or of picking up the opportunity and running with it. Again, fortunately, I chose the latter.

As soon as Kiefer made his remark, I realized that, for all of my reading, books had been for me nothing more than a long exercise in satisfying curiosity. Nothing tied them together. I read randomly with no purpose, no sense whatsoever of where it was leading or could lead, and had not yet found the golden thread that ties reading and thought into a meaningful whole. I remember staring at Kiefer without saying a word as this revelation rapidly formed in my head. He told me later that my protracted silence made him wonder if he had just scuttled our friendship, but it was quite the contrary. After my moment of inner shuffling, I replied, "Help me fix that, Kiefer."

He loaned me two books. One by John Cardinal Gibbons, a tried-and-true (if today intolerably stuffy) introduction to Catholicism, the name of which I've long forgotten, and another by Blaise Pascal, *Pensées,* in translation.

The next few weeks were like the aurora of a bright dawn after a night of tornadoes. Cardinal Gibbons gave me detailed understanding of traditional Christian belief and practice, and Blaise Pascal opened the universe to me. I could not understand everything I read in Pascal, but I did gain one profound realization from him. I might not yet understand all the answers he was providing, but at least now I knew there were answers out there to be had. I was ecstatic. The captain noticed something had changed in me and smiled one morning as he asked, "What's going on with you, Fowler? Found a new girlfriend?"

Kiefer and I continued our nightly meetings, he the flattered guru, and I the absorbent mind who had waited long enough for the clarity he was giving me and that I seemed to intuit almost immediately would transform my life forever. Besides the breadth of his reading, which astounded me, and the conviction with which he spoke in his studied manner, Kiefer impressed me in yet another way, and I still recall his example today when I am negotiating workdays at a crowded desk. In him I found a lasting image of the dedicated, ideal scholar. Datus had read broadly, but Kiefer did virtually nothing but read. The CO appreciated his lonely job as a radioman on twenty-four-hour duty in a remote radio shack and never required him to appear for weekly inspection. It's a good thing, because I doubt if he could have passed the simplest of inspections, and in those days such muster inspections were detailed and tough. This lack of weekly discipline gave free rein to Kiefer's disheveled tendencies. His immense store of facts and endless philosophizing impressed me, but so did his disdain for daily logistics and incidentals. I saw him as an ideal expression of freedom and self-confidence. *This* is how I want to live, I told myself.

We spent hours talking about everything from the latest Walter Winchell newscast, which we listened to on short wave, to the meaning of the wall shadows in Plato's cave. At Kiefer's urging, I signed up for a United States Armed Forces Institute (USAFI) course on the history of Greek philosophy from the University of Montana. The USAFI was a dying remnant of the war years, and I got in just under the wire. I did remarkably poorly with the course, and the young professor or professor's assistant who marked and returned my papers from Montana didn't bother to buffer his dismay at some of my answers. At least, however, this foray into a subject still beyond me was feeding my now-obsessive passion to understand life in all its dimensions. My reading and thought were beginning to have a direction at last.

With the coming of Kiefer into my life, I immediately, once again, broke free of any interest in alcohol, and I doubt if I ever again showed up at any of the nightly movies on the base. We were too busy making ice cream, picking bugs out of our daily supply of fresh rolls from the Subic City bakery, and talking well into every night. He had found a conversation companion in his lonely radio shack, and I a seemingly endless supply of new insight.

The source for this insight was the Roman Catholic church. At this stage, I didn't have to know anything more than that Kiefer had answers, the church had answers, Pascal had answers. And, God knows, I had questions. After two months of reading, I certainly didn't yet have any grand and detailed *Weltanschauung,* but I was so convinced that what I was hearing made ultimate sense that I wanted to sign up to become a Catholic. Who could doubt that the gaps in my knowledge would be filled in by future study?

It was with that assurance and enthusiasm that two months after meeting Kiefer, on July 6, 1947, I caught an afternoon boat across Subic Bay to Subic City, Zambales, a city the world would hear about in the 1990s when nearby Mount Pinatubo would awaken. In the bombed-out, roofless shell of a local Catholic parish, and sponsored by an elderly Filipino who worked on base, Rosendo Ding Soriano, I was baptized a Roman Catholic.

The old Spanish-style church building sat in the heart of an area watched over by the navy Shore Patrol and strictly out of bounds to sailors because of its oversupply of prostitutes who had helped two armies march through their city. Some of them, the navy warned us, had ended up not only with an array of venereal diseases, but also with leprosy. My former drinking buddies laughed at the irony of my going into downtown Subic to get baptized. At the next Sunday bullshit session, one of the guys remarked "I know that area well, but I'm always too busy in there on more urgent matters to remember to get baptized." My heart sang all the way to the church and back. The challenge of dodging SPs only added to the excitement.

Nothing could touch the new hope that had suddenly appeared in my life. I had just spent two months reading everything I could get my hands on about Roman Catholicism, but it was Pascal who finally convinced me that becoming Catholic and launching upon an all-out search for conscious union with the Eternal was what I wanted to do. Pascal pushed me far beyond my previous goals of mere psychological and social healing. He told me there was much more than these to hope for.

In college two years later, the irony and what I like to think of as divine humor of this whole episode hit home when I found out that Blaise Pascal's *Pensées* was on Roman Catholicism's *Index of Forbidden Books.*

What can I say about my new church and what it meant to me in those days? It was undoubtedly, I told myself, Datus's special gift. For the next several years I thanked him for helping me find it. Catholicism told me I was of infinite worth, using tightly reasoned ways to do it. It began feeding me what seemed an endless supply of intellectual treats. If eventually I had to admit it did little to heal my emotional wounds, I still recognize with gratitude that it did distract me from them long enough that I could get moving in life again. At last I could continue my education and growth. Most of all, Catholicism promised me that one day I would find *lasting* healing and wholeness, and more: union with Bliss itself.

My new church hooked me in the one talent alone that by now I knew I had: a good mind. I read voraciously, and from Pascal and Abelard, Cardinals Gibbons and Newman, Francis de Sales and Francis of Assisi, Teresa of Avila and Thérèse of Lisieux, the Catherines of Siena and Genoa, I learned about dimensions to life that reached beyond my wildest dreams. Life suddenly made sense, suddenly was secure; it was tolerable after all. From day one, the church's long tradition intrigued, fascinated, thrilled me, and in the process rewarded my mind with understandings about life and the universe, about God and about me. The whole fabric of the universe seemed, for the first time, to be safe, and sublime. Given my intellectual development at the time, I could not have found more suitable answers for every fear and uncertainty I'd ever felt. My new insights about everything, from my father to God, from the navy to the developing cold war, from opinions on the sub base to those of the ancient Greeks, from praying to sex, came together in a coherence that thrilled me. I was dealing with freshman insights, it's true, but I was still a freshman, and no pride of an Oxford graduate could have surpassed the pride of this plebe now proudly announcing that he, along with nearly two thousand years of major historical figures, was Catholic.

Catholicism told me that I was nothing less than a son of God, and then it went on to say that I could actually come to experience that reality here on earth. And it insisted with reassuring authority that it would teach me how to do that. If my panicked prayer in the base library that had started all this good fortune was blasphemous, as I still feared, I was sorry. But I was glad that I'd prayed it all the same, for suddenly and undeniably I was being shown options far more rewarding than booze or sex could ever be, options powerful enough to overcome any degree of loneliness.

In the years that followed, the Catholic church would continue to provide me with answers to increasingly refined needs, a cogent view of the cosmos that helped me not precisely *solve,* but at least *understand,* my problem. It gave me the guidance that my emotional and intellectual floundering so much needed. And, to cap it all, it assured me of a glorious, transcendental, and eternal resolution in the end.

As had happened when Datus appeared, my new mentor, the church, arrived with just what I needed just when I needed it. It brought solicitous, mothering guidance, and the significance is not lost on me that, following a common Catholic practice, I called the Catholic church Holy Mother Church for many years, with the emphasis on *mother.*

It's understandable that when this mother's answers were no longer adequate and I left her, she protested loudly. She had no way of knowing—and found my effort to explain inadequate—of the warmth that remained, and remains, in my heart for those days when she took me in and gave me shelter from the storm.

Like some mothers, she failed in one important way: she insisted that I needed her coddling for the rest of my days. She didn't know when to let go. She didn't understand that if many do accept her excessive ministrations and overly detailed guidance for all of their lives, it's not because this is advisable, but because such simple submission is so much easier than the hard work of finding personal wholeness and autonomy. If church managers vigorously press for such submission, it's because it is so much easier to manage than self-directed spiritual maturity. In her zeal for helping, the church encourages—demands—an infantilism that many of her "children" never come to recognize.

After ten months in the Philippines, I was transferred to the submarine base at Pearl Harbor in what was then known as T.H., the Territory of Hawaii. Eight months later I was assigned to a submarine, the *USS Sea Devil, SS400,* whose squadron of subs was stationed at Pearl. The boat was to make its way back to Vallejo at the top of San Francisco Bay to be decommissioned, and I to Alameda Naval Air Station to be discharged.

The men on the boat were, for the most part, career submariners who had served during the war. Their camaraderie was real, and they admitted me into it without hesitation. I enjoyed my brief time with them more than I had expected. I could feel myself getting well again, and it showed up in a new ability to lighten up. The *Sea Devil,* however, was a diesel boat, one of the old fleet types, and living conditions were crowded. It was not at all an ideal situation for somebody trying to meditate every day and to use every spare moment to read. I grew more and more anxious to return to the civilian world and get on with life.

My father knew Montana's Senator Mike Mansfield, and my commanding officer, himself a graduate of Annapolis, joined Dad in trying to convince me to go after what they felt was a reasonably assured appointment to the United States Naval Academy. Contact with a senator, apparently, through some miracle of bureaucracy, could expedite, if not ensure, such an appointment. Enthusiasm for a different kind of higher education and slowly hatching thoughts of possibly studying for the priesthood kept me from pausing to consider the opportunity even for a moment. No one else, though, seemed to understand my reasoning.

By the time I was released from the *Sea Devil* in Vallejo and sent to Alameda for discharge, I had applied to the bishop of Helena to begin the long studies for the priesthood. The old Catholic pastor in my hometown in Montana wrote me an ecstatic letter. I would be the first ever from his parish to become a priest. He wondered what miracle had transformed me while I was in the navy. He didn't say it, but I knew he remembered me as the rowdy, often drunken student for which I had built a reputation. I never got around to telling him my story, and that was wise, for as I got to know him I realized that he could not have understood.

I had not yet thought of becoming a monk for the simple reason that I didn't yet know that monks hadn't long ago disappeared with the rest of the Middle Ages. I was now certain, though, that I wanted to be a priest. If studying centuries of wisdom as a sailor was rewarding, imagine what it would be like, I told myself, to undertake what would be at least eight years of training at a seminary. If knowing the church from the outside was so rewarding, think of what it would be like as a priest functioning on the inside. The priesthood did not yet have any overtones of spirituality for me; I did not yet see it as a special way to serve God and be of use to his people, as I later would. All it meant to me at this stage was what it could do for me: better and more extensive training and a lifestyle that would supposedly ensure an inside track to the most sublime knowledge for the rest of my life. Spirituality was still a theory; another facet of the intellectual life.

When I was finally discharged from the navy in late April 1948, I left neither hard feelings nor close friendships behind. I had almost been eaten by sharks while swimming too far from shore on the windward side of Oahu once, but, fortunately, they had already had lunch—or my angels quickly convinced them they had. That escape may have been a symbol of how close I had come to losing myself to despair during my first venture into the world. But, instead, I came home as enthusiastic about life as I had once been in the warm presence of Datus. My time in the navy turned out to be a huge success.

No race horse has ever chafed more in a starting lineup than I did as I awaited final discharge papers at Alameda across the bay from San Francisco in April of 1948. I celebrated my new lease on living by going to an Ezio Pinza concert in the city's Opera House, the site of the recent signing of the United Nations Charter. Little did I suspect what the city that sparkled at me across the still-clear waters of the bay had in store for me.

I spent a day in Oakland buying civvies and then, discharge finally in hand, donned them and boarded the City of San Francisco for a Pullman ride to Montana. By preference, I sat alone for meals in the diner, and for the first time in my life felt as if I deserved the china, linen, and silver. It was a good ride.

10

Starting Over

The moment I walked into my family's ranch-house kitchen—home again as heroically as possible from the nonwars—I found myself even less contented to be there than when I had left two years before. It was clear that my father and mother were honestly glad to see me, but their preoccupying distress about my new Catholicism was evident. Within a few minutes they asked me about future plans I had mentioned in a letter from Pearl Harbor. I confirmed their worst fears and said I did intend to enroll at a male-only, private Catholic college. And, yes, I would be studying to become a priest. Silence settled on the house. They had no way to cope. I had no way to cope. We had never known how to talk about important things, and since this matter was important, all three of us escaped into silence. I furthered my escape by going out into the yard on the plea of getting reacquainted with my dog, who, of course, didn't give a damn if I was Mormon or Catholic as long as I was still around to love her.

Some wonderful moments did pass between my parents and me that summer, wonderful enough that they filled me with deep emotion more than once as I realized that beneath our inability to connect, we did genuinely love one other. I remember being hit hard as I began to realize for the first time what life at home could have been all along had we known how to talk, had we *dared* to talk. But now it was too late.

After a number of strained first-days home when I too freely criticized her Mormonism as I carried on about the wonders of my new Catholicism, I began to realize what an ass I was being around my stepmother. I noticed that whenever the two of us found ourselves without religious tags around our necks, Mother and I were easily back into nonstop, lighthearted conversation. We found ourselves having good times together again, moments of genuine sharing. I helped her iron clothes on Sunday afternoons, as I had often done, and went grocery shopping with her on Saturdays. My criticism of her religion, however, had clearly muddied our special closeness in a way that for years I resigned myself to thinking irreparable. Our relationship did finally recover, but only shortly before she died many years later.

Mother never once openly criticized my choosing to go to a Catholic college or deciding to become a Catholic priest. But I had briefly belonged to her Mormon church in high school, and on one occasion she grew unusually solemn, almost pensive, as she told me how concerned she was that I had forsaken "the truth," a thing perceived by Mormons as particularly and eternally dangerous. And then she added with her most heartfelt smile: "But God is merciful, and I know you have a good heart."

Throughout all this she remained a good listener and let me talk openly about my problems with my father. Sometimes she shook her head at something he had said or done and repeated in dismay, "That man, that man!" My own characterizing of him and his actions was a bit more colorful—not infrequently cloacal and profane under my breath. She understood the stress and usually, when I muttered too loudly, acted as if she had not heard what she at other times called my "dreadful navy tongue." Her response became predictable: "You'll rue the day you said that about your father. He tries, you know." I didn't know.

Dad and I did manage to get close a few times. On one occasion he forgot himself and was suddenly outgoing and easy as he questioned me at length about what it was like to be on a submerged submarine, what were the sounds, the smells, the feelings on the boat. Both of us momentarily forgot our learned roles and were lost in animated exchange. Then, suddenly, as if remembering he—or we—didn't deserve this much good feeling, he recovered his distance with ease: "Why in hell do you want to go to that god-damned college where there are no girls." I saw nothing in his words except their harshness, and I walked angrily away, giving as good as I figured I'd got.

One Saturday afternoon he asked me to accompany him to meet his friends at the local bar that had replaced Johnny Stone's Tavern. Today, wiser, I would go with him, but then, self-righteous and showing it, I told him that since I was on the way to being a sem-inarian, I had no intention of being seen in a bar. He lowered his eyes and fell silent. Whenever he didn't explode, you knew some-thing had truly gotten to him. I was instantly sorry to have hurt him, but I had no idea of what to do about it. Besides, I was too newly pious to feel very responsible. Piety has always been such a handy excuse for the selfishness of insensitivity.

Dad was not completely without humor, even with one he often called his knuckle-headed son. One evening we found ourselves out in one of the barns, and I was blathering on over something I was currently reading about God. Using the special term by which he habitually referred to God, he interrupted, "If that stool over there by the wall will jump up and down, right now, I'll believe all that shit about the Old Boy Upstairs." Before my cool could snap on, my head snapped sideways to stare at the stool. Gotcha! The stool didn't budge, fortunately for my nerves and his preferred lifestyle. Dad instantly broke out laughing. I knew he'd won one and I laughed with him. I remember how good it felt, as if there was some kind of new life between us giving signs of birth. But then, for an instant only, we exchanged glances, and in the same nanosec-ond that our eyes met we both looked away, embarrassed, and the laughter died. It was as if we'd been caught stealing cookies, tiny fa-vors of a good life we weren't allowed even to sample.

———

As the summer of 1948 drew to a close, it seemed clearer than ever to me that my world was in a different galaxy than that of my parents. We had spent four months together, and I still felt I could tell them nothing of my personal life—nothing about my love for Datus, about my experiment in the search for love in the Philippines, about the excitement I felt for the intellectual life that Catholicism held. The most intimate thing they knew about my personal life was that I had left Peggy and was no longer interested in dating girls. I didn't even try to explain that and remember thinking that the explanation should be self-evident to them. I was so engrossed in a compulsive reading and reviewing of Latin for placement exams in September that, apart from the fun moments spent with Mother a few times each week, I enjoyed no recreation with my parents that summer.

I still felt a great loneliness in my life, and it was during the first few weeks out of the navy that I initially consciously convinced myself that dating held no promise of filling that loneliness. I was attracted to partnering with neither female nor male, whether for conversation, for a beer, or for a brief romp in a haystack. Several times former high-school friends asked if I would like to meet some girl and bring her to one of their parties. I doubt if I paused to consider the possibility at all. The fact that I planned to study for the celibate Catholic priesthood was my plausible explanation: a consciously high ideal certainly, but an unconscious form of neurotic escape from daily life all the same. I was now oriented to getting well, it is true, but I was still filled with towering self-doubt and a sense of inadequacy. In high school I had bluffed an adequacy, but all the high-school support systems were gone now, and it was easier to bow out of relationships than to try to forge new ones, especially when, as I was convinced, an altogether new and superior level of living lay ahead.

There were a few times, however, during what I believed would be my last summer "in the world," when I asked myself if, perhaps, I should check out dating one final time. Even though I no longer masturbated at all, a few times I was honest enough to ask if I was truly ready for a lifetime of celibacy. The answer was always the same: my appetite for feeling okay far outweighed my appetite for sex. I understood the celibate clergy to be my most likely, if not only, route into healing, and I determined that henceforward "passion" for me would involve spirit, not body.

A great space had opened up in my life in the navy, and I was busy exploring it. In no way did I know it at the time, but becoming a Catholic in the tidal-wave, compulsive manner that I did was an indicator of a severe personality crisis. As I've since realized, religious conversion can be the conscious front for an unconscious drive to escape from whatever is disagreeable. That doesn't invalidate the authenticity of the religious experience, however, for, as spiritual masters have often said, God comes to get us where we're at. But it does mean that while I thought my greatest passion was for understanding and truth—and an honest passion it was—the far greater energy, the far more powerful passion driving my plunge into religion had to do with a deeper, more lasting, more frantic hunger. I was driven to feel secure, to feel authentic, to feel parred with others at last.

If we are to grow, we have to begin from where we are, and for me that meant I had to begin my journey to freedom and wholeness from a place deep in neurotic guilt. I had to begin from a state of almost complete self-rejection. Any understanding of what was really going on stayed mercifully out of sight until the time finally came when I could face it honestly and without undue flinching.

With a daily diet of the mystics, of Teresa of Avila, John of the Cross, Brother Lawrence of God, I honed my goal ever more clearly, what it really was that I wanted to find and know and "make love to." The mystics told me it was the Source, the Ultimate—God!

Driven by these surprising but frequent bedfellows, neuroticism and spiritual idealism, every apparently alien aspect of life paled by comparison. The words of the Christian mystics that I had scarcely understood two years before with Datus began to have a mesmerizing meaning for me. I had brought home a substantial collection of spiritual books from Bagley's in downtown Honolulu, and now I had time to read them. The mystics became the joy of my life. The reason was simple: spiritual books provided specific definition to the new hope that was mine, and mystics raised the stakes.

I began finding strength and increasingly explicit encouragement in meditation. My earlier experience of meditating with Datus had suggested the way. Now, somehow, amid the hubbub of opinions, likes, and dislikes—inside me, in my family, and in everyone else—I began to hear in meditation, for the very first time with any consistency, what *George* thought and felt and wanted and didn't want. There was a part of life, a part of *me*, that I was able to find only in meditation. I began to suspect there was a gem somewhere down inside of me longing to be mined and brought up to the sunlight. I was busy sinking shafts. If the path I had charted was one of neurotic escape, at least it was *my* path and *I* had chosen it.

My closest confidant that long and lonely summer home waiting for college to begin was, as before, my dog Mitz. When I had first arrived at the gate leading into our yard after a two-year absence, she instantly recognized me and came running. Now again she was completely content to lie beside me no matter how long I sat crosslegged in my bedroom or out on the prairie. Sometimes she would lay her head in my lap, periodically turning her eyes upward into my face and wagging her tail as if to send a message of both puzzlement and unqualified support. Two years before I had sensed she felt my pain; now I imagined she shared my excitement. The only thing she could not share was going each day to 6:00 A.M. Mass. But she was always there when I got back, greeting me each time with an enthusiastic affirmation I received from no one else.

We walked coulees and far stretches of prairies as I thought of how successful my time in the navy had been, how suddenly life had become so good. I felt unbounded hope and a rising joy where two years before I had walked in deep grief and complete confusion. I didn't doubt for a minute that I was drawing closer at last to what Datus had been talking about. I lamented the fact that he had not had the joy of being Roman Catholic. He was no doubt smiling and biding his time.

At last, in early September, I arrived at Carroll College. I immediately felt at home and earned straight A's from the start. Unlike high school, I was now immensely interested in such subjects as philosophy, history, psychology, Latin, Greek that, very much unlike high school, demanded hard work every day. I was back in my element, feeling zero attraction for booze, sex, or anything besides books and meditation. The quiet dignity of the fraternity-free campus was pure delight, and I was not once late for mandatory twice-daily chapel.

Even more than academics, what I needed at that point in my unfolding was to be under the guidance of someone who understood spirituality and meditation, somebody I could talk to. I had apparently forgotten Datus's words about how we need more than intellectual clarity. We need, *I* needed, not just the understanding that comes from study and thought about the how and why of the universe, but the *experience* of the universe that comes in meditation. A physics professor, Father Bernard Topel, came along to help me find precisely that.

I hadn't been at the college more than a couple of weeks when Father Topel, the priest who enjoyed a reputation as being the most spiritual priest on campus, came to my room on what seemed to be a casual visit. He told me later that he came explicitly so he could offer himself as my spiritual director, which he did. "I've seen you spending extra time meditating in the chapel and sense a contemplative hunger and energy in you," he told me. "I think I can help you along." I felt flattered, gratified. The subsequent two years under the guidance of this priest, later to be selected by the pope as bishop of Spokane, were immensely helpful for the simple reason that he was, before all else, a dedicated meditator.

———

Meditation, or what I fondly hoped was meditation, had begun for me soon after I met Datus in the winter of 1945. It waxed and (more often) waned from then until it finally took off in earnest a couple weeks after meeting Kiefer in the Philippines in late April 1947. "Taking off" in those early days—and for the first few years—meant thoughtful, quiet time devoted to spiritual reading and efforts to understand what I was reading. Not infrequently the reading was punctuated with sitting or kneeling like a dolt, waiting for something to "happen." Eventually, that somewhat strained and effortful silence became familiar and then refreshing. Eventually, but only years later, it became a dance of the heart.

I have practiced meditation daily since 1947. As I write this in 1994, I realize that meditation has been the single most consistent enterprise of my life. I have today come to a wonderful place, and there is not the slightest doubt in my mind that meditation is the reason for it.

By the time Father Topel began giving me my first extended—and what I suppose must be called professional—guidance in the art of meditating, I needed no urging from him about its importance or the wisdom of faithfulness to it. By that time I had already begun to find some sort of vague, impossible-to-define experience in meditation that set it apart from concentration, from deep thought, and even from the occasional emotional high of intellectual insights that come to all who are now and then calm enough to invite them.

Meditation, I had begun to learn—and a lifetime of its practice has confirmed this countless times—is not inner or even wordless prayer, not elevated thinking, not freedom from distractions, not a clever way to sit or breathe or any of the other techniques so often taught as if they constitute meditation. *Meditation is, first and foremost and essentially, an inner experience.*

In the years to follow I would learn that even if one thinks the most sublime thoughts given to humans to think, has the most sublime insights, and comes up with the most astounding theological, metaphysical, or spiritual breakthroughs, none of this can rightly be called meditation. Meditation isn't doing or thinking or feeling; it is an *experience*.

On the other hand, one may be peeling potatoes, making love, drinking a beer, be in a church or in a privy, and have that inner experience that takes one out of the ordinary stuff of daily life. Insight may accompany it; clarification and relief may accompany it. Healing of any variety may accompany it. But meditation is none of these. It is the *experience* itself.

And what is that experience? It is the experiential realization of the Ultimate Reality that we call—variously and indifferently—God, Brahman, Existence, Being, Life, Light, Nagual, or anything a thousand other traditions may devise. The experience may last only as long as it takes an iridescent hummingbird to catch a sunbeam as it whisks past our eyes. Or it may come to overwhelm us for days. In either case, the experience is, clearly, unmistakably, an *experience* and not a thought, a transcendental touch, or a mere poetic high.

The difference between hearing Father Topel discuss meditation and hearing most others do so is that for most it seems synonymous with recollection, quiet time, thoughtfulness, concentration perhaps. For Topel it meant *contact*. It meant the touch of the very Christ-life, the Buddhahood, the very Essence of us. When the mystics of the race tell us that we are all One with one another and One with God, for most people they seem to be speaking in metaphor. Most listeners nod in respect and quickly move on. For Father Topel, the Oneness of all things—us included—that the mystics speak of implied an underlying concrete Reality that is to be recognized so that it can be tasted.

Under Father Topel's weekly guidance, I began to have brief intimations of what lies beyond praying. Praying implies an *I* as set apart from a *Thou* to whom we address ourselves. Meditation does away with this separateness and replaces conversation with realized union, with recognized—and eventually experienced—Oneness.

The curtain never really parted for me at Carroll, not even for an instant, but now I know that I made significant progress there just in realizing that a curtain existed that might one day part. The hummingbird never flitted past me, but I at least knew that such iridescence existed somewhere out there in the garden.

In Father Topel, I had once again found a needed teacher and model for what I wanted to learn just when I was ready to learn it. On this occasion, though, my model was not so much one to be imitated, but rather a reminder that I was on a fantastic journey and that, yes, what I was seeking did actually exist.

I told Father Topel everything—except the nature of my relationship with Mike in the Philippines. I have wondered many times how he would have handled that information. Would he have withdrawn his support of my desire to be a priest? The slightest word from him and the bishop would have dropped me like a burning coal. Had I told Topel about Mike, would he have said it didn't matter? Topel the meditator most certainly would have understood, but would Topel the churchman, soon to be bishop? I'm fairly confident the meditator would have won out, but I was too insecure to take the chance.

It was through him that I first learned it was still possible to be a monk. In Honolulu I had picked up a copy of Saint Benedict's *Rule for Monasteries,* written in the early sixth century. The simplicity and idealism of the lifestyle Benedict described affected me—and attracted me—profoundly. But I presumed what he was describing had long disappeared. One day in casual conversation I mentioned to Father Topel that it was too bad I'd not been born a thousand years before so I could be a monk. He looked puzzled for a moment and then, realizing my erroneous presumption, exploded in laughter: "There are *hundreds* of monasteries to choose from!"

He helped me plan a trip around the United States for the summer of 1949. The circuit included Benedictines, Discalced Carmelites, Franciscans, Passionists, Trappists. It surprised neither of us that at the end of the summer I chose the Trappists for my future. They still followed Saint Benedict's *Rule* to the letter. What seemed particularly attractive to me was the singleness of their purpose, well exemplified by their carefully preserved perpetual silence. Silence seemed like a particularly significant symbol of the urgency of Trappists' pursuit of the very thing I wanted to pursue: clear and open and blissful union with God. With them I could be sure of finding the same experience that my great diet of reading the mystics assured me they had found. After visiting the Trappist Abbey of Gethsemani in Kentucky in July, I visited the Trappists a second time, in August, at Trinity Abbey in Utah, where I met Brother Matthew amid the roses.

I was filled with gratitude for the past and excitement about the future when I packed my bags at the end of a second year at Carroll. I was scheduled to enter Trinity Abbey two weeks later. Without a trace of hesitation or remorse, but with considerable emotion, I walked away from a place where I'd been happier than anywhere I'd ever lived. I hadn't grown much emotionally there, for it was still my time for sowing and not yet for harvesting. But I did grow in every other way. I had become an avid and informed student of philosophy and now understood much more of Pascal's *Pensées* that had proved to be so far beyond me when I was in the Philippines. Unlike when I left the navy, I left behind many good friends at Carroll, but I wasn't looking back. I was off to a Trappist monastery.

Years later my parents told me they saw only rejection of themselves and their home in the happiness I showed during my two weeks at the ranch before departure for a place I planned never to leave. "After all, what possible attraction could there really be in going to a place like that? Your excitement had to be because you were leaving home." Dad's level of consciousness at the time was such that he looked with admiration on my former high-school friends who were still spending Saturday nights at Little America and other drunken dance halls we had frequented as students. Them he could understand. Me he could not. I didn't try to explain. Had I tried, I would still have had to start with Datus. And what could I have shared of what Father Topel and I talked about? Which of my books could I have asked either of my parents to read? Today I would try any or all of these options anyway. But then I didn't.

Since after a five-year period Trappist monks take a vow never to leave their particular abbey, and since it didn't seem likely that any of my family members would ever come to visit me in a Roman Catholic monastery, I expected never to see home or any of them again as I prepared to leave. This good-bye had all the earmarks, indeed, of being a final one. When the day of departure arrived, I remained absolutely resolute. Resolute, but, to my surprise, overtaken by unstoppable tears all the way into town and to the bus depot. What bothered me, what seemed so very sad, what seemed the unfairness of it all, was that as far as my parents were concerned I was leaving not for Utah—not even for Mars, which at least they knew existed—but for a reality that they couldn't begin to comprehend. My Aunt Ruth had come from Washington state to say good-bye to me and was the only consolation I found in my family as she drove me away from the ranch and into town. I hoped she would be able to be an equal consolation to my parents, youngest sister Joyce, and half-brother Ron when she drove back out to the ranch. Perhaps she alone among all of our family was able to appreciate both sides of the Fowler impasse that day.

Datus was very much in my mind as I boarded the bus to my mountain valley monastery.

I wonder whether he was laughing or crying.

11

A New Kind of Reveille

Until the mid-1960s, when the annual meeting in France of the world's Trappist abbots authorized a change, reveille in a Trappist monastery was never later than 2:00 A.M.—1:30 on Sundays, 1:00 on days of major liturgy. It wasn't a far-off bugle that did the deed, but a thirty-pound bell hung, it seemed, just outside your eardrum. I've been roused by both bugle and bell, and there's no contest. The bell doesn't merely suggest or even demand that you get up; it does the work for you and *lifts* you off your cot.

What Trappists call their bell for rising hangs at one end of the dormitory of cubicle cells. It isn't rung by rocking, but by pulling at a leather leash hung from its tongue, which is then clanged against its inner side. This hellish engineering leaves considerable room for subjectivity on the part of the junior monk charged as bell ringer for the year. Every January as the new ringer assumed his duties, he seemed to go through a couple weeks of fundamentalist zeal for a certain brand of early morning justice. If he had to get up a few minutes early to awaken his beloved brothers, it was only equitable that those brothers, beloved or not, get off their cots *now!*

Even so, early rising seemed to be viewed by most monks more as the beginning of another day of inner adventure than as a hardship. Except when deep in a cold or flu, few ever gave evidence of having difficulty starting the day in the middle of the night. Early rising is like monastic living as a whole: it sounds a lot harder than it is.

The ambience of 2:00 A.M. is different depending on whether you are meeting it as you get up or leaving it as you go to bed. I've done both, many times, and the difference is dramatic. From the first morning I smelled the Utah night air sliding into the monastery valley from the surrounding Wasatch Mountains, I recognized it as sister to the air of the Montana prairies and loved it. When birds in the cloister garth began their own chanting about four, still another dimension of charm was added. By the time the sun arrived on the scene, the day for both monks and birds had been in full swing for some hours.

The abbot insisted that I spend a second year at Carroll College after my first visit to the monastery before he would admit me as a postulant. It was a normal requirement—"to try the spirit." Finally, in June 1950, I passed for what I was sure was the last time through the gate that had promised me its *pax* on my first visit the summer before. Three days of twiddling my thumbs in the guesthouse followed—another requirement, another final frustration to help an irresolute recruit change his mind.

Was I irresolute? Did I wonder if, just maybe, my father was right after all? Did I reconsider the forfeiting of all future travel, vacation, recreation, possessions, freedom, family ties, sex? Not for a minute. I was so consciously eager to find God and his bliss—and so unconsciously eager to escape my sense of personal poverty—that I had not a trace of hesitation.

Finally, on the third day, a couple of hours before vespers, I was unceremoniously ushered into the papal enclosure—so-called because for centuries monasteries had been forbidden to women under pain of excommunication by the pope—and I became a postulant, the community's newest aspirant, and a Trappist monk (of sorts) at last. A month later I would give up my worldly clothing, receive the all-white habit of a novice, and begin two years of basic training, sort of a medieval boot camp. Then, if I still wanted to continue, and if the community voted to accept me, I would make temporary vows for three years and exchange my white scapular for a black one. After that, with now a total of five years under my belt, and again after a community vote, I would chant my final and solemn vows in front of the gathered monks and become a full-fledged Trappist.

The first thing they did was cut off all my hair. I was rid of that red stuff at last! It didn't escape my notice that a closely trimmed red or blond cranium looks much better than those that once sported the black hair I'd envied all my life. Black stubble left a head looking downright grungy. Shaved blonds and redheads looked steam-cleaned by comparison. I had arrived! I was going to be all right after all.

During orientation that first afternoon, the father master of novices alerted me that after the bell for rising I would have only fifteen minutes to get my clothing on, dash cold water in my face, and get into my newly assigned choir stall in church. The next morning when I had made my way to where monks do this early morning cold-water face-splashing trick, I forgot the part of his guidance about there not being time to brush my teeth and started to do so. The observant father master frowned and shook his head. Lesson number one. I remember being a bit disgusted.

The collection of psalms, prayers, and other texts monks recite in monotone or chant in Gregorian plainsong is called the divine office or, more simply, choir duty. The portion in the wee morning hours is the night office. Getting it launched each morning was as moving for me when I left the abbey seventeen years later as it was that first morning in 1950.

Until the night office actually starts, there is only one small light burning in the huge abbey church, near the abbot's stall. The near darkness is filled with the muffled sound of rustling choir robes as monks move into their stalls. Then the bell ringer rings again—

one of the bells in the tower and more gently this time, as if repenting of his recent zeal—the lights come on, the monks stand. Choir duty for the day begins.

It doesn't take long to learn how to function in a monastic choir. You stand, face the high altar, and respond to the plaintiff monotone cry of the *hebdomadarius,* a priest-monk who leads the liturgy for the week: *Deus, in adjutorium meum intende*—"O God, come to my assistance." All respond, *Domine, ad adjuvandum me festina*—"O Lord, make haste to help me." All then turn to face the center of the choir, bow deeply, and add the Latin doxology:

> *Gloria Patri, et Filio, et Spiritui Sancto. Sicut erat in principio et nunc et semper et in saecula saeculorum. Amen.* [Glory be to the Father, and to the Son, and to the Holy Spirit. As it was in the beginning, is now and ever shall be, world without end. Amen.]

The choir is divided into two, each half on opposite sides of the church's nave, with choir stalls facing inward. The two half choirs customarily stand facing each other, chanting texts sometimes together but more usually alternately back and forth. At assigned times, both turn to face the high altar and recite or sing designated verses. Everyone sits, bows, stands, kneels, and at times leans back on little seats built onto the bottom of each stall's hinged bench and meaningfully called *misericords,* a term taken from the Latin for mercy. I quickly learned how they got their name. It is truly a thing of mercy to lean against them after hours of standing during the longer liturgies.

What adventures I was to have in that choir over the years. Sometimes in summer we would sweat profusely beneath our heavy robes; other times we shivered inside them when they couldn't compete with wintertime's mountain blizzards or becalmed subzero nights embracing the abbey from outside. Once when one side of the choir could scarcely hear the other because of a raging windstorm, the huge window over the high altar blew in and sprayed eighty monks with plate glass. It says something about this group of men that nobody ducked. Nor was anyone cut. There were years when the chant went well and was a joy. Years when, because of the loss of a talented organist or cantor, it went poorly to the point of being an interminably cacophonous agony. There was the excitement of having new oak stalls installed (curious phrase), and the weariness every year on Good Friday morning when we monotoned without break the entire Psalter of 150 psalms over a period of several hours in honor of the hours on the cross. There was the high adrenaline and jauntiness of the vespers hymn *Urbs Jerusalem* sung several times a year. It had been a military marching song of the Roman legions and had been baptized with new Christian words in an early century. There was the purity of the oldest chant and the concocted, pompous artificiality of those parts of it composed by a Roman bureaucracy after it took control of what had until then been the spontaneous outpourings of simple hearts everywhere.

No ritual or romance of outer circumstance, however, can compare with the weekly, monthly, year-by-year *inner* experience that comes with being in a monastery choir. The ritual eventually becomes second nature. Piece by piece most of the Psalter and other texts are memorized. As attention is thus freed, the inner occupation of a gentle and overpowering vision—wordy and reasoned only for a time—takes over. It's not a true vision at all, but an experience so real that *vision* seems its only accurate analog.

What is it you begin to "see"? Not lights or saints, one hopes. Not anything at all if you're lucky. Rather, you begin to experience the perfect harmony and proportion and benevolent nature of the universe. Ultimate meaning lying integral and uncompromised within any and every event. Life—*the* Life— within every person and thing. If the word *peace* weren't so run to death and misapplied to what often amounts to not much more than the satisfaction of getting one's own way, it would be accurate to identify this experience as the coming of peace. But it's so much more. A totally different "peace," too, than what we expected, because before it comes we have nothing on earth with which to imagine what we are expecting to find. Before it comes, limping metaphors are the best we have to understand it. I'm getting ahead of myself, however, and all this must be kept for a later chapter when it will no longer be the half-formed, hardly defined hope of an uninitiated junior monk.

All of the Trappists' ancient choir routine changed a year or two after I left the abbey, when English replaced Latin and Gregorian chant was replaced by a hodgepodge mewing by monks trying to find something, anything to chant in English. Until then, however, and for as long as I was at the abbey, the daily liturgy was grand, dignified. It was how we started and ended each day, as it had been for more than fifteen centuries.

During my first months in the abbey, I kept busy learning rituals, the Trappist sign language, and a sizable book of daily usages. Knowing the ancient monastic signs was immediately critical, because while keeping silent was considered essential, some form of communication was equally necessary in order to follow instructions at work. Even communicating by signs was forbidden in many places and at certain times, but speaking was forbidden always except when asked a question in class, when in the confessional, and when, with permission asked each time and customarily while kneeling, speaking to the abbot. Everyone took silence seriously, sometimes too much so. Years before my time, a major building burned to the ground one night at the Trappist Abbey of Gethsemani in Kentucky because the one brother who awoke and saw the beginning flames out a dormitory window would neither speak nor make signs to alert anyone during the so-called Great Silence of the Night (signs strictly forbidden).

Much more than being officially occupied learning usages, I was unofficially and more obsessively occupied trying to absorb the fact that my lifestyle now was what had been followed for centuries in the great medieval abbeys for which I had felt so strong a fascination, even as a child. I, George—now renamed Bernard—was living the existence set forth in the sixth century *Rule for Monks* that

I'd blundered upon in Honolulu. How could my good fortune possibly be any greater?

But from my first day in the abbey, something absorbed me far more than rhapsodizing about an ancient lifestyle. I was unaware of it myself, and apparently there was no one around astute or unvested enough to recognize it for me. I thought I was busy learning sign language and usages, but what I was mostly busy at was learning to turn my self-management over to others. I had come to the abbey to find myself, and I immediately set to work to make sure I never would.

If the formative realities in my Montana family didn't help me find an identity of my own, and if the navy's boot camp had worked hard to reduce me to preconscious responses, monastery life in the 1950s did all that with one sophisticated improvement. The regimen of the monastery got *inside* of young men's hearts and minds and seeded an explicit religious motivation for *conscious* self-abjection. I could resent my father's putdown and despise the navy for its style of training, but here in the monastery I was told to respect these same actions as the best of all paths to the highest of all fulfillments: holiness.

Many years later in San Francisco, several former monks and I shared the astonishment we all felt that we hadn't realized what was happening to us. We recognized the self-submersion, of course, because it would have been impossible not to, but at least those of us who stuck it out didn't know how to assess it. We missed a basic and horrendously fallacious principle that is still at work in much of Christianity and that was only present in higher relief in monasticism. A major part of organized Christianity, like the monastic life, openly justifies the subversion of the personal and social values of this world for the sake of the next.

Rome has traditionally called Trappists, Trappistines, and other cloistered monks and nuns its favorite children. Why wouldn't it? They're the most diligent of anyone in the church in giving up every trace of self-expression and self-determination. Rome's

gauge of excellence is the care individuals show for minutely prescribed church directives and, by consequence, for having no self-
determination in anything of consequence. Who in the Roman
curia would not love monks and nuns of the Trappist variety,
men and women who had given over every semblance of self-
direction to the church?

Being a Trappist novice was like having a doting mother who
cares not a whit whether her son grows into maturity, but only that
he respond to every whim of mama, be no trouble whatsoever to
control, be the model conformist in school, and then magically
graduate in a manner that will make mama proud of her totally
capable young man. The only thing that matters in this brand of
institutional formation is, as one rakish translator of church doctrine put it, "pie in the sky when you die by and by."

The year I entered the monastery was a holy year in Roman
Catholicism. It will be difficult for anyone who didn't live then to
appreciate how different from today were the attitudes in that era toward churches, especially among Catholics. Catholicism was counting its burgeoning membership with glowing gratification. It was
the day of the nationally broadcast Monsignor Fulton J. Sheen,
who spoke across sectarian lines and regularly made cases for despising the progress of this world for the sake of the next. It was the
era of Pope Pius XII, who routinely held audiences for world-class
scientists, historians, and scholars, many of whom listened to him
as to an oracle when he expounded on virtually all topics. It was an
era of increasingly widespread education, when Catholicism was
reaping the benefits of a backlash against the anti-intellectualism of
so many Protestant denominations—*and* when the intellectual
riches of the Catholic tradition blinded many from noticing some
less-evident accompanying corollaries.

The thirteenth had been the greatest of all centuries, intoned
the church, and society was on the way to restoring that Rome-
dominated era and culture in all its glory. God's Kingdom—the
Holy Roman, Catholic and Apostolic church—was at last resum-
ing the world leadership she had lost at the time of the unfortunate

revolt of protesters in the sixteenth century and during the lamentable Enlightenment that followed.

During the years I was in the abbey, priests and monks were obliged to swear and sign a solemn oath against the "errors of Modernism." And they did it with vigor—I did it with vigor. I signed it twice: before solemn vows in 1955 and again before ordination as a priest in 1958. By 1958, however, I did it with the beginnings of a grimace.

There is probably no more monumental witness to Christianity's intrinsic and long-standing fear of progress and change and its practical rejection of human resources than this Catholic oath against Modernism. It, and the requirement for it, were instituted in 1910 by Pope Pius X, understandably later canonized a saint as the quintessential institutional man. Protestants didn't have a Pius X or his oath to deal with, but in their own way many of them had the same problem. The evangelicals and fundamentalists among them had so rejected belief in the validity of human reason in favor of a literal reading of and belief in the words of the Bible that any possibility for "errors of Modernism" was ruled out. They added this anti-intellectual stance to an even more basic one that they held in common with Catholicism: disdain for this world as a mere place of bivouac and testing on the way to a reward in the sky.

And what was the Modernism we swore to forever oppose? A whole conglomerate of ideas, any and all of which the church feared might shake the familiar paradigm of there being one church meant to define guidance and doctrine for the whole human race. Nothing was ever to change, we swore, in how the church long ago defined itself. We would never grow enthusiastic about even the possibility of an ongoing deepening of the human race's understanding of eternal things. We would forever hold that the ultimate truth was already and finally, completely, contained in unchangeable church doctrine. We would never wander by wondering if faith might actually be something more than intellectual assent, never err into believing it might be something that could involve the *whole* person. Most of all, we would never

doubt the supremacy of a papal authority that was to tell everyone what they could, should, and damn well better believe.

The monastery held this reactionary, simplistic, self-submerging
view and multiplied it into every detail of life. All answers were
provided. Quoting Jesus in a manner as ridiculous as it was arbitrary, the abbot regularly reminded his monks that anyone who
obeyed the abbot was obeying God, and anyone who did not, was
not. Every single action was assured of being right if it was prescribed or permitted by Holy Mother Church, which, tugging
confidently on her own bootstraps, proclaimed in a loud voice that
it was God's voice we were hearing. As did the abbot she had set
over us. This overseeing by the church and our divine-right abbot
was total.

A minuscule monastic practice of that era illustrates this self-
reduction well and deserves careful preservation as the outrageous
prank of uproarious angels that it is, a prank played on overly
pious men, a monument to the inane extremes reachable by organized religion.

During my years in the abbey it was the custom for monks to
file singly past the abbot and bow profoundly to him when leaving the abbey church after the last bit of choir duty of the day. The
bow was a sign of our belief in him as God's representative. For
the first thirteen years that I was in the abbey, there was a detail in
that ceremony that probably went unnoticed by visitors. While
bowing to the abbot, we would, if nature demanded, raise the
sleeve of our cowl to our lips to request his permission to visit the
toilets before going to our individual cells for the night. He would
grant divine endorsement for this blessed event by nodding his
head. I have never, before or since, urinated with such a conscious
sense of heavenly support! Today, when nature calls, I simply go
somewhere and peacefully pee, never even considering the possibility of asking permission from anybody—so far have I fallen into
the errors of Modernism.

Somebody telling me when to urinate was not exactly what I
needed in my life then. But since I thought it was a question of

spiritual growth to embrace everything put before me, I eagerly
conformed and obeyed and waited with anticipation for my su-
periors to spell out ever-greater detail as to how God wanted me
to hold my face while I thought the thoughts they told me He
wanted me to think. That description, unfortunately, is fact and
not fiction. And it was the practice of a whole monastery of men,
not just of one admittedly neurotic fledgling. If Trappists in those
days carried dependence to extremes and turned the church's expectation into caricature, and we certainly did, it was from conscious hunger for holiness as much as from unconscious neurotic
self-diffidence. I recognized the diffidence only in myself then, but
in retrospect I notice there were no senior monks around free
enough of the same drives to pull junior monks back from such
silliness. Monks far more mature than I were asking permission to
urinate right alongside us newcomers.

Indignant Catholic churchmen will hotly deny the picture I've
just painted. Unfortunately for their position, there are countless
inactive priests, ex-monks, ex-nuns, ex-lay people—"recovering
Catholics," as many call themselves—who have abandoned the
church, and sometimes all religion, simply because what I'm re-
counting here was so oppressively true.

Few women will feel the need to be so defensive, because they
had no share in running the church in those days and so have nothing to defend. (I remember a world meeting of abbots in the mid-
sixties that even pondered the question of how often Trappistine
nuns, who were allowed no role in ruling the Trappist order, could
launder their stockings. The abbots legislated a decision that was
then published in all Trappist and Trappistine monasteries in the
world.) With the exception of a few abbesses and mother superi-
ors, women in the church have always been on the receiving end
of its solicitous micromanagement, and share no blame for the
foolishness of its extremes.

Our abbot had two favorite and frequent complaints. He complained in front of the whole community almost daily when one
of his flock failed somehow to show unquestioning conformity to

the church's, the order's, or his own dictates and style. With the same regularity, he lamented that he could not find sufficient numbers of monks mature enough to entrust with management of the monastery's material needs and economic survival. He never seemed to recognize the inconsistency of these two attitudes.

Apart from my reasoned and deliberate choice to practice such obedience, how did I *feel* day after day, year after year, as this plowing continued on my back? Friends have asked since if I didn't resent it. But that is to miss my point. I did *not* resent it, did *not* feel badly directed or abused by it, so deeply were my mentors and I convinced that I was doing my divine duty well. Slowly, over the years, monk after monk began to recognize the silliness of it all, and the monastery dropped from a high of eighty-three monks to about twenty-five in the years after I left. But until that awareness set in, we swallowed whatever they gave us.

I write candidly and admit the degree of my foolishness during these years in the abbey, because my story cannot be understood otherwise. One has to recognize illness to appreciate healing. My tale will, however, always say more about church management and organizational interests perpetrated upon monks and millions of Catholics around the world than it does about any individual. The first of the two abbots under whom I lived, Dom Mauritius, an old Dutchman of warmest memory, once told me in high approval that he had never seen so much zeal in a novice to accomplish the tasks set before him. He never once remonstrated with me about my lack of maturity.

12

Shenanigans

I didn't know it at the time, and, in view of my eventual solemn vows to God, would have been frightened by the thought, but I began leaving the monastery the day I entered it, exactly as students begin moving toward graduation the day they enter college. And in both cases, moving on implies more than just an accumulation of facts. It implies growth.

Novices in Trappist life typically experience a severe crisis soon after entering. Shorn of hair; wearing stiff, canvaslike underclothing and scratchy woolen outer garments both day and night; shorted of sleep on stone-hard straw mattresses; locked in a silence never punctuated by recreation, sports, or conversation; spending five to eight hours each day in choir; forbidden under pain of eternal hell to even think about masturbation; fed on a diet of bread and boiled vegetables with no meat, fish, or eggs, seldom butter, and only sometimes milk or cheese; the majority of new monks in my day quickly decided to run their vocational plans through the computer one more time.

Shortly before I left the monastery in 1967, I researched the personnel records it had become my duty to maintain. Roughly five percent of those men who applied to the abbey were eventually admitted, and, curiously, five percent of those admitted were still there five years later to make their solemn vows.

The crisis that hit most soon after they entered didn't even come close to me until years later—seventeen years later. When I finally did come to feel what many healthier men had felt within weeks of entering, I saw that what I had been doing all the intervening time was catching up with those who were individuated enough to leave sooner. I had once felt sorry for them, for those who "failed," as we called it. But I gained much from staying. For me, monastic life was at least as much therapy as it was education.

My appreciation of cloistered life changed substantially during my time in it. For the first eleven years or so, I loved it for its great dignity, its in-depth and protracted training, its open-ended potential for idealism, and, unknowingly, for the effective escape it offered to my lingering fear and guilt. Starting out in the neurotically pure delight of having my life run for me by others, and continuing for a time in the infantile joy and superficial semblance of peace that such submission provides the insecure, I slowly evolved until eventually I found myself running afoul of much of the edifice in which I had until then found my security. During my last six years in the abbey, I felt a growing and increasingly defined criticism for what many of my fellow monks and I had come to see as the confused priorities of local and Rome-based managers.

This growing criticism somehow peacefully coexisted with a lingering love for the daily unfolding of monastic living. Apart from how monasteries were being ruled and many of their outdated usages, I loved almost every minute I was a monk. One of the most difficult parts of monastic life for me was actually something trivial: the smell of bacon being cooked for the guest dining room every Sunday morning. I had never been a meat eater, with the exception of bacon, and now my predilection for it had to contend with its smell wafting through the cloisters every Sunday as I walked in single-file procession to the refectory to have my morning bread and barley coffee. There was one consolation: on Sundays we were allowed jam or, more rarely, butter to go with the bread. And in 1956, real coffee was substituted for that made from roasted barley. For all the years I was in the abbey, however, I could still smell bacon cooking every Sunday morning.

During my first two years there, I was a novice, dressed completely in white, except for the denim habits we wore when working outdoors. My college education was interrupted for daily classes in spirituality, meditation, and the history of monasticism, particularly of the Trappist order, officially named the Order of Cistercians of the Strict Observance, or, more simply, Trappists. After two years as a novice, the community voted to accept me as a member of the community, and I made my temporary vows and became a "simple professed." This meant that I was given the hooded black scapular that has been characteristic of Cistercians since their founding in 1098. At the end of that three-year period, the community voted again to accept me, permanently this time, and I chanted my solemn vows during the solemn Mass in the abbey church, vows *usque ad mortem*—"until death." I was now known as one of the "solemnly professed" monks. These five vows meant that I agreed that, for the glory of God and the salvation of souls, including my own, I would for the rest of my life on this earth be perfectly chaste, would own nothing whatsoever, would obey the abbot and church authorities in all good things, would never leave the abbey for any reason whatsoever except the need for hospitalization, and would never quit striving for perfection. When I sat down amid the senior monks on the evening of August 15, 1955, in my great white cowl, the outer garment that covered the black scapular and white tunic beneath it, I was a full-fledged Trappist at last, and fully determined to remain one until death.

During my three years of simple profession, I had continued my college studies. Philosophy had been a delight to me from the time of the USAFI correspondence course in Greek philosophy in the Philippines. It had intrigued me at Carroll College and did so even more in the abbey. We did our studies in Latin, and this gave us the very real advantage of being able to read many ancient and medieval texts in their original language. The monastery received no newspapers or nontheological periodicals, and it had no "secular" books, but it had a huge library of volumes about philosophy, theology, the Bible, and the history of thought. I read voraciously. Some months before my solemn vows, I was ready to leave the study of philosophy for that of theology.

The daily routine of choir duty, meditation, study, and work continued virtually without change from day to day over the years. Christmases and Easters came and went. Trappists in my era had neither televisions nor radios. A Korean War came and almost went before the abbot, who alone was permitted to read the daily *Salt Lake Tribune,* told us about it. A president was shot, and for some reason the abbot told us the same day. A pope died, and the abbot kept us posted on each detail of the election of a new one. Eventually the abbot even posted color photos from *Life* magazine showing the old pope's burial and the new pope's coronation. Postulants became novices, novices became junior monks, and junior monks became senior monks. More and more monks completed the long studies for the priesthood and were ordained. Brother Stanislaus and Father David were forever trying to find new spots in the church in which to build additional altars so all the priests could offer their daily Mass without having to queue for the few available. Until after I had left the monastery, the liturgy never changed as much as a word in its annual cycle.

Such a life would have been lethally boring but for the inner dimension, which was our whole reason for being there and what we were busy doing beyond appearances. The monastery was a place where one learned to contact God, where one ordered his whole life to do precisely—and only—that.

The surface of the pond was without ripple, but early in the 1960s, new currents were beginning to move beneath the seeming tranquility. Some of us were uncovering forgotten selves and sensed a heretofore unknown restlessness. The abbots of the Trappist order, with a few remarkable exceptions, reacted by marching smartly backward. One conservative side began digging in as the progressives began to dig out.

In fairness to the abbots and their cohorts of the vested, the contented, the uncomprehending, many of us were not discreet in how we exercised our new insights. We were like young adults sprung free at last on first dates after having been grounded for all those years when others our age had wooed their personal autonomy, lost their virginity to recklessness, and subsequently grown up. We were spiritually sophisticated, indeed, but in many other ways still children toying with first freedoms. The antics that began to fill our days were games of adult boys on the way, at last, to becoming men.

Some of the experiences that came splashing into our tranquil pond were innocent, some subtle, some outright puerile. Some arose from genuine conflict and were laughable only to a few of us. Some monks were learning to fly and others, not remotely interested in flying, contorted extravagantly—and hilariously—to avoid getting hit.

Unless one has been there, it's difficult to realize that a way of life as severe as that of Trappists is a dependably lighthearted one. Alertness to disproportion—to humor, that is—will never be lost on an individual or group when its spirituality is genuine. Honest spirituality always provides enough security to let one react spontaneously, and not infrequently spurs one to act outrageously. There was always plenty of humor in the monastery, and it would be unfair to give the impression that it was all severity and dissatisfaction. The disproportion that is humor had always been decidedly tame by sophisticated entertainment standards, and now it began to be creative.

Brother Ferdinand, for example, was the monastery tailor, known both for the fastidious elegance he inherited from his wealthy hotel-owning parents in Germany and for his surprising ways of skirting most rules, especially the rule of silence. One Sunday afternoon in the mid-1960s, a pious mole discovered him frolicking in a moment of stolen freedom and in what the old brother had imagined was a securely isolated part of the monastic lands. He had built himself a mud slide amid reeds growing along the bank of an irrigation canal and naked, covered with mud, he used it again and again for a splash landing in the canal. The peeping Tom reported him to the abbot for being "seriously immodest in his nonattire" and for breaking silence by singing songs that were, forsooth, clearly not chant. The abbot was significantly less than amused. Some of us, however, were thoroughly regaled and quickly, quietly sailed to the brother's support by reassuring him in our now rapidly expanding sign language that he was a model of the modern monk.

On another occasion another brother, Nicholas this time, prepared a mixture of peanut butter and fresh cow manure, put the concoction into a small prescription jar, and arranged that it be clandestinely delivered to one of the monks hospitalized in Ogden's Catholic hospital, Saint Benedict's. A note accompanying the jar informed the ill brother that the abbot had obtained this special remedy from Europe and now required that the brother spread it on his chest three times daily. Furthermore, he was not to let the doctors, nuns, or nurses see the medicine, lest they be offended by his use of something not provided by the local medical establishment. The monk obediently did as he was told. A few days later, Sister Mary Margaret, administrator of the hospital, phoned the abbot to say the doctors feared the hospitalized monk would have to be detained in the hospital longer than had been planned. Some kind of strange rash of offensive odor was appearing on his chest. When the full story finally came out, the abbot was aghast. His older council members were aghast. The rest of us were aghast, but only in the sense of being astonished at the devilish creativity of Nicholas.

The summer of 1966 was a watershed of what the abbot called rebellion. And he only knew a small part of what was going on in his monastery. Each Sunday, for example, unknown to him until much later, several monks showed up for noon choir duty clad in blue jeans with legs turned up so they wouldn't be seen beneath the choir robes. The jeans were chosen simply because they were readily available—and so clearly *un*monastic. They were borrowed from what the abbot believed to be a securely locked "secular clothing room," a place where the clothing of new arrivals was returned to them as they returned to the world or was kept until it was eventually given away after they made solemn vows. It took little effort to realize that these jeans, and the wearing of them, symbolized new freedom, earthiness, masculinity, toughness. As soon as choir duty was over, the jean-clad monks would walk by separate routes and with mysterious haste into the nearby hills. There they met, doffed their monastic robes, and, stripped to the waist in the hot sun, enjoyed each other's sparkling conversation and sometimes a good smoke provided by a cooperative guest, yet another arbitrary symbol of earthiness, independence, rebellion. There were three hours to wander and chat about absolutely anything that came to mind until the half-hour warning bell called everyone back for vespers. I joined this exotic crew in the hills one Sunday afternoon, wearing my first Levi's and experiencing my first nonspiritual conversation in sixteen years. The topic that day, I remember, turned on a book about cybernetics that Father Bonaventure had somehow managed to get, one all of us knew the abbot would not have permitted into the monastery stacks. I am fairly certain that none of us ever felt it necessary to mention these jaunts into the hills when we made our weekly confessions, simply because there was nothing wrong, in our revised thinking, to confess.

Ten months later I would leave the monastery. I have never felt the need to confess that either.

Sometimes fate seemed to connive with us to bring some flash of humanness, even outrageousness, into our lives. Trappist drawers in that era were canvaslike items that tied at the waist. Their drawstrings, too, were strips of this heavy material that were difficult to keep tied until they had been laundered often enough to lose their stiffness. One day at solemn high Mass, Father Brendan's heavy drawers came untied and fell down around his ankles as he presided at the high altar in full view of the choir of monks and a balcony full of guests. Brendan's creative dance was unforgettable as he struggled to reach through the layers and layers of the monastic and liturgical robes of his high function to hoist and retie his intimate apparel. Some monks were embarrassed. Some simply entertained.

Father David was noteworthy for his lack of skill at the rostrum in the refectory, where reading always accompanied the monks' daily meal. One year during Holy Week, when the text was a commentary on the trial of Jesus that preceded his execution, David droned on: "...and from inside the house of the High Priest Jesus looked out into the courtyard and saw Peter mingling with the soldiers and warming his hands at a brazier." Unfortunately— or fortunately, as one may prefer—David didn't carefully distinguish the last word and read "and saw Peter warming his hands at a brassiere." The refectory exploded in laughter, except for the abbot who sat at his high table trying desperately to set an example of appropriate decorum. David looked up from his reading and wondered what could be causing such an unfitting display during the most somber week of the year. This time he had even surpassed an earlier performance when he read to us that Jesus asked his disciples to observe the poor widow putting her two "mitts"—no longer "mites"—into the temple's poor box.

Father Anselm was one of the community's organists and could always be depended on to add a beat or insert a catchy chord if the chant was dragging or going awry. He had some sort of bladder problem that required frequent urination. During the liturgy of a solemn high Mass there is a moment when everyone stands at attention to listen to the singing of a selection from one of the gospels. On one particular Sunday this interval was too short for Anselm to make a round trip to the restroom before he was due back at the keyboard for the ongoing liturgy. Standing during this silent lull, with the long sleeves of his voluminous cowl hanging empty at his sides, he was heard urgently urinating into a bottle, which, it turned out, he had kept hidden in the organ chest for just such emergencies. When I was later speaking with the abbot, whose secretary and assistant I had become, I suggested that we might look into the possibility of getting Anselm a silencer. It was good to see the abbot laugh.

Despite all the abbot's narrowness in interpreting monastic usages—and in that he was only typical of abbots of his time—he was a naturally jovial person. For the six years I had my office next to his, I often heard him laughing with one or other of the monks who was visiting him. Like everyone else at the abbey, he had to be lighthearted in some sense, because stiff and serious monks don't last. Contrary to what many imagine, extroverts make for more adjusted monks. A silent life never punctuated by recreation or casual conversation and filled with prayer and studies, by its nature drives one inward and keeps him there most of the time. If a monk's natural tendency doesn't draw him back out, he may well fall into a pit and never make it out until a therapist fishes him out. I saw that happen more than once. Fortunately, some of us were able to enjoy Trappist silence without worry because our natural tendency was forever pressing us to interact, a smile of recognition here, a few signs there, and a natural, common buoyancy in general. Those of us who stayed somehow learned to enjoy the best of both worlds, community and aloneness, in an abbey dedicated to silence.

Some of the experiences of monastery life were perpetrated by frantic managers and were not in any sense humorous. The one that stands out in my memory as the most painful of all reveals an insensitivity and crudeness that defies suitable response.

After the decision was made one year to get rid of the flock of sheep owned by the abbey, Spes, a border collie who had been an indispensable part of their care, suddenly became dispensable in the abbot's scheme of things. "Monks are not supposed to have pets," was his frequent *ex-cathedra* explanation as he complained over and over that he had seen some monk petting the dog. His demand, however, could not be taken seriously, for the dog, as dependably loyal and loving as he was intelligent, had long since become closely attached to several of us, and we, certainly, to him. He was part of the family.

Every workday I had at least an hour of free time after leaving my office and before vespers. Spes was always at the appropriate abbey door waiting excitedly. Together we'd be off for a walk in the hills. A true friend, he seemed always on the verge of saying something.

One day he didn't appear for our walk. Nor was he there the next day. When he was missing for a third day, I asked the brother in charge of the abbey farm in sign language if he'd seen the dog. With a totally flattened affect, he signed back that the abbot had told him to take Spes out and shoot him and he had done so.

I stood speechless as Brother Cyril, who had been a Marine on Iwo Jima, walked indifferently away. Shooting things had been a horrendous part of his past, and it was not difficult to overlook his insensitivity. The abbot, however, had no such excuse. I felt a violent anger well up within me on the instant and, as by accustomed reflex, formed a simple prayer that was as unexpected as the news about the dog. "Holy Spirit, help me handle this!" was all I said. A third thing followed so quickly that it could have been the third count of a one-measure waltz. It was as if a whole treatise, with arguments and conclusions, were put before me in an instant. The moment Cyril turned to go, I saw the situation in a completely different light and with a clarity about the abbot that I had never seen before. There was much more involved here than the betrayal of a dog's trust and love. Cyril was not an appropriate target for my emotion, but neither was the abbot.

It didn't surprise me that I easily got past anger for Cyril, but it did surprise me—and I could have resented this had I permitted myself to—that I let the abbot off the hook so easily. The insight was that my emotion should be targeted not at the abbot, but at a religious system that had so corrupted his natural temperament, which, until he was elected abbot, had made him one of the most popular priests in the abbey. What deserved condemnation, I saw with a clarity I had never before experienced, was the demand in his office that had, here as elsewhere, overwhelmed his naturally warm humanity. It had pressed him into a mechanical insensitivity of which he would never have been capable on his own.

I heard another click on a scoreboard somewhere inside of me, a mechanism I didn't know was there, much less yet know its purpose. It was keeping tabs for that day almost upon me when monastic life, for all its beauty and ideals, would be judged by my heart and found wanting.

13

Reassessing an Education

Prayer was the monastery's and each monk's stabilizing anchor. The community survived despite whatever bits of humanity broke through here and there. It even survived the tumultuous changes that were no longer simply the insights of insignificant revolutionaries like ourselves, but, after the election of Pope John XXIII in 1958, were those of the reigning pontiff.

A few years after his influence began to be felt, some of us saw we could now drop our weapons as the new and unfamiliar things we'd been struggling for began to be official. The pudgy little man now on the papal throne even brought into line the heretofore arbitrarily all-powerful annual meeting of Trappist abbots in France and two particularly powerful old cardinals in Rome who, by insisting on their medieval opinions about how monks were to live, had caused Trappist monks so much grief.

The reign of the new pope, and what became known in the world press as his *Aggiornamento* (updating), occasioned countless changes to be felt in the abbey. It was suddenly permissible to criticize and then change usages that for many years, and in some cases for centuries, had been no more timely than buggy whips. Instead of praying three disparate sets of liturgies in choir (the traditional one plus one in honor of the Virgin Mary and another for the dead), we suddenly had but one. We stopped whipping ourselves every Friday morning. There were better ways to show compassion to Jesus in his suffering. Food improved, at least a little. Fifteen minutes were added to our night's sleep.

Changes were suddenly fashionable. Our new leader at the top was formulating the very insights that we in the hinterland had been feeling and fomenting in our communities for years. We recognized the same awakening, the same evolution—the same *revolution*—in the pope that we felt within ourselves. Some monks, of course, like many heavily vested cardinals in Rome and bishops around the world, were frightened by the whole specter of change and saw no need for it. Some with whom I lived all my time at the monastery have stayed on, and now, twenty-seven years later, are still there. I can only hope that, having missed their chance under John XXIII, they have at least by now found an appreciation for their humanity and personal fulfillment that most of us had either not dreamt of or felt it our monastic duty not to want, much less seek, in the pre-John era.

By 1963, the abbot, in his daily talks to all the monks in the chapter room and not yet influenced by Pope John XXIII's revolution, was routinely berating the community for its "rising spirit of rebellion," its "unconscionable lack of monastic spirit." Some of the oldest monks, long securely jelled in obedience, sucked their teeth in dismay and nodded their agreement. Those of us who were glad to be a part of the new church-wide happening sat listening to the abbot with feelings of indifference, resolution, even amusement. The dwindling number of novices watched the abbot in confusion, with no idea of what he was carrying on about. Since these new members of the community were carefully protected in an isolated novitiate from the rest of the monastery and its growing pains, none of us could explain the situation to them. We were not permitted to talk to one another, much less to novices.

What we were pushing had nothing whatsoever to do with rebellion. We were as earnest in our vows and religious commitment as was the abbot. Right beside him, we proved it daily by persevering in what was, at best, an extremely severe way of life. What we were seeking was growth, wholeness, *fulfillment,* and not change for its own sake.

But insights and influences had accumulated, and many in the abbey had started to take a second look at what they were doing there and why. We came to regard the strict rule of perpetual silence first with suspicion, and then with contempt. We had believed that curtailing communication with one another would result in a greater degree of communication with God, and it did help to develop our sense of God's presence. But over the years we had come to realize that a failure to communicate with others has its own counterproductive effect. It's not that we wanted to speak with God less, but that we had come to realize that communicating more openly with one another helps rather than hinders that divine exchange. As Father Gregory, a feisty monk with an acute intellect, pointed out to the abbot during this period, the "supernatural" life the abbot was forever demanding of his monks doesn't walk around by itself. It has no way to express itself except with and through the *natural* life: "just as it did in Jesus!" Gregory added. Spirituality, even the high mysticism to which we all aspired, is experienced in and through our natural lives or it is not experienced at all. Before Pope John, giving an honored place to human conversation and respecting the potential in us all for *human* growth was a sign of insubordination to abbots who were not given to being instructed. Most of us applauded Gregory and carried on more determined than ever to put added emphasis on being human while still being passionately monastic.

If our insights about renewal were characterized by diminishing patience and a weakening willingness to be subservient to outdated traditions in Trappist regimen, it was because the lid had been kept on the kettle too long and too tightly. Eating boiled vegetables and dry bread every day meant that every day we felt in our stomachs, if nowhere else, that our particular lifestyle required *exceptionally* defensible meaning to make it worthwhile. Lacking that, it was a neurotic prostitution of human nature, of *our* human nature.

Trappist monks had no movies, newspapers, television, radio, sports, novels, or vacations to distract them from the spiritual matter at hand. Even our program of studies was not like that of a typical seminary, where weekends offer a change of pace, weekdays include afternoon sports, and there is always the camaraderie of an evening meal. We had no comparable releases in the monastery. We lived close to each other, but were humanly very alone. There was no form of recreation whatsoever. We simply *had* to have substantially cogent reasons to keep going. Doctrinal bromides and reassurances of ancient abbots, bishops, and popes had long seemed adequate reason to carry on without question, but they were so no longer.

Church managers may or may not have been conscious of the risk they were running when they prescribed a singularly hefty study program for their monks. While they did tightly control the content of that study, the very extent of it ensured that our powers of reasoning were being honed and honed again. Trained minds blossoming in a developing race, newly critiquing all of yesterday's givens, ultimately undermined the unquestioning conformity church legislators had intended and for centuries had achieved.

It should have been self-evident to managers throughout the church that informed minds will eventually use their powers to sift and sort and analyze whatever information and directives have been poured into them. Sooner or later, even the most sacred cows are going to be given fairly detailed physical exams. It was inevitable that well-trained priests, monks, and nuns everywhere would begin arriving at informed and distinctly gutsy conclusions independent of whether these were intended by church leaders or not.

In organized religion generally, and in Roman Catholicism particularly, it was sufficient in previous times to defend a doctrine or demand by stating that Jerome, Augustine, Aquinas or some other traditional luminary had taught it. What was adequate persuasion in a more credulous era had become ludicrous by 1964. The church, after all, with the authority and threat that it now used to demand conformity, had once taught that the earth was at the center of a universe that revolved around it, that the earth was flat, and that the stars were spiritual entities with significant control over human lives.

Bring a crowd of military veterans into heretofore sheeplike cloisters and put them through elaborate studies, and you have set the stage for wrinkled brows, difficult questions, and finally a revolution where previously everyone had lived in hushed, unquestioning conformity. The boat will surely rock.

And rock it we did.

One day I asked Father Thomas, a professor of moral theology, why the church's rejection of birth control was held to be adequately justified by a simple appeal to natural law, when the same "law" is ignored in identical applications elsewhere. He furrowed his brow, and, pressured by a now curious class, reluctantly asked me to explain my question. Catholicism has always taught that to dam the flow of semen by condoms or other forms of birth control, or to "spill" it in masturbation, is eternally damnable and will send the perpetrator to hell. "Such acts deny the seed its natural, God-intended purpose" went the institutional wisdom. Why, then, I asked the professor, does the church not equally condemn our grinding of wheat to make bread and our crushing of grapes to make wine? Wheat kernels and grapeseeds are, just as clearly as human seeds, intended by nature to reproduce their own kind. Sacrificing the former for food flies in the face of natural law every bit as much as do condoms and spermicides. Could it actually be God's will that horses eat oats and thus deny those innocent seeds their natural reproductive goal—or is that practice, too, but a result of "original sin"?

The professor was aghast and, significantly, had no answer.

Shortly afterward the abbot called me into his office and spoke to me about their common concern for my faith. I reassured him I was full of faith, but while faith for me might at times exceed the reach of reason, I refused to let it ever contradict reason. I went on to wonder, in his presence, if most or all church doctrines and practices did not require reevaluation now that the human race was becoming more broadly educated and less uncritically credulous. The abbot heard, I think, not a word I was saying, such organizational filters did he have over his ears. He was a brilliant man, and, but for those filters, would have been out front with the rest of us rethinking the nonsense we have inherited from the church's past.

By 1960, when I finished formal studies for the priesthood, two years after being ordained (a common practice in monasteries where studies stretch substantially beyond the usual seminary curricula), I was a restless and well-trained monk. And I had only begun formulating questions, questions that I was addressing most of all to myself.

Studies had been demanding, but I still had ample time for substantial amounts of additional research in the abbey library. Even after my classes were completed, I continued to read voraciously, and the insights began to come once I started daring to do my own thinking.

A statement in a book by the French philosopher Jacques Maritain startled me one evening in a way I shall remember forever. I was sitting in the chapter room, the place where monks gather before going into the church for the final bit of choir duty at the end of each day. This is evening chapter, during which the abbot briefly addresses the community and then one of the monks reads from a spiritual or philosophical work for about fifteen minutes, a leftover from the centuries when only priests and students for ordination could read. I remember staring wide-eyed at the reader after he had read a sentence from Maritain that instantly became for me a major breakthrough.

I can no longer name Maritain's specific book, much less quote verbatim his actual sentence, but he wrote something to the effect that none of us will ever move beyond the mechanical, institutional, legalistic formulations of "faith" and get to its actual content unless and until we gain a contemplative experience of existence. In less metaphysical terms, he was saying that we must take care lest we forever prattle on in kosher formulae and never go after a far deeper grasp of the meaning and the experience of existing.

That chapter room event was my first indication that the thrust of my urgency to get well, to grow, would demand that one day I break out of every monastic mold of conformity. Maritain hooked something in me I didn't yet understand, and for most of my years in the monastery would have been frightened by had I understood it. But life is a process, and process is why we're here. Process takes time, and that's what time is for. First I gained fleeting insights, then fuller and fuller understanding, and eventually the time arrived when I was invited to act on that understanding. And finally I found I had the courage to act.

In the end, it was not studies or intellectualizing, or even the hours of chanted prayer in choir, but meditation itself that gave me such a new and undeniable experience of my existence that I dared to launch out on my own. From classes, reading, and consultation with my spiritual master I gained new conceptual tools with which to better understand Reality, yes. And these were priceless. But it was the actual *experiencing* of that Reality in meditation, as I have explained, that caused my tires to touch the road and carry me out of fear-based conformity to freedom.

The course of studies on the road to the priesthood at the abbey required that we inch our way through every page of the thirteenth-century *Summa theologica* of Aquinas and through much of his *Summa contra gentiles*. We plowed—groaned—through a soporific, four-volume, fine-print-Latin exposé of the theology of morality (as a certain Italian organization man, Professor Fanfani, understood morality, that is). Course by course we marched through the seven traditional facets of scholastic philosophy, and were always studying one aspect or other of the Bible. A few ancillary subjects like church history, canon law, and "sacred eloquence" (how to give a homily) were added. But to have said all that is only to have reproduced a page from a college catalog. It's to have said nothing about the real nature of monastic studies.

Listing courses doesn't mention the impact that meditative silence and choir duty seven times a day has on those studies.

When we start to meditate with regularity, something happens inside that absorbs, reshapes, and infuses everything we think and feel and do. Until then we may have thought our inner life was made up of thoughts and feelings only, with an intuition thrown in here and there. Meditation opens a higher and deeper, more expanded and more centered dimension—a dimension that begins to shape our lives long before we're conscious of it. When meditation becomes a significant part of each day, everything else in our days appears in its beyond-the-physical—"metaphysical"—and, properly understood, "spiritual" context. This isn't a conscious process, and we may not become aware of it for a long time. But it happens inevitably.

In a life lived in silence, the impact of philosophy, theology, and sacred writings quickly transcends all the specific data being learned. Study indirectly assists meditation, but meditation substantially transforms study. Study is suddenly more than a matter of learning facts; it becomes an integral part of an inner adventure.

Studying to become an ordained priest in a monastery is one thing in church managers' minds, but it's something else for the men they send through it. Monastic studies can precipitate more than what these churchmen had in mind—something, in fact, quite opposed to what they had in mind. The freedom that resulted for many of us after our protracted training didn't come merely because we had dedicated professors and a fine library. It resulted because of the meditative context with which monastic life supplemented the studies. Accumulation of facts doesn't set one free; what one does with, how one experiences, those facts is what sets one's heart dancing in freedom.

It was in meditation that I caught my first glimpse of the transcendental experience of Existence that Maritain had written about. And it was that experience, when more complete, that freed me once and for all from dogmatism, fear, dependence, and the obsessive gyrations of anxious self-perpetuation in institutionalized religion.

It is impossible to say when this happened other than to say it was the process of many years. Slowly—*very* slowly, for fear plays a powerful role when we start to reassess familiar faith—I began to see that my experience in meditation neither supported nor matched what the church told me about its big separate God. During my last year at the abbey, especially, I consciously met a Source within me that was far more like what Datus and I had read about in Emerson, Holmes, and the Hindus than what Catholicism had taught me.

The church, like Datus, had set out to teach me to pray, and even when it used the word *meditation,* it actually only meant inner prayer, mental prayer. In fact, willy-nilly, I moved beyond mental prayer and into the experience of meditation. I eventually saw that Datus, Kiefer, and Topel were correct and the monastery wrong about the ideal way to approach and respond to religious, transcendental fact—to God. Meditation is not a dissecting and deepening absorption of doctrine as Catholic practice, if not theory, presents it. Meditation is the experience of that Ultimate Reality, the *conscious* experience of it.

I could almost hear Datus heaving a sigh of relief when I began spending more and more time in private meditation, increasingly undistracted by the tabernacle on the high altar, totally turned inward to find there the Source and Self of all things.

Years later I found a Buddhist metaphor that aptly describes my state during my last year in the abbey. I was like a rock in a stream, smiling as it lets anything and everything float over and around it.

One of the retreatants who came to the abbey for a week of spiritual R and R during the spring of 1967 was General Westmoreland's chief of chaplains, back briefly from Vietnam. Free to talk to him as the monastery's retreat master for guests, I spent hours with him walking in the hills, he with his problems, I with mine. During this interchange with someone back from the

intensity of war, I began for the first time to see real-world implications to the insights I had gained. By the end of the week, I
suspected—also for the first time—what I had to do.

It took a special hour of meditation a couple of weeks later for
me finally to find the courage to tell myself, and only then the
abbot, that I had decided to leave the monastery.

That memorable meditation was a scary invitation that could
have been couched in words straight out of the Bible: Friend,
come up higher.

14

Intervention

It was the beginning of what seemed another predictable day at the abbey. From down the long cloister, I could hear the door of the scriptorium opening and closing as my brother monks moved in wordless silence to and from their prayers and books and endless writing. It was a familiar noise, a good noise. It was not even a distraction as I prolonged my meditation longer than usual after the night office. The aurora behind the mountains to the east of the abbey was just beginning to be faintly visible through the stained-glass window over the high altar.

For one who is absorbed in the business of a prayer that has become a wordless union with God, external noises are simply integrated into that reality. They register somehow on the superficial mind, which is to register on not much more than the senses, but they don't disturb the ongoing contact with one's most intimate Companion. Neither did the perpetually chattering birds out in the cloister garth now interrupt my silence as they had when I was a younger monk, when they and their racket had seemed a huge nuisance during my efforts to meditate.

As it had often done before, the abbey this morning reminded me of the troop ship that had once carried five thousand of us from San Francisco to Manila. At my spot near the altar dedicated to the Virgin Mary, which for centuries monks have called the Lady Altar, I seemed to be lying once again on the ship's topmost deck under a shawl of tropical stars, listening mesmerized as small motors, fans, and generators joined massive central diesels to chant a mechanical *ohmmm* out into the earth's oceans. My ship this time was a monastery riding high in the mountains of Utah, and it was sending its own deep-throated *ohmmm* out into a vastly deeper, infinitely broader cosmic sea.

I felt good as I lingered in a darkened corner in the church. Life had become a thing of peace, of fairly dependable happiness. That sense of calm was somewhat precariously possessed, it is true, but only because of the old habits of too much sensitivity and feelings of inadequacy that were still a part of me. In general, I enjoyed a sense of fairly detailed and confidently comprehended meaning about life, and what I too easily presumed would henceforward be its complete predictability. I figured I was now settled in as a permanent part of the purr of this ancient craft, and I felt good about being aboard—even if I did believe that some of its decks needed substantial swabbing.

Comfort, however, is not always in our best interest, and Divine Mirth was about to redirect my itinerary.

At first, I felt what seemed to be just an unusual, rather vague bodily disturbance, as soft as a loving touch awakening one from a pleasant dream. Rather quickly, though, it was as if my body were catching fire, so hot that it tingled—not a tingle of pain, but an absorbing sensation of great heat. For just an instant I felt panic as the heat grew to the point where reason suggested it must have health-related implications. As rapidly as that thought came, it was gone, and in its place I found myself incapable, as never before, of being troubled about it or anything else.

A statement I had read in the writings of Juliana of Norwich, the fourteenth century English mystic, and had even caught brief glimpses of in my own meditation, came to me now once again, but this time powerfully and with understanding: "All is well! All is forever well." The bliss that flows from this realization, and that the mystics speak of as transcending all the troubles of this world, had until that moment been only a theory to me, something I "believed in" simply because it was taught by great spiritual authorities. Now, for the first time, it became my experience.

The succession of bodily heat, reason's concern, and finally complete reassurance all happened within the span of a few seconds. As quickly as when lights come up in a theater, I saw the point being made. My tingling, burning body had accomplished in a few seconds what years of effort in meditation had not managed to do. Caught off guard, my mind's attention was so absorbed in the condition of my body that reason's reflex and analytical habits were shunted to the side. A lifelong predisposition to live in my head had meshed well into an almost bodiless life of study and thought in the abbey, and by the time of this experience at the Lady Altar, I was deeply formed in the habit of living almost entirely from my ears up. And now, unexpectedly, in a delightful and rewarding way that had never happened before, I was, as it were, surprised out of—beyond—my mind.

With greater perspective and more experience, I would later come to realize that in that moment I made my first real transition from a mental prayer that had simply moved the words of my mouth into my mind to a contemplation that uses no words at all, not even explicit thoughts. I moved from theorizing about Ultimate Reality to my first real experience of It.

It's not that this one episode forever and immediately jettisoned my old habits, but it was a new beginning for all future spiritual striving. My theology, spirituality, longings would still be based on theory and thought, but henceforward the reference point for God in my life would not be what books or professors had told me about, but what I had now experienced for myself. It was only one experience of one moment, but it was of such a nature that everything I had ever read or heard about God and unseen reality was changed forever.

Why at that particular moment? Well, why not? If not then, when? I'd been seeking such an experience for years, and the breakthrough eventually comes to all who seek it. Simply put, it was bound to happen eventually. And why the sensation of burning throughout my body? I didn't know it then, but after working with others on the same journey, I would later understand that surprising and unusual bodily sensations often accompany various stages of meditation and spiritual breakthroughs. They vary greatly, but they are common. The particular bodily distraction I experienced on this occasion was simply honed to my particular need. As my attention to thought was surprised by the distraction of a body that seemed to be catching fire, I was freed for a brief gap between thoughts to experience for the first time what silent attention without preponderant conceptual involvement is like. It was only a brief taste of the transcendent experience, but it was one that instantly and immeasurably multiplied my appetite for the experience of God. Meditation would never be the same for me again.

The mental shutdown that came to me that morning, accomplished so quickly as to leave no room for either choice or analysis, turned out to be only the preamble to the much greater shake-up that was coming into my life. During that instant when I was free of mental busyness, I found myself alive and well in my feelings in a new and astonishing way. I saw myself for the first time living in—coming from, assessing from, understanding from—my heart in a nonconceptual, nonanalytical, metalogical manner.

Unfamiliar? Indeed. Confusing? Only a bit. Frightening? Not at all. My new state was unusual, strikingly unusual, but as quickly as it happened, it was comfortable. And not without reward.

It was as if years in the convoluted reasoning processes of theology, philosophy, and psychology were for the moment set aside—not despised, not rejected, certainly not devalued, just set aside, bypassed, gone around. The One Life, One Mind, One

Being I had for the last year come to believe myself to be a part of, the Great Ultimate in which I had so long theoretically believed, was suddenly here. I was no longer just *thinking* about It as the Source of my own Life, Mind and Being, I was *experiencing* It to be just that.

My mind had been telling me for some time that Reality is in some mysterious manner One—mostly because all the mystics said so. Logic had then concluded that if all is One, then that One is clearly the only One there is. One is one is one. Each of us, therefore, must necessarily be a part of that One—one with the only One there Is. But this insight and conviction, like all faith, was only theory until it was experienced. What my head had been telling me in simple syllogisms, my feelings now experienced for the first time.

From my place near the Lady Altar, I could see the high altar where the Eucharist was kept in its little golden tabernacle. The Eucharist is what Catholics call the Real Presence because they believe Jesus is actually, physically present in it. From the moment I first read Cardinal Gibbons's explanation and defense of the real presence of Jesus in the Eucharist, I had not until this moment questioned it. And even now, what I found myself doing was not so much question it as begin to understand a deeper meaning in it. A new theology of the Eucharist seemed to be suddenly spelled out in my heart, and my heart, after all, was having the greater role in what was going on. My mind understood little yet, but my heart found itself sensing a larger dimension than Cardinal Gibbons and theology classes had ever taught.

A Real Presence of Jesus in the consecrated host? Well, yes and no. I now saw, felt, knew beyond any possibility of questioning that God was present not only in that small wafer, but in everything else whatsoever, wheresoever as well. Jesus was God's Son, of course, but *son* is a metaphor trying to represent the expressing—or, more clearly, and to clarify the Latin roots of that word, "outpressing"— of the Source Being as the young prophet Jesus of Nazareth and everyone and everything else. And in that sense, yes, God is present in the Eucharist up there on the altar. But He is equally present everywhere else as well.

The Sole Existence, the One Life, the Source Being is present in everything. There is one Life, one Being, one Existence that out-presses as all that is. The Eucharist may be a handy reminder of the universal Presence of God in everything, but it is only that, a reference point, a tool for ritualized worship and remembrance. In no way is the Real Presence in the Eucharist unique otherwise.

On the morning of the experience I am relating, I could never have explained what I just wrote. The substance of the break-through realization was there, but it would be some years before my mind would catch up with my experience. The realization was real, however, and from that moment, a problem disappeared that I had always had when trying to meditate in the abbey church. It had been confusing to find thoughts and spiritual feelings happening inside of me and yet, because of the theological conviction in my mind, having to refer all this inner transaction up to the Real Presence in the tabernacle on the altar. From this point onward, whatever was in the tabernacle was also in my heart.

With neither discursiveness nor argument, I found myself for an instant beyond all theology, all syllogisms, all doctrine. I was touching Bliss and, as anyone would, knew it instantly. Years later I would recognize Lao-tzu's opening statement of resigned frustration (aimed at all theologians, I guessed) in his *Tao Te Ching:* "The Tao that can be described is not the Tao." I suspect he had heard too many philosophers try to define the Tao. I myself had been busy for many years trying to do just that—and so had seen It as vastly more complex than It is. None of us can fully appreciate Lao-tzu's statement until we are *taken* beyond all description to touch what we have until then been circling within our thinking.

The experience itself lasted for a few seconds, the lingering glow of it, perhaps, for an hour, but it would take me several years to appreciate what had been taught in that brief time, to get my mind to step aside willingly and let the Wordless Event have the field. Wordless understanding and full acceptance were still off in the future, but the reality of the experience and the basic insight I have just described have remained indelible, unforgettable.

I knew, I felt—immediately, clearly, correctly—that my life had just been substantially changed. The *perceived* world that I had always known had just been illumined as being only an imagined separateness we have dreamed. If my mental prayer had just turned into meditation, my meditation was suddenly well along the way to becoming a dance.

The most unexpected result of this experience was that I found myself inwardly invited, almost to the point of being pressured, to get more energetically involved in the world's active process. After the morning's experience was over, it seemed not nearly so important to be off in a corner of the world and silent in order to cultivate a spirit of prayer and contemplation. The whole spiritual enterprise now seemed less fragile, more available. As days passed, the thought came to me again and again, with an unusual sort of inner urgency, that it might be time to leave my mountain valley, my abbey, my place of comfortable peace. It may be that I was now sufficiently healed of youthful neuroticism, or it may be that the theology of being a monk is flawed after a certain point of development. Or both. At any rate, it seemed clear that the abbey had now served its purpose for me. To remain longer would be escape or love of ease.

I began feeling a need to get out and start telling people about the inner side of religion I had now experienced. It's hard to keep a joy locked inside. I felt a new desire to help fix the human race *from the inside,* to remind people of the Ultimate Reality to which everyone must personally give permission if It is to enter their awareness.

In the two or three years before my experience at the Lady Altar, I had come to believe that the hurts, hungers, frights, and murders that run amuck in the human race would have to be fixed somehow—in a way I could not understand—from the inside.

Now I understood for the first time that all these problems are caused by a race asleep and thrashing about in its panicked nightmares. There will be wars and holocausts and genocides as long as God is portrayed and thought of as a tight-minded Legislator, a feudal Lord, an offended King, a hypersensitive Artisan—even if church managers condescendingly tack onto that ridiculous list the not-very-convincing footnote that He is also loving. As long as people dream on that they are insecure and needy and in some sort of eternal jeopardy, there will be atrocities. But as the human race grows up spiritually, and as individuals gain a personal experience of the God they have been worshipping in fear, they will recognize that much of their theology and philosophy is built on nightmares. That will be the day of the rethinking of presuppositions and of vested positions. That will be the day of peace. I suddenly found myself unwilling to sit it out in the mountains of Utah. I wanted to play an active role in the process of the world's awakening.

In its nightmares our race has piled up warnings, requirements, illusory explanations, and schedules of dues and punishments. And all the while the only real God—the Dancing One—has been forgotten. Nightmares have been preferred to the more gentle reality simply because people have never been told or found out for themselves they have another option. Church teachers have never quieted down long enough to find it out for themselves and to go beyond their seminary training that was wholly centered on the blatherings born of the fear of a young human race.

After this experience I realized that the only cure for everything from global problems to the sad face of one lonely person is that all sleepers must leave the counterfeit reality of painful dreams behind. I knew I had to continue to awaken myself, but I felt urged, too, to help others do so along with me.

The abbot was at a meeting of abbots in France when my breakthrough happened. By the time he returned two weeks later, I had made up my mind, and I still have a copy of the letter I wrote to him telling him of my decision to leave. In rereading it today, I see

how unsure I was despite my new clarity. "Dear Reverend Father
Abbot," it began in conformity to studied monastic protocol, and
then it waffled on in a defensive wordiness that was demanded not
by monastic protocol, but by my own lingering habits of diffidence. Although I had decided to leave, I hedged in telling him
so and floundered through a page and a half before getting to the
point. Even then, I didn't say, "I am going to leave," but "I think
I must leave. . . ." I was hesitant to tell him about a decision he
would view with contempt as that of a "fallen monk," the tag
commonly attached to those who proved to be "unfaithful to their
vows."

Although I had previously worked closely with him for six
years, he had by this time drawn away and was showing increasing disdain for me. I had clearly become one of his problems.
Neither my sermons in the chapter room to the assembled monks
nor my private conversations with him were ever proper enough.
His dismay was scarcely camouflaged any longer, and I suspected
he would see my letter as final confirmation of his all-too-evident
negative feelings about me.

Whatever he actually felt, my reluctance to talk to him about
leaving turned out to be unnecessary. Whether from relief at the
prospect of my going or in genuine support, he was courteous in
our exchange. I suggested that I go back to the navy, this time as
a chaplain, but he asked me to go instead to Notre Dame University
for a doctorate in liturgy, "so that if you decide to return you will
be of more use to the monastery." Fair enough.

As it turned out, Notre Dame was already into its summer session and would not accept a latecomer. Reluctantly, but kindly, the
abbot acceded to my desire not to delay until the fall quarter and
found me a spot in the summer session at the Jesuit University of
San Francisco (USF).

God bless the Jebies! I suspected they were going to be just what
I needed.

They were.

15

The World a Second Time

I was a well-educated, increasingly self-confident thirty-eight-year-old priest with an uncanny eye for ecclesiastical bullshit—and the testicular fortitude to call it what it is—when Brother Nicholas drove me to the Salt Lake City airport on a bright June day in 1967. I was off on an adventure I couldn't have fantasized six months before. Off to the City by the Bay for another graduate program in theology at the Jesuit University of San Francisco.

As we pulled away from the abbey and past the sign that was still promising its *pax* to all who entered, I remember being surprised at how easy it was for me to leave. I felt not a trace of guilt, fear, hesitation. *Au contraire!*—I was feeling vital, whole, in charge as never before. The singing in my heart made me think of those heady months with Datus twenty-one years before.

Many others had left ahead of me, and still more were to leave later. I was glad I wasn't leaving in bitterness as some had. The reasons some gave for going ranged from ridiculous and resentful to idealistic and informed. Peter left after reading that fish is good brain food and when the abbot proved unwilling to give the order to start serving fish. Augustine left simply because the celibate life was too lonely for him. Cyprian left because he resented even the two hours of daily manual labor that interrupted his scholarly pursuits. One young man left in a great huff within three weeks of his arrival when he found out he had been misinformed about monasteries being places where homosexual activity was part of the observance. A few withdrew to join other monastic orders where, they judged, their talents or spiritual tastes would be more effectively engaged. Two particularly admirable and memorable young men left to become hermits. Several stormed out in outspoken anger and seemed unable to pinpoint any specific complaint, although to most of us it seemed fairly evident that diet and early rising were the probably unrealized reasons. At least one withdrew simply because the abbot's personality rubbed him the wrong way.

With such memories in mind, I was grateful to feel warm sentiments toward the abbot and his council as I was leaving. If they saw my withdrawal as failure, and I was sure they did, I knew they did so honestly. But my lack of monastic submission was important to me for yet another reason. I saw it as signifying that I had moved into enough self-confidence that I no longer felt the need to fight back or defend myself against either the abbot and his council or the looks of cool disdain that I received from some of my brother monks during my last days in the monastery as the news spread that I was leaving.

As was the custom, upon my departure I reassumed my name of George and dropped the Bernard that I had been given the day I entered the abbey. I smiled to myself at how different the restored George was going to be to live with from the George who had arrived seventeen years before. My last memory in the abbey is of laughter with Father John, a monk some years my junior and who had been docile to the point of tongue-tied timidity in his early years at the abbey, but who, after ordination to the priesthood, developed into an outspoken reformer. In the last moments as I was about to step through the doors, he broke silence to tell me, with his best dimpled smile, that the abbot obviously didn't realize that little lambs sometimes grow up to be rams.

Without any doubt, the abbot was as relieved as dismayed at my going. With all of his generosity, he had nevertheless remained confused about why so many of his sons seemed unable to appreciate his doctrine about obedience, which, after all, was that of a Catholic church as much ours as his. He openly admitted more than once to the assembled monks that he couldn't understand what he called the lack of faith that some of us exhibited for what Rome called so solemnly and authoritatively his rightful place as God's divine-right ruler. As he watched me go, his relief was evident, but I'm sure his sense of duty made him also fear for my welfare—and probably for my eternal salvation.

I never once doubted your sterling intention and sincere dedication to duty, Father Abbot. It was not you, but the system you were working for that caused the problem, a system in which many of your monks were far less vested than you and your fellow abbots were. It was a system that demanded we believe what we were told to believe, repeat what we were told to repeat, do what we were told to do, and maintain an inner contentment throughout. When the mid-twentieth-century human race began to be more generally educated, and then more critical of arbitrary medieval authoritarianism, Trappist monks found themselves feeling the same urge as most others to evolve, to grow, to take a more active part in the providence and disposition of their own lives. For some reason, you did not understand this urge. The powers in Rome had always reserved the word *heretic* for those who, as the derivation of the word indicates, "choose" their own way of responding to God, as distinct from the way Rome has chosen for them. Church management in the 1960s saw much of what was happening in its monasteries and convents and parishes as akin to the age-old insolence of more familiar heresies. More than once, Father Abbot, you accused your monks of being unfaithful by being too independent in thought and action. You knew well that Rome stood firmly behind you, and that the Trappist hierarchy stood firmly with you. When the outdated charade of ancient and medieval conformity nonetheless began to crumble despite your efforts to shore it up, it should have surprised no one—although it did surprise you, Father Abbot—that individual monks began to graduate and disappear.

My neighbors on the flight to San Francisco saw only my shaved head and ill-fitting black suit and Roman collar and left me strictly alone. The flight was preserved for me as a time of deep musing, a time to see in new perspective exactly what had happened to me in the mountains of Utah.

Had I simply substituted neurotic attack for neurotic escape? Were my closest friends in the abbey and I, perhaps, really just irresponsible rebels? Or could it be that our restlessness in the last few years at the abbey did actually come from psychological and spiritual growth?

If Roman Catholicism had become my third mother when I became a Catholic in 1947, a far more intimate relationship had been established when I entered the abbey in 1950. I came as a young man deep in self-doubt and self-rejection and was greeted by a wealthy dowager whose only wish was for young people who would be her obedient lessers and to whom she made the promise that she would call them her favorites. I liked her richness, her dignity, her promises. She liked my mind, my ready subservience. She taught me everything I wanted to know, detailed studies in the classics, philosophers, theologians, historians. She taught me to read ancient documents in original languages. She taught me to be quick and alert in mental gymnastics of the most subtle varieties so that I could explain and defend her thinking. She gave me copious time for personal prayer and, having forgotten how to teach me to move beyond mental prayer to meditation, she at least provided me with an extensive library on Western mysticism, thereby unwittingly opening to me the world of meditation and release. For a long time I found her detailed directions a source of badly needed security and gratefully did everything she asked. For a time ours was, indeed, an idyllic relationship.

But, as Father John said, lambs do have a tendency to grow up.

As I have written earlier, once when I was in the navy in Hawaii I swam too far from the beach and found myself among sharks who, apparently, had already had lunch. In the abbey I almost lost my life yet again by accidentally contacting a 7,500-volt power line with an aluminum ladder. I escaped this second time with only a brief period of unconsciousness and three months in the monastery infirmary recovering from severely burned feet. Seated on that United flight to San Francisco, I began wondering what these close calls had meant. The Mormon doctor who came regularly from Ogden to the monastery to nurse my feet back to health told me one day, "You're being saved for something, Bernard. A few hours before you touched that line, another young man did the same thing seventeen miles away and died instantly."

It wasn't privilege I felt when he told me that or as I now recalled his words on the plane. I didn't feel special, but curious: Why me? Why him? Succumbing to my lifetime habit of always comparing myself with other men, I suspected that the other young man had probably completed his task and I had not.

What I finally concluded was that my life had progressed well at the abbey. Fear, escape, and endless acting out of insecurities buried deep in my mind and heart were where I had begun. Several times in the Jewish writings that Christians call their Old Testament, the texts say that "fear is the *beginning* of wisdom." I had started with fear, but by daily exposure to spiritual realities through chant, meditation, personal thought, and passionate study of the race's store of wisdom, I had inaugurated a refashioning of my psychological makeup, away from fear and toward love. I knew that this process was by no means complete, but I saw that it was at least off to a good start.

When a flight attendant asked if I wanted a cocktail, it took me but a nanosecond of deliberation to surprise myself and say yes to my first alcoholic drink since the Philippines, twenty years before in 1947. I responded, "Whiskey, please." The attendant started to ask what kind of whiskey, but after what looked to me like a chagrined glance at my general appearance, thought better of it and handed me her own choice, the tiniest bottle of Jack Daniels I'd ever seen. I almost gagged on the stuff, but I loved it for the self-determination it symbolized in my life.

Maybe what became particularly clear to me on the flight out of Utah was a needed perspective on the sincerity of both traditionalists and revolutionaries within the monastery and church, a perspective that applied to my monastic experience and has applied equally well in countless situations since. To see the driving energy and emotional involvement of those defending the traditional practices of the monastery and church in the sixties, or today, as a pure expression of selfless concern for others and religious truth is naïve in the extreme. But it is equally uncritical to claim that those of us who were restive for reforms were motivated by an unsullied dedication to truth. All of us, on both sides of the fence, were pursuing perfection. All of us, on both sides of the fence, were sincere. And every single one of us was at least partially driven by neurotic urges and influenced by blind spots.

A physician friend once made a case that no one can finish the long studies to become a priest or medical doctor without strong neurotic motivation as support along the way. I'm convinced he was right. I had been struck in the abbey by a statement made by Karen Horney, a recognized authority on the subject of neuroses, that a person who serves the poor may, in fact, be as driven by neurotic needs as the one who abuses them. Some neuroses, she explains, are socially acceptable and useful, and some aren't. Individuals with patterns that are personally painful or socially troublesome are often the more fortunate ones because criticism and social pressure will make them want to change as quickly as possible. When neurotic habits are acceptable or useful in others' eyes, however, we may too easily lie down in comfort and spend the rest of our lives with the approval of all, but without significant growth.

My own spiritual hunger and drive were genuine when escapism made it easy for me as a young man of twenty-one to give up family, sex, marriage, children, travel, and much else to embrace the hard-pressed life of a Trappist monk. My *conscious* motivation was spiritual and idealistic, but my subconscious drive was built on fears of inadequacy as a man, as a provider, as a viable unit among my peers.

The same double motivation drove the abbot, a former chaplain to Hollywood stars, to leave his popular ministry in the archdiocese of Los Angeles and join the monks in the hills of Utah. It was a heroic decision—motivated *consciously* by idealistic spiritual striving.

When we monks of varied backgrounds found ourselves chanting side by side in choir, working side by side in the fields or in classes, every one of us maintained decorum and a conscious effort to "love your brother as yourself." Judging from externals, we succeeded, and there were never any open arguments. And there's much to be said for this kind of external good order, even if it most certainly must not be taken as conclusive evidence of authentically high spirituality. External order provides an environment in which problems—and the high reaches of consciousness—can be worked at without the distractions of battle plans and carnage. It provides an environment for healing in every sense. Had I spent my Utah years in the midst of battle, I might never have become aware of the hidden levels in me that needed healing. It's even less likely that I would ever have begun to break through to what a long mystical tradition calls "higher consciousness"—awareness, that is, of the unseen parts of the cosmic and religious story that day-to-day personal consciousness does not see.

The problem is that external peace is too often, too easily, taken to be proof of inner wholeness, or even as authentic spirituality itself. Many times I heard our own or a visiting abbot make the point that quiet obedience and faithful conformity "no matter what" is the holiness in this life that leads to bliss in the next. That reductionism, however, is justified by nothing whatsoever except the tranquillity of abbots.

Many of us had confronted this huge oversimplification and falsification head-on in the early 1960s. Indeed, on this plane flying back into the world after many years of participating in what was, in effect, a bloodless and gentlemanly theological warfare, I realized that I had been participant in a significant moment of history. Pope John XXIII had kicked it off, but then, still smiling as when he had arrived, he left it in the hands of less clear-sighted church managers to complete.

It took me more than half of my years in the abbey to realize that bliss is not the automatic product of a passive, static conformity built on a denial of personal will and freedom. It took me that long to realize that beneath a deceptively unruffled monastic peace there lived within me a man who was clamoring to get out and live. And, contrary to most outsiders' idea of what makes a man leave a celibate lifestyle, the "living" I longed for was made up of vastly more powerful urges than a sublimated—or repressed, if you wish—appetite for sex.

It took me years to realize that the recognition my buried self was longing for could not be obtained from others, but only from myself.

Monks fall into two categories: those who pursue studies for ordination to the priesthood and those who do not. I was one of those who chose the path of studies. This meant that my life would be punctuated by a series of interim goals. There would be two professions of vows and seven successive ordinations, only the last of which would be to the priesthood. Each of these events was a major objective to work for, an achievement to look forward to. They were not automatic; you had to work for them. They kept you busy and attentive, and too easily distracted from the deeper implications of the total process. I remember running enthusiastically toward each milestone as it arrived on the horizon and then, as soon as it had been passed, beginning to regroup and speed up to reach the next one. And then one day all the interim goals were in the past. Only then did I see the forest that surrounded the individual trees that had, one by one, been absorbing my attention.

I sat playing with my swizzle stick on the plane to San Francisco and became aware that interim goals had for a long time distracted me from my only important and critical goal: to find and become myself. I learned the hard way that there is in each of us an individuality and freedom that wants—and ultimately demands—to be activated. Only after the institutional goals were past did I begin to meet the someone who is more than just a compulsive achiever, the someone who is authentically me. That was when I found the thinker beneath the thought, the one who feels beneath the feelings, the man beneath the monk.

I was traveling several hundred miles an hour away from a monastery where I'd promised God I would remain the rest of my life. Within two weeks of arriving in San Francisco, I knew I would never return. I was a fallen monk who in less than three years would become a fallen priest. Nevertheless, aware of what I was doing and knowing God was with me every step of it, I was feeling a lightheartedness that exceeded the lightheadedness brought on by the unaccustomed alcohol in my blood. I had sprung free from external bonds and no longer had the slightest doubt that my journey would ultimately free me of inner bonds as well.

Exactly twenty years before this plane ride to San Francisco, I had island-hopped across the Pacific in a propeller plane from Manila to Honolulu. When jet contrails began appearing over the Wasatch Mountains and crossing air space above the abbey in the 1950s, I sometimes looked up and felt disappointed that I would never ride in one of those new kind of planes. I was still smiling when my first jet ride landed at San Francisco International Airport.

Ex-monk Augustine, a fellow student for twelve years in the abbey and now married and with children, met me and drove me to the University. He, too, was smiling as we met, and even before either of us said a word, I knew he understood me perfectly.

16

Jesuits and San Francisco

To fly into San Francisco in June 1967 was to fly right into the hippie movement at its best moment. I landed in the middle of a flower children revolution I hadn't even known was happening: "What in the world are flower children?"

Haight Street was several blocks south of the University of San Francisco campus, and by the time I was a week into my new graduate program, I was ready to explore what everyone was talking about as going on down the hill in the Haight-Ashbury district at the east end of Golden Gate Park.

A bejeweled, stringy-haired, and obviously stoned young man in red, yellow, and purple clothing was the first to talk to me: "Where ya' from, brother?" His open-faced sincerity and straightforwardness made me feel at home. My clothing baggy, my head shaved, my face gaunt, I was wide-eyed, unbelievably innocent, and feeling no criticism whatsoever for what I was seeing. That was easy because the emotions that sprang up naturally within me were warmth and trust for the brightly colored weirdness that gently elbowed its way around me. I found the loving greetings that came at me from all sides easy to believe, accept, and return in kind.

It's impossible to describe adequately the abrupt, almost violent awakening my senses experienced that first visit to the Haight-

Ashbury. Everywhere I looked there was color. That alone was new for someone just emerging from seventeen years in black and white.

I remember standing still, almost in shock, soon after arriving in the Haight-Ashbury district. But it was a shock of delight! Within the space of a week, I had traveled from a chaste, almost bodiless world of no color, no smell, no touch, little taste, repressed feelings, ethereal music, and silence, to a world at the extreme opposite on each of these points. The smell of exotic fragrances—and body odor—was everywhere. Everyone was clothed, often scantily, in outrageously mismatched colors, under which women made no effort to camouflage their nipples or men even their aroused genitals. Everybody was talking, hugging, kissing. No one seemed reluctant to be incarnate.

Soaring over it all, like a Beethoven or Bach gone mad, was the loudest, most unfamiliar music I'd ever heard. Familiar or not, I fell in love with rock on the first day I heard it. In its own way it was doing exactly what Gregorian chant does, only this time with a body. Gregorian chant had long since taken my soul, and now rock began asking my body to come along as well.

And then there was the hair. I had just come from a world of shaved heads, and suddenly all around me was more hair, beautiful hair, than I knew existed. I couldn't wait for mine to grow again, and I wondered how long it would take.

Within two hours, I was offered incense, flowers, hugs, and free sex. The abbot would have been gratified to know that I turned down the sex, but alarmed that I was there to accept the rest.

I arrived in San Francisco with no idea whatsoever about what was going on around me, what this hippie movement was all about. One thing I did quickly sense, however, was that there was an energy and demand for freedom, an authenticity and renewed enthusiasm for life moving through these so-called hippies that were remarkably reminiscent of what was happening back at the abbey. It was kin to what for some years had been birthing in my own heart and mind in the Utah hills. I sensed this similarity as clearly as I smelled the ubiquitous incense around me.

In the abbey we had carried no flowers or incense sticks. We had no marijuana and no sex, free or otherwise. Apart from such superficial differences, however, these young people milling around me in their smiling thousands were clearly acting out of the same honesty and spiritual enthusiasm that were common and characteristic commodities in my community back in Utah. The world views supporting the two movements were universes apart, it's true, but the revolutionary movements themselves were identical. There was one notable exception: one movement was young and vital, full of energy and naïveté; the other was old and badly adulterated, jelled in vested concern and jaded.

In time I learned, of course, that all that glittered in the Haight was not gold. But my initial impression proved accurate for as long as it lasted. Before I watched heavy drugs engulf the community two years later, there was much that was genuinely utopian in a midnight stroll among the hippies. I could relate to them, for I had just come from a place where love also ruled, and where rebellion against mindless observances and a demand for new beginnings were also coming to birth.

My chief preoccupation that first summer in San Francisco, however, was not down in the Haight-Ashbury, but up on campus. It was summer school, and USF was filled with priests and nuns from all over the United States and Canada. They were a type I had never met before, clerical and religious Catholic men and women such as I could not possibly have believed real were I not rubbing shoulders with them and daily sharing their ideas and ideals. They were, in their own way, every bit as revolutionary as the kids down the hill.

Pope John XXIII was by now deceased, but the renewal he had inaugurated was very much alive. The cardinals and bishops were, mostly, trying to forget what he had started and to bury it, but his new thinking ruled this summer campus with a vengeance. The graduate student body was unique in that it was self-sorted: it took considerable courage to come to a university that had acquired a reputation as being *way* out front in Catholic reform. The men and women who came obviously no longer felt constrained to wait for approval from Rome or from anyone else to make their Masses, their prayers, their daily lives meaningful in new and honest ways.

Some few priests and fewer nuns included setting celibacy aside in this struggle for authenticity, but for the majority of us our freedom simply meant creating new and meaningful liturgies, critically and sympathetically revisiting our Jewish roots and the ideas of the sixteenth century Protestant reformers, and, more than anything else, looking once again at everything the Catholic church had ever told us.

From my earliest days as a Catholic I had easily picked up the "one true church" snobbery that Catholics were so proud of. When I arrived home from the navy, it had been warmly encouraged by the old Irish priest who was pastor of Saint Michael's in my hometown. Father Maroney was simply a man of his times, and his Irish-immigrant attitude of open contempt for anything non-Catholic (especially anything English) perfectly suited my new enthusiasm. It was intoxicating to my old self-doubt that I had at last found something to be right about. When the dearest of my several aunts, Aunt Ruth, asked me in early 1950 if I would accompany her to hear a renowned Anglican priest speak at her Episcopal parish, I refused with great self-righteousness. Father Maroney later warmly congratulated me for my good judgment.

This "right-church" attitude only grew worse over the years as my seminary and monastery training progressed. Fellow seminarians and I lost all proportion—one could almost say all decency—when it came to passing judgment on other churches and religions, although I believe most observers would have called us rather noble-minded young men otherwise. In religion alone we became bigots and idiots, at the urging of, and under the guidance of, our church.

We laughed uproariously at "those poor evangelicals" and their biblical fundamentalism, and then turned ourselves to a weighty discussion of whether God's law obliged a person in conscience to obey a traffic light. We rolled in the aisles over the refusal by some orthodox Jews to eat an egg laid on the Sabbath, but then scowled anxiously over the problem of how big a drop of water had to be if swallowed after midnight on a day of Holy Communion before a Catholic would go to eternal hell for having swallowed it.

All of this is amusing now, and it was even amusing then, only we didn't see it. At the University of San Francisco in the summer of 1967, I began for the first time to see these attitudes in perspective as the absolute nonsense that they are. I studied the Torah under a rabbi, Protestant theology under one Protestant scholar, and the writings of Paul in the Christian testament under another. Before the year was out, I would concelebrate a nuptial Mass with a Southern Baptist professor in a Stanford University chapel. My times, they were a changin'.

I was dismayed that I hadn't long before seen the "We're right and you're wrong" hangovers from the sixteenth century for what they are.

When Cardinal McIntyre, the archbishop of Los Angeles, sent one of his priests to forbid me to marry two Catholic students in North Hollywood if I planned to face the people during the nuptial Mass, as rumor had led him to believe, I laughed out loud and did it anyway. The cardinal had his priest explain to me that to face the people while saying the nuptial Mass would be to turn my back on God. Such were the traditional wisdoms I was learning to despise—and ignore—at USF in the summer of 1967.

The graduate student body at USF didn't wait for Rome to let us replace Latin with English in the liturgies. We simply did it. We did anything we judged would make our religion and religious practices meaningful again. Some of the world's most noted theologians and experts, recently internationally recognized *periti* at the Second Vatican Council, were our summer professors at USF. For the most part they were as enthusiastic about our innovative thinking as we were. After all, they'd played midwife to most of it.

Some of them participated in our late-night discussions, and some even followed us across town to the Red Garter Beer Hall on the Embarcadero for great evenings of sing-along Dixieland music. It was a Red Garter custom for the band to play special songs during the evening in recognition of each identifiable group of patrons present. When it played "Anchors Aweigh," sailors, ex-sailors, sailors' lovers, sailors' relatives, and all would-be sailors would stand up, cheer, and nod their gratitude to an obliging audience of fellow revelers. The army, air force, and Marine Corps songs, too, brought numbers of people to their feet for cheers, bows, and a few boos. Each time the band played "When the Saints Come Marching In," however, as it inevitably did several times each evening, a great majority of the large audience would stand, cheer lustily, and begin making elaborately deep, outrageously solemn bows they had practiced for years in Catholic liturgies. The bulk of the Red Garter's patrons in the summer months were priests and nuns from USF, out in plain clothes for an evening on the town. When we were finally seated again, we'd order another beer, crack some more peanuts, and thank God yet another time that we were blundering our way across Jordan.

My years in the monastery had been a time to get my head on straight. San Francisco was to be my time to get my *life* on straight. It was a time when I learned to rejoin the human community. Utah had been where I got my inner life in order. California was where I did the same for the rest of me.

Being in the world didn't intimidate me at all, but something about being there did surprise me. After a month of floundering around with a slowly recovering shaved head and in ill-fitting clerical garb that was not capable of recovery, I found myself quite popular anyway and almost in need of a social secretary. I had found an off-campus job as chaplain to a convent of seventeen joy-filled nuns caring for two hundred elderly people at Saint Anne's Home on Lake Street. They presented their new chaplain with a three-room apartment on the top floor of their institution, and a new car. A former monk and close friend, Bill Petrie, married and living in the city, gave me lessons in freeway driving, and suddenly I was mobile.

I was the first Trappist monk most people had ever seen, for, unlike several others who had left various Trappist abbeys and come to San Francisco, I had not yet terminated my status as a monk and was still officially a Trappist. Many referred to me as "the monk from Thomas Merton's order," and I was invited more places than I could possibly fit into a student's schedule. This was especially the case after they (and I!) found that I had a certain easy manner and ready humor in giving sermons and talks that sprang as much from passionate convictions as from long training. I was paid well for these talks on both sides of the Bay, and this unexpected enterprise generated an unexpected abundance of income for me. By the time my full head of hair had grown back—as red as ever—I had replaced my drab garb brought from the abbey with clothing more to my liking and my size. I still wore the Roman collar for Mass, but, in keeping with the practice of most priests at USF, seldom otherwise. By Christmas, six months after leaving the abbey, I was an active member not only of the campus, but also of a good bit of the City by the Bay as well. The woman I was later to marry would one day complain with some chagrin about our nonstop social life: "I didn't realize I was marrying a city!" I had been waiting to live most of my life this way, and now I was cocked and primed and ready to go—and going most of the time.

When I left the monastery my inner life was strong enough that it didn't get lost in my newly found excitement. During my first two months on campus and before I moved into the convent, I arose every day at 4:00 A.M. and was in the massive USF Collegiate Church to say Mass by 4:30. There I met and became special friends with an old Jesuit brother, Brother Emmanuel, who managed the sacristy, the room in which priests' liturgical vestments and utensils are kept. His smile reminded me of Will Rogers, his words and style of Brother Matthew. Nothing seemed to perturb this slightly rotund, gentle, smiling old gentleman. He was always at the church before me, freshly shaved and smelling faintly of Mennen aftershave. When his duties as Sacristan permitted, he even served my Mass himself.

For the first couple of weeks at USF, as I crossed the fog-shrouded summer campus on my way to the church in the early morning hours, I thought I heard a pipe organ playing vague and unrecognizable music somewhere off in the distance. I had not been told that the Jesuits had a school of music and concluded it must be so overenrolled that student practice had to be scheduled around the clock. Eventually it dawned on me that what I was hearing was the moaning of foghorns on ships coming and going through the Golden Gate and on various coastal stations along a shoreline I had monitored on a submarine's radar when returning from the Pacific in what now seemed as if it had been several life-times before. Brother Emmanuel laughed when I told him about the imagined school of music and all-night pipe organ. San Francisco is always foggy in the summer, and that beautiful, fog-shrouded, predawn summer campus has forever caused fog to be for me a thing of magic and mystic warmth.

Studies—for the most part unchallenging and not at all as in-depth as they had been at the abbey—eventually came to hold only a small part of my attention. Every single day held something new, whether learning to drive on a freeway, going to Santa Cruz to swim in the surf, shopping for new clothing, spending most of a night in a rap session, or meditating in the elegant prayer chapel at the largest synagogue in town, Temple Emmanuel, just down the street from my convent home.

One surprising enterprise I found myself engaged in was warding off the amorous attentions of a nun who was apparently doing ad-vance research on her plan to crash her way out of her convent. I had now been faithfully celibate since 1947. No sex with myself or anyone else for just over twenty years. This lusty nun caused me to take a deeper look at that celibacy. My ultimate refusal of her offer was not as simple as that first refusal had been when sex was proffered in the Haight-Ashbury a week after I arrived.

Like most priests and nuns at USF, I was not about to go to bed with anyone—"fall into the sack," was the campus phrase—unless and until and only if I had made a carefully deliberated choice. I was, however, very definitely now consciously in the process of making that choice along with many others.

There were more elements pressing the possibility of sex on me than the fact that it was always available. I was eating three—spiced—meals a day again. My body was waking up. Far more compelling, my *nose* was waking up. I seemed to be smelling perfumes everywhere. It made me laugh as I recalled the afternoon when Spes, the monastery sheep dog, came up against female fragrances the first time he found himself confronted by women on the visitors' side of the monastery wall. It couldn't have been their skirts that confused him and sent him into paroxysms of barking, for all the monks wore what in effect were skirts. It was the female *smell* that drove Spes almost crazy. And now fragrances were doing the same thing to me. I was seeing *and smelling* shapely figures all over the place, and—God save us!—even sitting next to them at meals and in classes. The abbot had warned me there would be days like this. I didn't bark as Spes had done, but that's only because he was more honest.

It was during this time that I saw the film version of D.H. Lawrence's *Women in Love*. It moved things deep inside of me that I had forgotten about. Much later a friend would give me a quote from Lawrence in which he talked about his controversial erotic paintings, and it summed up the effect this movie had on me during these first months out of the abbey. "I paint no pictures that won't shock castrated public spirituality," Lawrence had written.

Without understanding it at the time, I was reacting to the "castrated" state of the church's spirituality. Later I would do extensive research on where and why the requirement for a celibate clergy had arisen in Catholicism, from where and why the proscription on birth control and masturbation, from where and why its negative attitude toward sexuality and bodilyness in general. During that first year in San Francisco, however, the renewed rumblings of my libido were still suppressed, and my first insights on the topic were still intuitive, preconscious, and usually scary. I kept my celibacy intact, but with effort. Sister Mary What's-'er-Name of the Disintegrating Veil had to look elsewhere for help in her proposed intimate lab work. About two years later, when she had finally left the convent and was living with a loving partner, I met them both for dinner one evening, and my previous indignation at her former hard-sell approaches softened. She had been acting as she felt she had to just as I acted as I felt I had to. Both of us were simply trying to undo aspects of our past.

As I recall those early months in San Francisco, it seems that virtually every element of my life was significant. Two, however, stand out as singularly so.

It dawned on me as my first Thanksgiving out of the monastery approached that I was free to fly to my parents' new home in Logan, Utah. As it turned out, commitments kept me in the city, but I began planning a visit at Christmas. My parents were elated. So was I. When I first arrived in San Francisco and phoned to tell them that I was there and would be leaving monastic life, they could scarcely contain their joy and relief. My Mormon stepmother proclaimed proudly that she had prayed me out of the monastery and that I should stand by because the next thing she had in mind for me was "a really very nice little wife."

My stepmother had visited me several times at the abbey, my sisters and brother one or two times each, but my father had consistently refused to come. Eventually, though, in 1965, two years before I was to leave for San Francisco, he gave in to family badgering and one day, unannounced, showed up at the monastery all by himself.

Our meeting was strained for a few minutes. It was the first time he had seen me so gaunt and with a shaved head. Our conversation warmed up noticeably when I borrowed a jeep from the brothers to drive him around the abbey's ranching operation and show him things to which he could relate.

At one point I noticed tears running down his cheeks—the first I remembered—and before I could ask him what they meant, he told me that all those years he had suspected monasteries were places the Catholic church provided for its homosexual priests to indulge their needs. Then he added: "Why, I wasn't in this god-damned place ten minutes before realizing that isn't the case!" From that moment, our relationship was on a rapid mend.

I had been ordained for seven years by then, and his estimate of the abbey was helped no little when, as he told me, he noticed everyone addressed me as "Father." That pleased him. Maybe his son had accomplished something worthwhile, after all. I was show-ing him through the abbey building at one point and had entered the huge tailor shop where all the habits, cowls, and strange Trappist undergarments are made. Brother Ferdinand, the tailor, was notorious for his inability to keep the strict rule of silence, and he and Dad immediately launched into a long conversation. Dad would talk the rest of his life about that wonderful Brother Tailor who was such a fine gentleman "even if he had come from Germany."

Now, two years later and in San Francisco, I looked forward to going home for Christmas. The trip promised to be a great healing between my family and me. And, in fact, it turned out to be ex-actly that. For the remaining thirteen years of my father's life we were increasingly close friends. In his mind it only remained for me to give him the final gift of a wife for his oldest son. I would do that soon enough.

My stepmother told me that to his last day he never stopped bragging to his friends about his special son whom he could at last understand. My half-brother, Ron, who was only three years old when I left home for the monastery, once told me that I was always an unknown quantity to him as a child. He only knew me as the picture on the piano and as the older brother to whom our father often referred—"George always used to say" or "George always did that this way." I had too easily presumed that Dad had simply written me off when I went to the monastery, an ex-son who was no longer in a position to inherit and take over running the family ranch as he had done from his father and as he had hoped for me.

The second significant event of that first year in San Francisco began when I received a long-distance phone call from the abbot of another American Trappist monastery. He asked with some urgency that I come immediately, without explaining why, and said he would reimburse me for my transportation costs. I left the next day, and when I showed up at his abbey, he asked if I was willing to do him and my Trappist order a favor: "Will you write an article for *The National Catholic Reporter* that will expose Antoniutti?"

The Roman Cardinal Ildebrando Antoniutti was head of the section of Vatican government that rules persons in the church who have taken vows. His rule was notoriously high-handed, arbitrary, and openly counter to the direction that had been set by Pope John XXIII and the Second Vatican Council. It was probably as well intentioned as the Crusades and Spanish Inquisition, but it was a similar crime against humanity nonetheless.

The National Catholic Reporter was particularly heralded in the 1960s as the only dependable bit of Catholic press free of official censorship, the only periodical that could or would expose those events in the church that the rest of the Catholic press, bishop-controlled, would not make public.

The abbot I was visiting had contacted the editor of the *Reporter*, who had welcomed the chance for an exposé of the notorious cardinal, provided only that the abbot had documents to back up any accusations that would be made in the article. The abbot did, of course, have the communications from Rome that had been sent to him and the other abbots—all with the demand that, under pain of mortal sin, they be kept secret—meaning that hell was the threatened sanction. The abbot I was visiting knew I was familiar with these documents from my time working with my own abbot in Utah.

I stayed up all that night putting the facts together, and the January 11, 1968, edition of the *Reporter* carried an article titled "How Rome Squelches Abbots." It was signed by a name the paper itself had chosen, *Monachus Indignans,* Latin for "An Indignant Monk." Elsewhere in the same edition the newspaper published the full text of one of the offensive letters Antoniutti had authored to Trappist abbots throughout the world.

Shortly after the article appeared, Dom Gabriel Sortais, the abbot general of the Trappist order, was on a plane from Rome to Spain when a radio message was received on the flight deck ordering him to get off at the plane's next stop and return to Rome immediately. A friend from his office later reported that when Dom Gabriel had returned and been ushered into the cardinal's office, the offending newspaper was spread out on the cardinal's desk and he was crashing his fist into it, demanding to know how his secret correspondence had been betrayed to the American press and who the indignant monk was.

American Trappists generally, and even a couple American abbots, were regaled by the whole affair. I received reimbursement for my transportation expenses to the abbey and a substantial fee that I could use the next time I went to the Red Garter for more training in being human.

The full implication of this Antoniutti episode is largely lost now in the 1990s, but in the late 1960s it was still somewhat unbelievable that such a thing could have happened. I mention it in this book because it is representative of the time, but also because it served as the final stroke to whatever loyalty I may have still felt for church-managed monasticism.

I had by now realized that living as a monk or nun in the Western world had become an institutionally suffocated effort, primarily oriented to survival of the status quo. In the Antoniutti incident, I saw that fact spelled out in high relief by the church politicians who were keeping the whole thing going. Significantly, the abbot who had asked me to write the article and reimbursed me for my efforts left monastic life himself soon afterward and married about the time I did.

I remember wishing I could return to my own abbey just long enough to give one more sermon. I would have so liked to share a perspective on the Trappist life that one could see in San Francisco but not from within the walls of a cloister. Life did not have to be denied; the body did not have to be whipped; good food was not a danger. Life in this world could be affirmed and entered into with energy, with joy, with self-determination, *and as an integral part of mysticism and spirituality.* It did not have to be feared and disparaged and denied. That sermon, however, was one thing that both I and my own abbot were now certain would never happen.

In the meantime, in San Francisco and far from Rome in more ways than geography, I had become a distant cousin to the Jesuit community at USF by having become brother and spiritual confidant to some of the young-at-heart Jesuit priests. The older and conservative Jesuits were known as "old dads" by my new friends, and I became aware that their community was having growing pains similar to those of the Trappists. There was a difference, however. Being in the world and very much *of* the world, Jesuits had at their disposal all sorts of resources that Trappists, locked away, did not have.

These young Jesuits made a deep and lasting impression on my heart as well as on my mind. They were every bit as dedicated to spiritual values as any monk, but they managed to marry to this dedication an outrageously fun-filled ability to enjoy the life and earth that God had given them. They somehow managed to go swimming, snorkeling, traveling, playing sports, partying, all without losing their close involvement with God. In my training, unlike theirs, such endeavors had been labeled worldly and counterproductive to the highest spirituality. I was busy learning from them that involvement with the world leads to wholeness, not to spiritual compromise.

My most important lessons at USF did not come in the classrooms. They came in the Jesuit faculty lounge, to which I was often invited, off on a beach, or in the Sierra Nevadas—often with a bottle of wine, a hunk of cheese, and a loaf of French bread—with a few sharp-minded, warmhearted friends, Jesuits and otherwise. I particularly remember one Sunday morning when I offered Mass in Sequoia National Park with a group of graduate students crowded around a fallen tree that served as my altar. When the Mass was over and as we continued standing in the awe and warm camaraderie of the moment, a young Jesuit looked up into the towering giants and sang the title line of the currently popular "Winchester Cathedral"—replacing the word *Winchester* with *Sequoia:* "Sequoia Cathedral." Our cathedrals were, indeed, being redefined and new ones recognized. Some of our most honest worship had just happened out in a high-flung Sequoia edifice that traditional eyes would never have recognized as being every bit as holy as Saint Peter's in Rome. I could only wish such an experience upon all my brother monks back in the abbey where Mass was said each morning in corners of a darkened church, more often than not with only the priest and one other lone monk present as server. I had graduated there from a five-year course in theology, and now I was embarked on another two years of the same, but this time my program had dimensions in it that the previous one didn't even know existed.

I went back to the monastery briefly at the end of my first summer school and the beginning of the fall quarter. The abbot delicately suggested that perhaps now I had "worked it out of my system" and would be willing to stay where I "belonged." I'm sure he and some of his council thought I'd been away from the world so long that I must be now finding it quite overwhelming. If they only had known in what way I found it overwhelming, they would never have imagined I might return to the cloister. Without defense, without explanation, I quietly told the abbot, "No." That was that. He was gracious and said the abbey would continue to pay for my graduate program.

Back in San Francisco and after each day with my new friends on campus, I would return to my convent of nuns. There I'd find myself involved, yet again, in the happy, outgoing exchange of simple human friendship. I often stood back in my thoughts and wondered if all this was really happening to me. The nuns were bright, humor-filled women, and I thoroughly enjoyed them and their colorful mother superior, Mother Charles, whom the younger nuns and I called Charlie.

I had no inkling of what was coming next in life, but I could no longer doubt that it would be exciting and with purpose.

I would never have guessed it would include two lovers, one a man and one a woman.

17

Clarifying Things

About ten years before these first months back in the world, an incident happened late one summer in the mountains of Utah that I found myself thinking about frequently as challenge after challenge came to me in San Francisco: "If I can learn to handle a snake, I can learn to do anything."

Most of the monks at the abbey were out in the fields helping harvest a last crop of alfalfa. At one point the grass in front of me rustled as a snake made a hasty retreat. I instinctively drew back. We did have rattlesnakes in Utah, but in the green grass where we were working at the moment, this particular snake could only have been a harmless garter or bull snake. I realized all that, but any snake might as well be a king cobra as far as I was concerned.

All my life I'd had an unshakable phobia for snakes. The simple thought of one would cause a shiver to pass over my body and make my toes curl in my shoes. My oldest sister, Bernice, exploited this fear when we were kids on the ranch and more than once chased me with a snake; sometimes it was dead and sometimes not. Once when I had borrowed a little green jacket of hers one too many times, she cut the head from a small garter snake and made sure I saw her put it into one of the jacket pockets. I never touched the garment again.

In the abbey hay field, almost thirty, I still feared snakes as much as I had as a child. A monk working beside me, Father Brendan, taught me a lesson that day that would heal me of this silly phobia once and for all. That healing, in turn, served me in San Francisco and would serve me all my life as a reminder of our power to change anything once we totally engage our will.

When I jumped back from the rustling grass, Brendan looked at me in astonishment and then calmly and with affectionate disdain told me in sign language that such a reaction was unfitting in a man of God who believes in the sacredness of all creatures.

That did it; my time had come. A master had arrived for a needed lesson. I was ready to grow. It was the look on Brendan's face, perhaps, that motivated me to act on the plan that formed in my mind. He had hooked my shame, if nothing else.

A few days later, still in the harvest fields, I spotted another snake, a bull snake about a yard long, and I was determined to do what I had to do. Bull snakes are curious by nature and, if approached slowly, do not retreat as will most other varieties. Slowly I reached out and picked him up as I had seen another monk, Father Bonaventure, do more than once. I was astounded at how smooth and muscular he felt. I held him for a moment and then let him slide, in curiosity or escape, into the sleeve of my habit. He slowly worked his way inside my clothing and down next to my skin until he came to rest wrapped around my waist just above my tight belt.

Several times as all this was happening I had an instant of what I suspect was real potential for psychotic panic, instants when I had a conscious choice: deliberately stay intact, or unglue completely. I quietly told myself with great firmness that I *would* take control of my life, and I stood steady.

After about ten minutes, I carefully removed my guest, sat down crosslegged on the ground, and let him coil up on my lap. Again the possibility of panic came to me like wave after wave of a stormy surf as I looked down and actually saw a *snake* coiled in my lap.

Familiar hysterical patterns cried out to me, "There's a snake in your lap!" My mind held firm, though, and I still remember as clearly as if it had happened yesterday the pleasure I felt as my heartbeat finally grew calm.

Apparently my odor and feel had come to seem safe to the snake, and he quit testing the air with his tongue. He stayed peacefully in my lap, and then, to my amazement and great satisfaction, I saw him close his eyes. When I finally put him on the ground, he didn't move away, but nosed curiously around my shoes. He felt safe. More to the point, *I* felt safe. Both of our worlds had suddenly improved. In the end, it was I who walked away from him, clearly conscious of a huge victory. Father Brendan, who was again working beside me, had observed all this and acknowledged it with a slow, smiling nod of recognition. It had been a justifiable quarter-hour respite from harvesting.

Snakes have no more effect on me today than purring kittens. I've handled them many times and always with the pleasure I find from any other animal. But they hold a special charm for me. We share a secret: one of them taught me an important lesson once.

After the initial novelty and distraction of my new life in San Francisco began to wane, I realized more clearly than ever that I still had a great deal of personal work to do. I was not nearly so self-confident and socially at ease as most others. I found myself often feeling phony as I took part in the social life of my new community. I had lots of fun—put on a good act, as it were—but almost all of it was compulsive and driven. I didn't *feel* at ease, so whatever I did seemed somehow less authentic than what I saw others doing. I might be doing the same things that friends and fellow priests were doing, doing them just as well as they, and to all external appearances seem to be having as much satisfaction and fun as they. But in my introspective moments it seemed to me that most others were doing their jobs and having their fun in honest freedom, while I was still full of self-doubt and uncertainty. My actions were not deliberately faked, but they seemed mechanical and never the result of a creative, free, totally confident, and honest involvement.

I felt I was seeing genuine emotional freedom and social health in others, how it would look without my overlay of fears and their artificial restraints that I had learned in childhood and at the monastery. I fantasized with great longing what it must feel like to be so free, so self-confident, so at ease. The task that I knew I had before me was to reduce all this new insight and the benefit of these examples to practice. I was adamantly determined to dump all remnants of old habits of self-doubt and self-disdain. I repeated again and again, "If I can handle snakes, I can do anything."

There were now many small successes in my life to encourage me that I did, indeed, have the potential to heal completely. I was able to speak easily and well in public. I partied, to all appearances, easily and well anywhere. I didn't flirt and usually limited myself to two cocktails or glasses of wine, but I danced every chance that came along. I found myself having countless new friends who invited me to go more places than I possibly could. Significantly, the day after he had lunch with me when visiting my convent of nuns, San Francisco's Archbishop McGucken sent me a letter giving me permanent "faculties" for functioning as a priest in his jurisdiction. This document meant that, unlike most priests temporarily residing in his jurisdiction, I no longer had to apply on an annual basis to have my faculties renewed. Somewhat inconsistently, I was pleased that I had managed to be in such good standing with the local guardians of the church. Criticize it as I did, the church remained important to me, and I obviously continued to feel some sort of need for its approval. I was still a novice at looking for approval primarily from myself.

Early in 1968, not quite a year out of the abbey, I sat up late one night in my convent apartment and decided I had to take care of my problem of neurotic self-doubt with as much finality as I had once taken care of the snake problem. I was more resolute than panicked and told myself over and over that I wasn't going to let *any* habits of old fear linger in me any longer. I determined to go after *complete* wholeness with *total* effort, and no holds barred.

As a part of this resolution, I began consulting a Jungian analyst, Dr. Katharine Whiteside Taylor. She quickly became a trusted guide and dear friend. Early in our relationship I began, at her request, to call her Katharine, and we came to love each other deeply. She always scheduled me as her last client in the afternoon so we could have tea together and she wouldn't have to terminate my session at the end of one hour to make way for another. Twice a week for eighteen months we worked on my dreams, and soon enough it was abundantly confirmed that I did, indeed, have much work to do. My unconscious was making extravagant efforts to tell me that there was a valid person inside of me clamoring to get out.

One of our sessions fell on my fortieth birthday, and I mentioned to Katharine that the saying "Life begins at forty" seemed as if it would turn out to be literally true for me. Clarity, purpose, and strength seemed to be coming at me from all sides. She was seventy-two at the time and smiled as she reached across the table, patted my hand, and told me it had begun for her at forty, again at fifty, at sixty, and recently all over again at seventy. In her charming way, she was underscoring my enthusiasm and giving me an important teaching: every signpost in life is significant, and all of life is an unfolding process of growth.

Katharine exerted a powerful influence on my life in more ways than helping me understand what I was being taught in my dreams. She became a role model to a degree that only Datus had been before her. Here again I found a live, present, unqualified example of personal freedom and self-actualization who not only lived fully, but could also spell out how she managed to do it. In working today with others who are struggling to find their identity, to self-actualize, to individuate, I find the California jargon of that era seems still to be as helpful for them as it was for me in the late 1960s.

Sometimes Katharine held grand-style parties of thirty or more in her small and exquisitely appointed house. She would appear on each occasion in another of her long, slinky, beaded or sequined gowns from the 1920s and would dance as vigorously as any of us late into the night. There was never any alcohol or drugs at her parties, but it was a standing remark that everyone stood a risk of OD'ing on life at her place. On a long weekend at the Westerbeak Ranch, a Jungian retreat north of San Francisco, she led a large group of us each morning in a dance to the rising sun just as it was making its way into the sky over the wine-country hills. As I moved in this group of swaying, bowing, sweeping, joy-filled bodies led by a wisp of an old woman who could just as well have been thirty years younger—and who had the regal dignity of a medieval abbess—I felt that I was in a world completely alien to the one I'd always known. I found myself wishing that all of my brother monks could be there swaying and whirling with us. Mine was now a reality of which they had not the tiniest inkling, and—this would have surprised them—God was as much a part of this world as of theirs.

Being a priest in San Francisco in the 1960s was heady, exciting. As self-awareness began to come to me and as I began facing up to needs long repressed, it was also increasingly lonely. I didn't see my need as sex, but companionship. I felt sure I could control myself with regard to sexuality, but I wasn't so sure I could with regard to loneliness.

I'd been dealing with loneliness all my life, but the longer I was out of the abbey, the more I was pressed for close companionship. The pace quickened in San Francisco, as I began moving enough out of youthful compulsiveness to become aware of just how lonely I truly was. Many bishops and priests passionately—and honestly—defend celibacy and an unmarried lifestyle simply because they've never slowed down long enough and been honest enough in quiet meditation to meet their real selves and recognize their pathetic loneliness.

They will reply to such an accusation with a complete array of traditional bromides about Divine Love being enough for them: "He who has God needs no other," for example. It's certainly true that some individuals do find that their mystical union with God precludes the need of—and in some cases even the possibility of—intimate and absorbing human companionship. Show me a bishop, abbot, priest, or nun whose celibacy is backed up by evidently superior levels of honesty, gentleness, charity, selflessness, and fulfillment, and I will agree that celibacy is a successful path for that individual. When, however, I see the usual frantic and frazzled, competitive and escape-ridden, short-fused and at times even criminal lifestyles of some celibates, I cannot but think celibacy is far too costly a price for such destructive loneliness. The church has tried to legislate an individual charisma into a reality for all its priests, and it simply doesn't work.

Visiting rectories around the San Fransisco Bay Area and observing the lifestyle of many parish priests at close range didn't help at all. More than once I felt that many of my fellow celibates were as married as any man—not to another human being who could love in return, however, but to golf clubs, liquor cabinets, or other rubber dolls of counterfeit intimacy. Not infrequently, I saw priests take the frustration inherent in this charade out on their housekeepers and parishioners, totally unaware of the implications of their actions. I was hearing priests' confessions on a regular basis and knew they were, with few exceptions, faithful to their promised celibacy, but I have since often found myself thinking "More's the pity!" A good roll in the hay would have been the most real, most therapeutic event in their lives since entering seminary. Logic kept pressing a question on me: Which is the greater misfire: to make love to another human or to a bottle, to a golf game, to institutional posturing? I was not yet ready to jettison my own celibacy, but evidence was mounting that it really didn't make much sense.

My increasing criticism of the celibate requirement for priesthood was as persistent as it was spontaneous, but for my first year out of the monastery I fought such thoughts as seditious and felt guilty about them. They rode me relentlessly, and I couldn't throw them. After all, I wouldn't remain a student forever, and I had much at stake. What options was I going to have if I remained as a priest in San Francisco after I was finished at the university? From what I saw in priests' lives around me, the outlook was pretty glum. I had no intention of dedicating my life to bigger and better parishes or to the frenzied running of schools. My options seemed to come down to this: either be willing to worship idols of busyness and organizational perpetuation, or find some kind of human companionship that will make substitutions unnecessary.

I was awakening as a man, and with this awakening came the honest needs of a man. I think one of the reasons I was so determined not to get sexually involved with anyone was that I feared sex might prove to be as real a substitution for, and as deep a distraction from, my deeper need, loneliness, as obsessive golf and church management were for so many other priests I knew.

A combination of experiences brought my need for companionship home and made me finally face up to just how lonely I was. They also paved the way for me to be free enough, self-guided enough, to get sexually involved later in Europe when an appropriate opportunity presented itself.

During my second year in San Francisco, I became acquainted with a young Jesuit professor at USF, Father Ron Merrifield, a professor of physics with additional duty as chaplain to an off-campus, now-defunct "halfway house for homosexuals," Emmaus House. The church was trying to woo gay men into leaving their "lives of sin," and Emmaus was an experiment being tried in both New York and San Francisco.

The house for this experiment was just down the hill off the south end of campus, and I began accompanying Ron when he went down to say Mass, hear confessions, and be available as a counselor. After we'd been doing this for a few weeks, he was reassigned to Loyola University in Los Angeles, and it didn't surprise me that I was asked to take his place as chaplain until a permanent replacement could be found.

The young men at Emmaus made their way into my heart almost from my first visit. Their warm and honest friendliness walked innocently into the middle of my loneliness and made me feel it more painfully than ever. I didn't feel insecure around men, as I still did around women, and so I was less defended against their affection when it came. Soon enough, I found myself having to face not only their affection, but my own sexuality more explicitly than ever before in my adult life.

The Emmaus residents quickly became warm, sensitive, and loving friends, and they happened to be gay. I was a father figure who neither damned nor despised them and one who could scarcely camouflage his affection for them. They loved me openly as they would the father many of them had never been permitted to love. I found my emotions hooked in ways for which I was prepared not at all. Many times it was difficult not to reach out to embrace a bright-eyed, mostly confused, and frightened young man who, in those days before gay liberation, was caught between his innate or acquired orientation to same-gender intimacy and his church's threats of eternal fire. I avoided any explicit show of affection for them as much as I could because I clearly realized that I couldn't trust myself as to where it might lead if the first line of defense—restraint—were compromised. My years of monastic discipline came in handy.

As it turned out, I never did have an explicitly sexual encounter with any of them, but I suspected then, and know now, that the only thing that held me back was a realization of how great such a breach of trust would be. I was supposed to be helping them *not* act out their homosexuality. Whether I wanted it or not, though, whether they realized it or not, the affection I felt for them began to spill over more and more into sexual feelings. I still bought the church's bigotry and fear of homosexuality, and these new feelings ignited a huge disturbance in me, producing still greater fodder for the confessional. More and more anger piled up, however, anger that I was being forced to control what increasingly seemed like a legitimate desire to get close to someone. Some degree of growth is implied, I guess, that while I often confessed doubts concerning my vow of celibacy, I never confessed anger about being in such a bind.

Dismay and pain were in my heart every time I left Emmaus to drive back to my one-person apartment at the convent and away from a place where I was finding a closeness with individuals who opened their hearts to me as none ever had. People had been calling me Father for years; these young men were making me feel like one.

I had never thought of myself as gay, especially after the experience with Mike in the Philippines, but now, thirty-eight years old, a chaplain at a convent of nuns in one part of town and at a halfway house for homosexual men in another, I met a man who made me wonder if I was gay after all, or perhaps even wanted to be. With him, loneliness was suddenly gone, but at the price of celibacy and maybe of heterosexuality. As our relationship deepened, I was not sure for a time whether I cared much if I forfeited either or both.

Tom appeared at the Green Apple Bookstore on Clement Street, halfway across town from Emmaus. It was the best source of used books in San Francisco then and had become one of my favorite haunts. I was talking with the owner one afternoon when another customer approached him with a question. The newcomer introduced himself, and it turned out he was a thirty-four-year-old physician. It didn't get by me for an instant that he was striking and trim. His hair was slightly tousled, adding to the effect of nattiness and charm. When the store owner left to attend to other customers, Tom and I continued talking. We found we had many common literary interests and eventually, since it was late in the afternoon, decided to share an early dinner at an Italian restaurant down the street.

Near the end of a prolonged meal of sparkling wine, matching conversation, and a remarkably easy mutual familiarity, Tom invited me to come to his apartment in Sausalito—honest enough to tell me openly what he had in mind: bed. I was dumbfounded. I had not seen it coming. It was as if Mike's arms of twenty-one years before were coming around me from behind and falling below my belt once again. I hesitated this time, too, but only long enough to damn inwardly my uncertainty and loneliness alike. I was surprised, angry, grateful, irritated. Then, with my heart beating so hard that I was out of breath, I agreed to go with him. I thought of Mike as I followed Tom in my own car across the Golden Gate Bridge. Apparently I had not learned my lesson well in the Philippines. No matter, I needed some kind of intimacy in my life if I was going to survive, and Tom seemed a particularly likely source. I was so eager for a swim that I was willing to dive without having plumbed the pool.

Tom turned out to be a delight, from first to last. He wasn't Datus, but neither was he Mike. He took time to light candles, put on a reel of Beethoven quartets, and pour his best Merlot before lowering the lights and sitting beside me on his tan leather sofa. His career provided him with enough discretionary funds that if he wanted something, he simply went out and got it, and he obviously knew well what to go out and get. Fine furniture, modern oils, an extensive collection of music, even his crystal wineglasses revealed a man of refined taste.

The first sentence out of his mouth when the chitchat was over was that he was looking for love, not sex. In quiet, measured, upbeat confidence, he spoke with spirit about his adamant determination to jettison loneliness from his life once and for all. It was only a matter of time, he said, until he would find the right person, and he wondered if we would eventually agree that I was that person. He was as lonely as I, but, unlike myself, was clear that he planned to solve it with a man and not a woman. I had only reluctantly decided to solve it at all, and was still totally confused as to whether it would be with the help of a man or woman.

Tom was Catholic, and when I told him early in the evening that I was a priest, he simply remarked, "I've always wondered if priests don't need to be loved, too."

I later realized that I had moved too quickly in agreeing to Tom's invitation, and that I had acted precipitously on a matter about which my conscience was still completely confused. I knew I had to solve my loneliness, but I had not yet deliberately decided to do that through sexual intimacy with anyone, least of all with a man. I had always said—and sincerely intended—that I would never move contrary to my vow of celibacy until I had come to a deliberated and conscientious decision on the matter. And now, hastily, with no deliberation, no pause for breath, as soon as a bright and handsome man beckoned, I followed him home without so much as a whimper of protest.

"Where was your conscience in all this, priest and monk vowed to celibacy?" I bitterly asked myself on the return ride later that night. "After all, you have to say Mass for a convent of nuns at 6:00 A.M. How can you do that now that you've spent a good part of the night in bed with a man?"

It's much easier to direct a tree before it falls than it is to move it after it's on the ground. There was nothing I could do about my smarting conscience as I offered Mass in the convent chapel the next morning. I arrived in the chapel early and knelt in the back while the nuns were reciting their morning prayers—my own only prayer being that God would forgive me for being about to offer Mass in my condition. Soon after it was over I was making my confession to a fellow priest at the university. He said something that helped me extricate myself from the deep disturbance and remorse of conscience I was feeling: "You know better than to do a thing like that, George," he said simply, "but you also know that the bigger fault was to do it on impulse. Go home now and figure out what it is that you want out of life."

His words carried the beginnings of peace in them: "Figure out what it is that you want out of life." I'd struggled a thousand times in the past months as I faced the "danger" of a sexual liaison with someone at Emmaus, and I'd always walked away with celibacy intact. Now it became clear that celibacy was not the issue. I had already realized at Emmaus that celibacy itself wasn't holding me back, but my sense of duty to the men there. As I thought about it more carefully, my disturbance over the previous night's experience with Tom was not about what had transpired between us, but about the fact that I had not taken time to let my conscience acquiesce in what I was doing.

There were not the same restrictions with Tom that there were with the men of Emmaus. He was fully adult, knew what he was doing, and was not in a stress situation that I might be exploiting by being intimate with him. He was intact, mature, fully competent, self-directing. By the end of the day following Tom's and my first night together, I had concluded that my experiment in intimacy was as likely to be legitimate as anything in my life might be at that time.

I phoned him and was at his apartment in time for dinner that evening.

I knew Rome's syllogisms on the subject of homosexuality by heart. Homosexual sex is wrong, filthy, dirty, immoral, against the natural law, and so on, ad nauseam. By this time, however, my own intuition had so often contradicted and been ahead of Rome's positions and institutionally vested understandings that what I had begun to check for guidance was no longer some jingo composed in Rome, probably hundreds of years ago, but what my own good sense and spiritual insight were telling me.

Today, as I review this episode in my life, I feel that had I turned aside from this opportunity to get close to someone at last and without harm to anyone, it would have been a betrayal of common sense *and honest spirituality*. There was a conviction clarifying within me that church directives about sex, brainwashed by the teachings of generations of a tradition that was nursed on fear and conformism, and whose judgments are formed almost entirely by precedents from a less-educated, more naïve past—that these directives should not be given priority over informed good sense and a personal conscience nurtured by meditation and thoughtfulness.

As I drove home from my second late night with Tom, I was sure I was in love with him.

There was one fly in the ointment, however, and it was a big one. Once again, sex with a man proved unsatisfactory. Disappointingly so. The architecture of two juxtaposed male bodies just didn't work for me. Intimacy, yes. Gentleness, yes. Closeness, sharing, tenderness, caressing, yes. Even the touches of foreplay. But when all of these led further, as they inevitably did, I was still as unsatisfied in 1969 as I had been with Mike in the Philippines in 1947.

Nevertheless, Tom's and my time together was exceptionally happy. We drew very close. And I learned something from him that the vast majority of people, clearly, still don't know: most gay people do not spend all or even a large part of their time obsessing on their genitals. And if some cruising types seem to do so, even for those it's usually only a phase no different than what is accepted as standard for cruising heterosexual jocks in high school and college—and a lot of adult businessmen. Most gay and lesbian people are as involved in the daily things of life as are any others.

With Tom's unwitting help over the next couple of months, I found myself coming to the same determination he had about finding companionship, although not until much later did I match his confidence and verve in doing it. The best I could manage at the moment was to continue courageously in our exotic, erotic training program in a humanness that the seminary and monastery had somehow overlooked.

We'd been seeing each other for somewhat more than two months when our relationship was interrupted by my unexpected trip to Europe. We didn't get together again after my return because by then a woman I had met there had clarified for me, once and for all, where the compass of my most intimate preferences pointed. I called Tom soon after my return, and we talked on the phone a few more times as well. The last time we talked was when he told me about a companion, a young professor at San Francisco State College, who had moved in with him. Just before hanging up this last time, we thanked each other for the weeks we'd had together. It was an honest gratitude in both of us. I had been another step in his search for a companion, he a major milestone in my search for mine.

Switzerland, Molokai, Berkeley

In the last days of my master's program at USF, Katharine said she would, if I wished, call Zurich, Switzerland, and see if she could use her connections there to get me a place in the summer session at the Jung Institute in that city. My finances were in good shape, so to my astonishment and with my gratitude she called. Before I knew it, I was on a flight to Zurich. She also arranged for me to consult there with a world-renowned analyst named Jolande Jacobe, who had been a personal collaborator of Carl Jung. Katharine had studied under this *grande dame* of Jungianism while working for her doctorate in Zurich. She prepared Dr. Jacobe for my coming, and I was received as a friend.

Switzerland was beautiful, exciting, and not at all friendly to students, even to those of us on our best behavior and in the forty-year age bracket. It was the summer of student riots in Paris, and we were treated as suspects on the streets of Zurich and Geneva. We weren't even allowed into France. The only warm welcome we felt was across the borders in Austria, Germany, and Italy.

Despite her reputation, Dr. Jacobe was a disappointment and proved to be not nearly so insightful as Katharine. She seemed more interested in telling tales about the good old days working with Jung than in working with me on my problems. She lost my respect completely one day when she recounted in intimate detail the personal problems of a priest client of hers whom, as it turned out, I had known some years before in the United States.

In retrospect, apart from one unforgettable series of seminars by a husband-and-wife team of Swedish professors, I didn't gain much at the institute. Europe, however, had a gift for me vastly more significant than classes or consultations with an internationally famous analyst.

For two years back in the States, and especially for the eighteen months I worked with Katharine, I had been deliberating concerning what I should do about my vow of celibacy. My experience with Tom had begun impulsively, irresponsibly, but in the end it did help me realize that there was little value left in celibacy—either in itself or for me personally. It certainly made one thing abundantly clear: I needed companionship. But it only confused me more than ever about whether that companionship was to be with a man or woman.

By the time I left for Europe my thinking had come together, and I made a calm and surprisingly anxiety-free decision to go ahead and jettison celibacy, deliberately this time, if and when an appropriate opportunity and a right person came along.

Not only Catholic, but even Jewish and other non-Catholic friends have many times asked in amazement how I could have so easily set aside a solemn promise that I had made to God. First of all, I did not *easily* set it aside. The decision had not come quickly or without much soul-searching.

Promises made to God do not become, once they are uttered, cut-and-dried juridical commitments that must last unchanged forever. Vows to God are expressions of dedication and intention made at a given moment in given conditions of a person's spiritual development. If the conditions of the one who makes the vows were never to change, then his or her obligation to those vows would never change either. But if the realities in a person's life do substantially change, then the obligations of another day and situation change accordingly and proportionately.

In a similar situation, it's all too easy and theologically puerile to dictate blithely that once married, forever married. A good divorce is better than a bad marriage any day. Yes, of course, the union should be given every effort at survival and/or recovery. But if the love bond, which alone is the basis for the bilateral contract called marriage, is indeed broken—and for whatever reason—then that fact should be recognized, declared, and the two lives should move on along separate ways, taking advantage of lessons learned. Divorce is not defeat; it is a life experience that, like all others, carries lessons for us. Religious vows are not unlike marriage vows.

By no means are religious vows ever ends in themselves. The only purpose and end of religion or religious observance of any sort is closer union with God—or, more accurately, a greater awareness of the perfect union with Eternal Being that by our nature we already necessarily have. Promises made to God that we will or will not do such and such are made *only* to draw closer to God. Practicing poverty or obedience, maintaining celibacy, and faithfully staying in one convent or monastery for the rest of one's days, as Trappists promise, have no value whatsoever in themselves. If and when and in so far as these observances and promises help us center on God, they are priceless. If they don't ever make sense to some people, or no longer make sense to those for whom they once did, they become useless and, more often than not, counterproductive. I believe it was the seventeenth-century French bishop, Bossuet, who once characterized the nuns of the Cistercian convent of Port Royal on the edge of Paris as being "as pure as angels and as proud as devils." Their celibacy was intact, but that effort obviously stole attention from something of far greater importance.

We do not live in a universe ruled by iron-clad, inflexible specifics. We live in one of unfolding Eternal Process, one ruled by Divine Mind and Heart, and the most iron-clad rule of all is that we are not only permitted but urged to take charge of our lives and use the mind and heart God gave us to respond as self-directed, responsible individuals. The days are gone when religious—and marriage—vows are to be observed at the cost of personal growth, fulfillment, happiness, dignity. That sort of unbending legalism may make sense in the world of a child or of a young race, but children grow up and the human race, too, is no longer infantile. We all have both the right and responsibility to make first *and successive* choices that suit and further our spiritual growth as our lives unfold. This holds true when our successive choices run afoul of dated attitudes and meaningless laws still perpetuated by those who grow at a different pace or have other interests at heart.

During my last session with Katharine before I left for Europe, she and I had a bit of fun selecting a code phrase—"pleasant Swiss evening"—that I was to incorporate into a letter to her if, while there, I did, as she put it, "get into the bed of bliss with someone." She kindly told me she knew wisdom would be with me and that I would decide responsibly, but that her own personal hope was that I would "be so lucky as to meet someone who will be so lucky as to experience your sensitive and waiting ability to love." I was deeply affected by her statement and knew she was right: I did have a restless potential to love someone in ways that would include, but stretch far beyond, genital sex.

Louisa was a petite, soft-spoken, just-stepped-out-of-*Vogue* sort of woman, one who since childhood had known the privileged life provided by the "old money" of many generations. She took for granted limousines, exquisite jewelry, the finest clothing, and the best suites in the best hotels. I was charmed by the respectful manner in which she spoke to waiters and taxi drivers and that several times during our travels she sent picture postcards to her household servants at home. Unlike some wealthy persons I've known, Louisa wore her money easily and didn't pause to caress it as it passed through her hands. I once watched her give a substantial handout to a begging family in Lugano with all the care and respect a thoughtful person would use to give money to dearly loved relatives. She had a fineness and nobility I admired openly, and she once told me she appreciated being with a companion who recognized her as the person she had worked so hard to become.

Saying that Louisa turned out to be the companion who arrived in my life at the right place at the right time might sound as if I imagine she had been put in my path just for me to use her. But the fact is that all the wheels of reality work together in mutually perfect timing, and she several times reminded me that I had also arrived with equal timing in her own life, emerging as she was from a year-long period of grieving over the sudden death of her husband.

Our relationship began when I accidentally backed into her in a quaint Zurich shop that sells only umbrellas. She accepted my apology with one of her special smiles and a slight nod of her head. The very next day, as luck or a loving Providence would have it, our paths crossed again in another store. This time I was a bit more attentive, and we exchanged a few sentences about the coincidence of this second meeting in as many days. I asked her if she would join me for a cup of coffee. She was precommitted, but agreed to meet me for lunch the next day. Even after the first meeting the day before, she had become a thought I could scarcely dismiss, and after this one I could think of nothing else.

A second lunch followed the first one, then a dinner, and then a dinner followed by an opera. And punctuating our meals were walks along the Limmat and through Zurich's old churches and parks. I found it all a bit scary, but I was determined I would not take time to back off and figure things out. Louisa later told me that she was surprised at how quickly we drew close.

I was not accustomed to have a woman pay my way, and I protested the first time she reached for the bill after one of our early lunches. She looked at me with her intense brown eyes and quietly said I was foolish to take money, or its source, so seriously. As simply as if it were routine, she pointed out that as a student I was undoubtedly on a budget, and that she had more money than she needed. "Be realistic and permit me, then, to make our meeting less stressful for your budget." From that point on, she paid for everything. And there were many "things" to pay for. We became inseparable, often meeting for breakfast at her hotel, having lunch at exotic spots that she seemed to locate with some kind of sixth sense, and then dinner at restaurants where I myself could scarcely have afforded a cocktail. I was relieved that she never patronized me, never offered to buy me anything personal, except once when she rented a tuxedo for me for a gala affair that required white-tie formal dress.

I was struck by her affluence, but of a sort other than material. It was her easy pride in herself and the effortless security and un-affected humility with which she expressed it that captured my at-tention. I was as charmed as astonished by her freedom from feelings of guilt and fear. Even during our first lunch when I learned she was Catholic and told her I was a priest, she simply congratulated me on the years of effort that implied and then asked if it bothered me to spend time with a woman. I assured her it did not. She smiled and said, "I'm glad." We never mentioned it again. As long as I knew her, she graciously maneuvered through every external circumstance without dismay or disturbance of any kind that I ever witnessed. She was an elegant, lovely, self-aware woman and a constant delight as a companion.

She was also a good lover.

After Louisa and I had been together for several days and had fenced with increasingly explicit sexual innuendos, we finally de-cided to take our growing friendship into bed. After my explicit proposal, she invited me back to her hotel suite as naturally as if for a cup of coffee.

The experience that followed was—immediately—something very special and very new in my life. Sex had never before carried for me any of the overtones and meanings that it suddenly now had. My "gotta-prove-myself," animal-like humping in high school was the only imagery that I had ever had with which to fan-tasize sex with women. Now, suddenly, making love proved to be just that, something else entirely from anything I had ever known.

It was no longer that of a boy with a high-school fledgling nor of a confused man, somewhat reluctant, with another man. Now it was a thing of perfect proportion and beauty and fragrances and softness, intense and gentle, unhurried and somehow scarcely physical, and at the same time the most delightfully physical thing I'd ever done. And I was with a woman of the world as lovely and sophisticated as I could dream of. The nervousness I felt on our first late-afternoon tryst lasted two or three minutes at most, and it never returned. Louisa and I seemed as natural in bed together as if it had always been planned, as if we had known such a relationship for years. Her presence seemed more a thing from a sanctuary than from a bed of passion. But passion there certainly was, and when I left her suite to go back to my lodgings, I was more centered than I'd ever been in my life. Katharine Taylor had been right: the mingling of bodies in love carries with it a dimension that, not unlike meditation, one has to experience personally to be able even to imagine. Late though it was when I got to my room, I wrote to Katharine before going to bed: "Dear Katharine, You would not believe the pleasant Swiss evenings we are having...."

Of the various places Louisa and I went in Austria, Germany, Switzerland, and Italy, Rome was the highlight. We contracted with a taxi driver to be our personal tour guide and asked him to show us the usual tourist spots. Louisa was quick to realize that the ancient places in that great city meant more to me than mere tourist curiosities. For years I had read and spoken more Latin than English in choir and classes, and it was long since like a second language to me. In the process, I had also been steeped in the culture and history of the Roman Empire. And here we were in the capital of that ancient empire. I found myself walking the very Senate floor where more than two thousand years before, in a text I knew well, Cicero had made a case—and lost it—for his friend Milo. Over there was where Julius Caesar once marched into the Forum with some of his legions returning home from Gaul. I was able to walk on the very floor of the vestal virgins' convent, which it once would have cost me my life even to gaze upon. I stood in awe in cavernous public baths and imagined the din of the huge crowds of good citizens coming to refresh themselves on sultry Roman afternoons and evenings. Several times Louisa found other things to do so I could seat myself in silence within some ruin to let the ancient stones whisper to me.

One afternoon she asked if I wanted to go the next day to an audience with the pope. I looked at her in surprise and said, "Are you kidding!" We spent the next morning in the delights of our hotel suite instead, and that evening at dinner I told her that my decision of that day—my *choice* of that day—seemed to symbolize uniquely my recapture of my life from the church. She said nothing, but when I had finished speaking raised her wineglass, and the expression of her sweetest smile told me she understood.

I rose particularly early one morning and made my way alone from our hotel to the Coliseum that had been pictured on the cover of my first-year Latin grammar. The guards had not yet come on duty for the day, so I climbed over all the barriers and cautiously made my way to the topmost bit of that ancient structure. In some strange way, sitting there as the sun rose over this mystic and now smazy city, I felt as if I were, or had been, an intimate part of the ancient world of this imperial *Roma*. From atop the Coliseum I could see a great metropolitan expanse that seemed to be clattering as much with ancient chariots and people clad in tunics and togas as it was with honking taxis, befouling diesel buses, and impatient commuters. It was as if the dimension called time were suddenly missing. I was outside of it. I was free of it and no longer locked in a sequential reality.

The sun crept over the horizon exactly as it had when Augustus was down there being roused by his slaves after they had prepared his morning bath. The sun was rising just as it had in A.D. 455, when Vandals wandered through these streets, past this same Coliseum, first in reverent amazement and then in murder and fiery pillage after one of them had his awe-filled face slapped for having dared to stroke the white beard of a supercilious senator.

I watched the ancient capital awaken for almost two hours before returning to the hotel and my special friend. Louisa was having coffee in our suite. This lovely lady was my playmate in a garden of delight where the games included pleasures of the body, but also so much more that is human and companionable and full of creative adventure. I poured myself some coffee and took a seat across from her to share my Coliseum adventure. When I was finished, she smiled and rose to come nestle beside me and remark softly, "And the best part of an experience like that is that we can never find the right words for it. Correct?" She was right, exactly right.

We enjoyed our time together enormously, and yet neither of us ever spoke as if our relationship were meant to last. Theoretically, at least, I was free and could have stayed with her, but while I now knew where I stood on the issue of celibacy and loneliness—I wanted none of either—my mind was still not sure where I stood regarding my role as priest. I still loved being a priest, and—whatever the church might say—priesthood and celibacy were two separate realities for me. Louisa, too, was free, but she had her own life and never gave any indication that she wanted me to be a permanent part of it. We were both on vacation, as it were, from life as we knew it. We both had tears when we said good-bye at the Zurich airport and she boarded her flight to Madrid. Our vacation from life was over. We were going back, better, to our separate parts of the world. We have never contacted each other again.

Making love with a beautiful woman did not disturb me as I had long fantasized it might. I was, after all, a changing person, if not yet totally changed. I wasn't wholly free yet, but I was on the way. As with other close companions of the past, whether sexual activity had been involved or not, my heart blessed the day I met Louisa. Each of these persons—Peggy, Datus, Mike, Matthew, Tom, Katharine, Louisa—was a gift from God. I can only hope that I was as much a gift to each of them as they were to me.

The hold the church had on my private life was being replaced inexorably by a sense of wholeness and independence. The progress was linear. First, I'd had to realize—be honest enough to admit, that is—that I was lonely despite my touted priesthood and proudly venerable monasticism. Then I had to admit that I could, and should, do something about that loneliness. Then I had to decide if I could live with celibacy or would live better without it. Emmaus, Tom, and Louisa were major milestones and turning points in the resulting decisions.

My priesthood alone remained without resolution.

After Louisa left, I still had a few days before I would return to Frankfurt, Germany, to catch my flight back to California. Classes at the institute were over for the summer, so I used one of my remaining days to take a train ride back into the Alps. Another lesson awaited me. Another aspect of my unfolding still needed attention, and Switzerland had an answer for it.

Louisa left no doubt in my mind that I was a heterosexual, but while my lingering habits of self-disparagement might be only a fraction of what they had been as a youth and younger man, some old patterns of thought remained. Another young man, Pierre this time, would help me recognize that my stubborn obsession with muscular male bodies was still alive in me despite all that had happened in the past year.

Late in the afternoon after a long day's hike in the Alps, I was waiting in a small Hofbrauhaus for my train back to Zurich. I ordered a sandwich and a beer and had only begun to eat when a twenty-year old French student from Paris introduced himself and asked if I would mind if he sat with me so he could practice his English. He said he knew I was American by the way I had ordered *"Ein Bier, bitte."* (So much for my weeks of trying to go native.) We launched into a lively exchange that was to last for about three hours.

Unlike the train that never seemed to come, my attraction to, or at least excessive admiration for, his princely frame arrived right on schedule: immediately. From my first sight of Pierre, I was agog over what struck me as his striking masculinity. Not traditionally good looking, he was nevertheless something of a lusty Greek god in his lanky muscularity and dimpled, laid-back easiness. My reaction to him surprised me, just emerging as I was from several weeks of glorious heterosexual sex with a strikingly handsome woman.

My God! Was I gay after all?

As Pierre and I talked, laughed, and guzzled our beers, I seemed to be watching our interchange from the back of my mind. It was as if a second person were in there trying to analyze what my attraction to him was all about. His proportion of form was distracting me from our conversation. It was clear I didn't want to seduce him, and I didn't want him to seduce me. So what was the fascination? What was all this about if it wasn't about sex? My confusion and ongoing analysis lasted until the very last moment before our train was ready to depart.

Just as we were boarding, he to sit among other students, I to find, hopefully, someone with whom to practice my German, I hit gold. We had just shaken hands and laughed a final time at his faulty English, my faultier French, when, as he turned to go, I realized in a flash what the confusion had been, not only this afternoon, but all my life.

It wasn't Mike's or Tom's or now Pierre's or any other man's muscular maleness I wanted, *but my own.* I hadn't ever really wanted to impinge on them sexually. I'd tried that and been disappointed every time. What I really wanted was whatever it was they had that their proportion of form symbolized for me. Their masculine proportioning was a symbol, a *sign* of what I wanted, and not what I wanted in itself. I wanted their seeming wholeness, self-possession, self-presence, self-establishment. I didn't want *them,* I wanted *me!* My problem was that simple. I'd failed all these years to see that what I wanted was not the symbols themselves, but what the symbols stood for.

This insight has stood the test of time. One more silent click was heard in the universe as my life inched another notch forward on its path.

It was only one insight, however, albeit a major one. It wasn't a magic flight all the way out of my long conditioning and history. In some ways the lesson would have to be repeated again later at the Lincoln Memorial in Washington, D.C. But for now the pressure was off. Male beauty would still turn my head, but no longer more than it would find itself turning for female beauty. I no longer confused admiration for a body with a desire for sexual contact. There's a great freedom in this distinction, once realized. It leaves plenty of room for guiltless admiration when shapely figures saunter past. It's not that much different than visiting a beautiful floral conservatory and feeling no desire whatsoever to steal blossoms.

One of my theology professors, Father Jerome, confided once that since he was a young seminarian in the Franciscan order, he had refused to go to a beach because he couldn't go without "staring myself right into hell." Except for Pierre and my insight in the Swiss high country that afternoon, I might still today be just as silly. I wonder if I would ever have realized, as apparently Jerome had not, that when you can't take your eyes off the beauty of a Siberian tiger preening in the sunshine at the zoo, it doesn't imply that you want to take the beast home to bed.

As I look back in perspective on the spring and summer of 1969, I realize that I gave up much more than celibacy during that period. By the end of the summer, fear of sexual intimacy in my life had been overcome once and for all, and at long last I could see it as just another part of human wholeness. The fear and contempt of sexuality that, in his lingering guilt and Manichean hangover, Augustine of Hippo had overlaid on Christianity in the early fifth century was finally out of me. Datus had said, "I don't surround my eating, tooth brushing, or bowel movements with taboos and hush-hush rituals, so why should I do so for my sexuality? If I don't surround my hands or ears with shame, why should I do so for my penis?" At last, twenty-three years later, neither did I.

I discussed this realization with a priest friend after my return from Europe, and I compared sexual functioning to a handshake. Shaking someone's hand, I argued, can be an act of greeting, respect, or promise, or it can be used to confirm a lie or to reassure falsely. Why should the use of a penis be seen as any different than the use of a hand? Sexual functioning in itself is neither good nor not good; it all depends on how and where and why it's done. In no way is it better to avoid sex than to have sex. In no way is celibacy preferable to a sexual activity that honors love, honesty, fairness. My priest friend worried that I might be just rationalizing my affair in Europe, but five years later, after he had himself left the priesthood and married, we had the same conversation once again. This time he argued my case even more strongly than I had. Rome, of course, is still impervious to both reason and human experience on this matter, as on so many others, and continues to sleep soundly as increasing numbers of its priests go awry in all sorts of deceitful or even criminal substitutions for healthy sexual functioning.

My humanity had awakened and was beginning to stretch. I began looking around with a new sense of purpose. I saw everyone in a new way—women at last included. Having dropped my defenses around them, I was now able to relate to the female half of the human race in a new and wholesome manner and as easily as I did to the male half. I suddenly found I had many female *friends.*

By the time I returned from Europe, I was primed for a permanent relationship that, as Tom had said about finding his companion, I now knew was bound to happen sooner or later. I began hoping it would be sooner.

From the viewpoint of my life's fulfillment, I could not have met the woman I would eventually marry at a more timely moment. From the viewpoint of the Church of Rome, she could not have come along at a more inopportune one, for I certainly was, in the church's word, "vulnerable."

Vulnerable at last! Thank God Almighty, vulnerable at last!

———————

After returning to San Francisco, I almost immediately caught a plane to the Kalaupapa leper colony on the island of Molokai in Hawaii. My friend Jerry, on staff there, was having some sort of crisis and had urgently asked me to come. His crisis turned out to be not very serious, but the week I spent on that island was another gift from the universe for more reasons than that it was seven days in a paradise of warm sands and body-temperature ocean. It proved to be my time to consolidate what had happened in Europe before I had to return to the academic world in the Bay Area.

The colony happened to have one of its frequent dances scheduled for the evening before my week there was over. By custom or, as some said, by law, a rope was stretched across the dance floor; infected people were to dance on one side and the noninfected on the other. Jerry and I and a few of the lepers with whom I had become friends after several long evenings of conversation, soon removed the rope, and for a few hours I happily danced with as many lepers as staff persons. Late in the evening, an unhappy staff doctor wryly told me, "Well, Father, now we'll just have to wait twelve years to see if you've got yourself infected with Hansen's disease, won't we." As history turned out, he need not have worried.

What I carried away from Molokai was not disease, but memories, images, and loving feelings for and from the gentle people who live there, people who seemed to exemplify the inner glow I was just beginning to feel myself. They were a fragrance lingering from my European caper. Their love reassured me once again that love is, truly, the substance of life and is, indeed, as beautiful as it is pleasurable.

Just before I boarded the small plane that was to carry me back to Honolulu from the sandy beach at the colony, a little elderly leper, Rose Kato, handed me a small card she told me she had spent a good bit of the previous night preparing. She did this without the help of fingers, which, along with her ears and toes, she had lost to leprosy as a teenager. Her elegantly delicate gift was made from bits of sand, tiny shells, and dried plants carefully glued onto a folded card to form a tropical island scene. Inside she had written a note asking that I take a bit of her back to the mainland "where I have always wanted to go and never could." Both of us had tears in our eyes as we hugged good-bye. As I turned to glance from the four-seater plane rising from the beach, I saw her standing beside Jerry who had an arm around her shoulders. She was waving one arm and drying her eyes with the other. I wondered if the varieties of love that were appearing in my life would ever stop. The young Japanese-Hawaiian pilot saw me wipe my eyes and said simply, "My grandmother was a leper, Father."

Another plane back to the mainland, and I was packing my things at the convent to move into an apartment in Concord, across the Bay and east of Berkeley. The apartment and my next year's education were to be paid for by a grant that I had obtained to study graduate psychology and do an intern year in pastoral counseling. From the apartment in Concord, I would juggle my work at the psychiatric ward of the Veterans Administration Hospital in Martinez and classes at the Graduate Theological Union in Berkeley, a consortium of graduate theology schools associated with the University of California there.

As it turned out, interning in pastoral counseling was to be the least of my interests in the coming year.

19

Lori

She struck me as something of a Tinkerbell of a nun—although it was evident from the first that she was clearly her own self-confident person. I'd never before seen eyes like those of the bright-faced woman that sparkled back across the table at me on the first day of a Berkeley seminar in October 1969. It wasn't just that her eyes were big. They were alive—they talked—they laughed—they danced! I was completely taken by them, and then by her. And, I couldn't help but notice, her fragrance rivaled that of Louisa.

Sister Loretta Ann, a petite Victory Noll Missionary sister for twenty years, campus minister at Purdue University for the past six, and now a fellow student in Berkeley on a Danforth Foundation Fellowship, told the class she preferred to be called Lori. She looked across the table at each of us—and me—in a way that was personal and intense. Her gaze never pushed roughly into my space the way the aggressive Sister of the Disintegrating Veil had done at USF, but it was intense. At first Lori's eyes distracted me, and then *she* did. I sensed right from the start that the pope wasn't going to be happy about the relationship that could develop here.

I didn't know what to do with those eyes that kept catching me looking at her. I was a priest and shouldn't be noticing eyes like that and looking at them as often as I found myself doing. A seminary training geared to celibates had warned me against this sort of innocent beginning. One thing was immediately certain: this little nun was certainly going to make this seminar different from any I'd been in before.

From that first day, Lori created outrageous emotions in me—fun and dancing of a kind I'd never experienced. It was as if I'd suddenly discovered a new room in my house, one I'd never known was there. Certainly one I'd never been in before. A room reserved for happiness only.

Lori was clearly charming the professor and every student present. I was dismayed—although the seminary-trained part of me was grateful—when I felt sure that I'd be lost in her crowd, never particularly noticed by her. My self-doubts were not as strong as they'd been in the past, but they were still strong enough that I couldn't find it in myself to imagine that this delightful woman would single me out for notice in a class of twelve men. I couldn't hope for that even had I wanted to, I told myself. After all, nuns do not usually "single men out." Even so, it still seemed to me that it would be especially pleasant to have those eyes looking my way more often than they looked in anyone else's direction.

I shared the ride into Berkeley each day with Fred Aigner, a new friend just beginning the same graduate program and a neighbor of mine in Concord. On the way home after that first seminar, I was eager to talk about what was going on in me. And so, with long-practiced care for calculated objectivity, I asked him in studied cool, "Did you notice that woman sitting across the table from me in the seminar this afternoon, Fred?"

Showing not a trace of concern for my embarrassed monkishness, Fred exploded in laughter as only someone can who has no investment whatsoever in the careful niceties of career celibacy. He fairly shouted, "Yes, Georgie, I noticed her, and I noticed that you noticed her." Delicate Fred. He'd been lying in wait. Damn it! Didn't he realize I was a Catholic priest? Young and married and Lutheran, he obviously saw no dangers at all in male-female attraction. In honor of his mentor, Martin Luther—an ex-monk married to an ex-nun from my own religious order—Fred had to be enjoying the fact that suddenly he was himself dealing with another ex-monk taking aim at a "soon-to-be-ex-" nun. I laughed at his outburst, but was too concerned about its implications to be amused. Was my attraction to Lori, then, that obvious?

I loved Fred and his wife, Sally, from the moment we met. At the apartment complex where we lived, we often spent all Saturday with other neighbors playing Marco Polo in the Olympic-sized pool. Fred and Sally quickly became a breath of health and balance in my life, and over the next few weeks they played a significant role in keeping me honest.

Lori disturbed me so much because I sensed that in her I was attracted to much more than a possible amorous frolic. If my intuitive sense about what I was feeling for her was correct, she could easily lead to dramatic changes in my life that I was not sure I was ready to face. It was one thing to have decided never to return to the cloister in Utah. For that Rome was only upset. And it was only slightly more upsetting to Rome for me to have forfeited celibacy. For doing that, with either man or woman, Rome would only slap me on the wrist and send me off to confession. But it would be quite something else, far more serious, and would involve automatic excommunication and the loss of my right to function as a priest were I to get married. A new kind of shiver started moving up my spine each time I saw Lori and her big eyes. I began to dread—as well as look forward to—Dr. Bob Leslie's seminar.

There have always been married priests in the Eastern Orthodox church, even in some of the few parts of it that have remained under the jurisdiction of the pope. Rumor had always had it, too, that a diocese hidden away in the hills low on the Italian boot also allowed its priests to marry. (No one I ever met could prove or disprove this, so carefully was the mere possibility hidden by Rome.) My own options to marry as a priest were far more restricted. Theoretically it was possible that, after mountains of paperwork and a delay that often stretched into years, I *might* be allowed to marry with the blessing of the church. No guarantees. If it happened at all, however, it would be at the price of ever functioning again as a priest and of much supercilious abuse from the Roman curia.

My other possibility, and the only one that I would realistically consider at all if I decided to get married, was that I would simply marry and say to hell with all the bureaucracy. That would mean a special type of automatic excommunication, as well as suspension from ever functioning again as a priest. As Lori and I kept trading glances across the seminar table, I didn't like my options.

It's true, I had by now rejected many positions that Catholicism teaches and expected me as a priest to teach. I totally disagreed with its "Come home to Rome" attitude toward Protestants, its disdain for oriental religions, and its condemnation of "evils" like birth control and masturbation. But my heart was still warmly attached to much that I knew in the church. I had never really thought about the possibility of forfeiting everything that was still precious to me about Catholicism.

Granted all that, I had to admit also that I was being pressed by a deeper element in life than the preservation of good standing in the church or any sentimental attachment to it. With a consciously calculated risk and an irrepressible, almost reluctant enthusiasm, I decided to pursue, ever so cautiously, a relationship with this little woman with the big eyes who seemed always to manage to sit directly across from me in the seminar.

To my thrilled—and unthrilled—surprise, it became evident after the first week that she had, indeed, singled me out among the men in the class, not in a flirtatious way but simply in a specially attentive, particularly charming way. I was flattered, delighted—and scared as hell. Against my better judgment, or, more accurately, against that of my church, I pushed on. I had an intuitive trust that everything would work out well in the end if only I managed to be honest and open along the way.

The eleven weeks from the day we met until the day we were married were the most wonderful and the most difficult weeks of my life.

Lori and I shared with each other all the good things that were going on in us during those excitement-filled days of Pope John XXIII's reform. I told Lori about my past in great detail and eventually about how she seemed to be pulling it all together into meaning for me. I told her about the girls in high school, about Datus and Mike and Tom, even about Louisa. She didn't blink.

Very soon, I knew that the question here was not whether Lori and I would or should go to bed together, but whether we should make a life together. On our first date, I instinctively knew that she would not even consider the bed idea, but from the moment I first mentioned the possibility of a life together, she seemed interested. I came away from that conversation wondering, "What in hell am I doing?"

A week after meeting her when I heard her mention to someone that she'd not yet been across the Bay into San Francisco, I offered to take her over in my new Grandé Mustang and show her "my" city. On that first time with her alone, a time we would subsequently refer to as our first date—a word we would never have thought of using the day it happened—I put my arm around her shoulder as we crossed the busy street in front of the Cliff House at Land's End. Surely the abbot would approve of this scoutlike concern on my part for an innocent nun's safety.

That was one small step for a man to take, but a giant leap away from his celibate lifestyle. From that contact on, the need to make a major decision was no longer theoretical, but an immediate and pressing reality. Our closeness felt so good, intimate, totally right, despite the screaming of my training that told me it was wrong, sinful, totally risky.

The simple act of putting my arm around Lori's shoulders precipitated a review of my life situation. I had not yet been completely honest with myself about my untenable situation and had fantasized that I would be able to find some spot teaching in a university or as a chaplain in the Veterans Administration or in one of the armed services and would be able to slip by unnoticed. That first date with Lori was a reality check. It let me know in no uncertain terms that greater honesty than what I'd suspected was to be required of me. I'd been dreaming that I would be able to function as a priest even though I no longer felt that a great portion of what Rome and the archdiocese were asking of me made any sense whatsoever. Contrary to what Catholicism demanded, I openly counseled some couples to get a divorce and, to some of my priest friends' horror, came up with the dictum, "A good divorce is better than a bad marriage." I routinely told young men to quit giving a second thought to their imagined sin of masturbation. I refused to absolve it when they mentioned it in the confessional. "There's no sin to absolve," I would explain to them to their astonishment and openly expressed relief. It is not that I was being indifferent to my obligations, but just that I felt constrained to execute them at a level deeper than with rote, programmed formulas. I was about to learn that I would now have to start applying that sort of total honesty to myself and to my own problems as well.

After we had a cocktail together in the Cliff House lounge, perched out over the Pacific surf, I bought her a locket —"just a souvenir of our day together in San Francisco, you know." Then I bought myself a ring for my pinkie—"just to remember a pleasant day, you know." My feelings were moving me to spontaneous expression, even though I didn't yet dare look directly at what those feelings were.

Our first cocktail together turned out to be unexpectedly prophetic. I forget what drink Lori ordered, but, as new at choosing cocktails as I was at dating nuns, I ordered some god-awful concoction that I wouldn't even taste today. It was called witch's brew and was made from a variety of sweet liqueurs as heavy as oil. The swizzle stick in it was a small, upside-down broom holding a little paper "fortune" in its plastic straws. I stuck the note in my billfold and still have it. Isaiah was never more prophetic:

> Your heart is a hunter and is quick to give chase. But why waste ammunition at long distance? The time is near when you must backtrack and take more careful aim. Remember, even the most elusive game responds to a mating call.

We laughed when I read it aloud, but I was inwardly aghast. Lori seemed to laugh simply, honestly: only that. She didn't seem to have any of my hesitations about what was, after all, a fairly straightforward, if tardy, life development. She later told me that she knew within the first week of our meeting where our relationship was going and that she never once had any qualms about it.

My heart was, indeed, already "giving chase," even though my training was crying out in alarm to have me run in the opposite direction.

"Long distance?" Not at all; she was right here beside me.

"Backtrack?" Indeed, if that's what you call restructuring your whole life and your relationship with a church that has dominated the adult portion of it.

"Game?" This "game" was sitting across the table from me and showing no signs whatsoever of being "elusive."

But it was the "mating call" of the note that bothered me most of all. That sounded dreadfully close to being a new commitment in conflict with my present one.

We drove back across the Bay Bridge to Berkeley and had our first meal together in her student apartment on the edge of campus. Lori had had a turkey cooking while we were in San Francisco and that evening served a Thanksgiving dinner with all the trimmings. When an amused dinner guest, himself a married priest, asked what we were already giving thanks about, I was not amused. Was I to be pressured from outside as well as from within?

Lori had invited this priest and his new, ex-nun bride to share the meal. Earl and Eleanor LaBerge, two people who have remained our closest friends over the years, kept smiling in knowingness as they watched us play a familiar, dutiful little churchy game called "getting acquainted without getting involved." When they returned to their apartment, they told us later, Earl told his wife that we would be married before Christmas. He was sure of it, and I was busy backpedaling to prove he was wrong.

———

A bald fear began kneading me day and night. A choice was being forced upon me by nobody but me. It would have been easier had it come from someone else. I had learned to resist the demands of others, those of my family, my abbot, my bishop, my fellow priests, even my own body, but never the demands of logic. Many nights in the weeks to follow I sat alone with a cup of cocoa, wondering what Datus would advise me to do. At some level, of course, I knew what he would say, but I wasn't *sure* that I knew it—or that I wanted to know it.

For a few months in the abbey years before, I'd had an occasional nightmare about having left monastic life and been unfaithful to my vows of poverty, obedience, and, especially, chastity. Those nightmares in the late 1950s are the only ones I've ever had as an adult. And here I was in waking life, a priest dating a nun, apparently on the road to fulfilling my only nightmare.

Lori was my heaven; a wavering loyalty to my priesthood and church was my hell.

Fred and Sally sat up with me late into the night sometimes, patiently listening to what, as I think of it now, must have been totally new and utterly confusing territory for them. After all, it wasn't as if I was trying to decide whether or not to burn something down or kidnap, kill, or maim somebody. I was only trying, with disproportionate agony of conscience, to decide whether or not to marry somebody. How foreign that must have sounded to healthy Lutheran ears. They listened, they questioned, they helped me sort everything along the way.

All three of us recognized that Lori had clearly begun to light up my life. Because of their own deep faith and gentle spirit, Fred and Sally understood my dilemma as well as if they were cradle Catholics. But they went further. They brought a new kind realism and life-affirming, *self*-affirming freedom to the decision-making process.

They understood well that one of the realities I had to deal with was that I had made some weighty "solemn-vow" promises to God. They helped me put these vows into a new kind of perspective and to remember again that life is a *process* which, thank God, remains forever open-ended.

I had worked this out before, but now again and with vastly more at stake than simple celibacy, I had to explain to myself what "solemn vows" meant to me. The only purpose and meaning of the vow of poverty is to help ensure that we keep God in our minds and hearts as our highest wealth. It has no value whatsoever as simple assurance that we own nothing. Obedience to external authority is useful only if and in so far as and as long as it helps us be responsive to our own highest inner insights and guidance. Celibacy has no meaning at all except insofar as it helps us for a time not to be swamped in physical pleasure at the expense of spiritual value and purpose. Legalistic, institutionalized expression of these vows is useful only when and if external observance serves the inner. It becomes counterproductive once the inner is activated and stabilized, in the same way that prolonged parental guidance turns harmful after a child is grown.

Lori was having none of these difficulties. Now, years later, she says she is still surprised at how quickly and easily she understood she could achieve the purpose of her vows while living with a husband just as she had for twenty years while living as a nun. It still feels good to hear her say that as soon as she saw what sort of person I was, she had no more doubts. The particular form her intention in life had taken, her vows, was simply no longer meaningful. Vows had served their purpose in her life. Her dedication to God could now take another form.

As Datus had done long before in trying to help me debunk some of my fearful attitudes about sex, she handled one of my greatest difficulties with an ease that both mystified and dismayed me. And this added to my difficulty. What was wrong with me? Why couldn't I get it together as she had?

Or was something wrong with *her?*

How could she be so lighthearted about a matter of such grave importance? As soon as I formulated this accusation, however, my heart knew the answer, that in some way or other she was right and

I was wrong. My abstract principles might be dismayed, but my heart and common sense were as lighthearted and happy as Lori.

I saw from the beginning that it wasn't economic concerns about forfeiting my status as a priest that pressed me. I never doubted I could make a living on my own. Something more spiritual was bothering me. It had been a difficult decision to give up my celibacy, and now it was proving to be still more difficult to give up my priesthood.

Could, as I suspected, this situation be an invitation straight from the Bible: "Friend, come up higher"?

As the days moved into weeks, Lori and I became inseparable. As we talked more and more intimately about where we were in our relationship, she seemed to be happier and happier. But while I enjoyed her company and was happier than I'd ever been, I wasn't able to shake my inner turmoil.

And then suddenly, about four weeks after it had begun, I awoke one morning with the whole matter resolved. I sat up in bed with perfect clarity. What had been causing my hesitation was a floating fear that in losing my priesthood and the church I might also lose my relationship with God, the one stable and reassuring element in my life around which all else moved.

With that dawn came the realization that I had all this while been buying the notion, taught so explicitly and in so many subtle ways in the seminary, that being disobedient to the church means you are, by that fact, disobedient to God. And to disobey God is to lose God. That loss would mean for me losing what over the years had given me the only bit of inner health, authenticity, personal validity I had. It would mean throwing away the one means whereby I was breaking free of old compulsions, frantic impulsiveness, and—the abbot's favorite word repeatedly driven into my self-assessment—"immaturity."

My inner life certainly, and my outer life increasingly, had begun for some years to have a sense of sublime security, joy, okayness. Was I going to lose these if I lost my membership and function in the Catholic church? I was at last feeling safe and happy and good. Would I lose these if I traded in the church for Lori?

Of course not!

Now that my secret fear was at a conscious level, I was able to dispose of it quickly. When I saw Lori later in the morning, I told her about my breakthrough, and from that moment there was nothing present to qualify the happiness I felt about her being in my life.

I decided to celebrate my new freedom and our decision to marry by having a dinner party, the first I'd ever attempted in my life. I had not the slightest idea of how to carry it off because I'd never once cooked a meal. Everywhere I'd ever lived there was always someone cooking for me, whether mother or Mrs. Maclean, navy cooks or brother cooks at the abbey, or nuns at the convent. Since moving to Concord I'd simply eaten at restaurants. Half the fun of preparing my first dinner, I promised, was going to be the challenge of doing something entirely different—something that verged, I knew, on being entirely impossible. But I was getting used to the difficult, and I was no longer paralyzed by the imagined impossible.

New pans, china, flatware, glasses, napkins, tablecloth, candlesticks were the beginning. Then came several dishes put together from a borrowed cookbook and with my most neurotic care for detail. The dinner was a huge success.

Except, Lori never lets me forget, that in a moment of inspired creativity I added salted peanuts to the green salad.

"Unorthodox and therefore fitting," is my routine reply.

20

The World a Final Time

Lori and I set a date for our wedding, and continued to fill our weekends—and every schoolday we dared—with trips in my baby-blue Grandé to places all over northern California. We had lots of friends, both in San Francisco and Berkeley, and they seemed as happy with our decision as we were. Everywhere we went people seemed to know about the upcoming marriage of a priest and nun.

It was a time of great warmth, of unimaginable happiness, a whole new world of having someone special next to me in the car. We drove countless back roads, and the Mustang always got us back in time for classes and studies, which had by now become terminally boring for both of us. We agreed that it was the first time in our lives either of us had found ourself plodding unwillingly off to school.

Besides planning for the wedding, there were more immediate considerations. The biggest was the fact that we were supporting two apartments, two phones, two heating bills, and a lot of gas running between Berkeley and Concord. Since we planned to get married, the sooner we moved into one apartment, it seemed to us, the better. We were each living on generous education grants, but it made lots of sense to do away with duplicate expenses since we'd soon be furnishing a new home.

We wince now at how small the one-bedroom apartment was that we found two blocks from campus, but then it seemed like a palace. It *was* a palace—our palace. When we pooled our household furnishings and bought a few extra things, we were set up for entertaining and quickly became an off-campus gathering place for many friends.

There were, of course, other implications that came on the heels of moving into an apartment that had only one bed. I tried to keep things in the right priority, but the very thought of our sleeping together had my hormones doing somersaults. An almost-forgotten sexual appetite had been awakened in me during the previous winter with Tom and later with Louisa in Europe, and I could relate to what one of the female graduate students announced at a party one evening as she lamented about how she missed her boyfriend in Orange County: "I'm so horny they can hear me honking in Los Angeles."

Several friends helped us with the big move, and after we had put everything away in our new home, Lori and I went down to Shattuck Avenue for supper. And then we were home alone for the first time. I was obsessed with Lori throughout this period of my life, but that evening I found myself distracted from even that obsession by what was to come. This was going to be the first time in my life I'd be making love more with my heart than with my erection. I truly loved this woman, with a quality of love different from what I'd imagined it to be with high-school girls, with Mike in the Philippines and Tom in Sausalito, or even with Louisa in Europe. I had, I think, truly loved Tom and Louisa, but it was a love I knew to be only an interlude. With Lori, my love was forever.

We sat talking for a time, close on the couch in the living room, and then, as naturally as if by custom, moved to the bedroom. It was just a few days before we were to be married.

Lori was as innocent and excited as a little girl opening a Christmas present. She had come to the decision to be here in bed much more freely, more consciously, and along a less-convoluted path than I. She has always trusted her intuition more easily than I. My way had been soul-searching, rational, complex, seminary-trained. Hers, none of these.

And then I learned I'd married a thirty-eight-year-old virgin. That affected me deeply. I would never have asked for that and had not thought to expect it. I certainly didn't deserve it, but it meant something special when it arrived unexpectedly. It was yet another dimension of this new-found happiness. As never before, I felt I was being loved with a love reserved for just me.

It would be too somber and serious, and not quite fair to the critical historical process, if I were to let the tale of that day end there. The clowns of all time would rise in vengeance. God's outrageous humor would be slighted.

It's one thing to say that Lori was emotionally, mentally, and spiritually ready to make love with the man she was about to marry, but it doesn't automatically follow that her body was equally prepared. I had never before known the need for a lubricant, but now I found myself stranded in the Sahara with only sand for my coffee.

My God! We were sallying forth to shake the cosmos, and the door was locked with no key in sight. It would have been a sacrilege to leave the sanctuary and the magic of the moment for a trip to a drugstore, and I realized I had to think creatively.

"Lover, do you have any Vaseline?"

"Whatever would I have that for?" she answered, confused.

"Anything like that at all?"

"I don't think so, honey."

Long pause. Come on, George, concentrate!

A great deal was at stake. I frantically called on years of training in mental acrobatics to help me in a situation the blasted seminary had not thought to consider.

And then at last, cool, calculating, resourceful reason came up with an idea: "Well, sweetheart, do you have any cooking oil?"

"Cooking oil? Whatever would you want that for now?"

"Yes, sweetie, cooking oil. Trust me. It's important. Do we have any?"

"Of course we do. In the cabinet over the stove."

The thought of using cooking oil in such an intimate application caused me only a nanosecond of dutiful hesitation over the possibility of infection, but long rationalizing at the feet of Aristotle and Aquinas paid off handsomely. More valiantly than Indiana Jones or James Bond ever could, I rescued my hormones—screaming idiots by now—as my mind made a solid case that cooking oil in a kitchen as clean as Lori's could not possibly be unsterile. The reasoning seemed impeccably cogent at the moment.

Mission accomplished.

The sweetest moment I recall from that night in Berkeley, though, was not while Lori and I were intimately engaged, but when, game over and trophy won, we lay together in silence. My passion was satisfied, but my feelings went beyond the simple satisfaction my hormones were at the moment toasting.

I'd just made love with someone I loved more than anyone, ever. I felt as if I had arrived at a new level of life.

And I had.

It's difficult to recount all that was happening in me. In no way did I feel I'd committed the ugly, remorse-laden, crudely sensual "sin" my church told me was the lot of priests who, God forbid!, have sex or, *far* worse, get married. In place of all that, the feeling of Divine Presence and love was tangible as I lay there trying to let the impact of my situation register. Having Lori beside me was like a crystal capstone of beauty and light in a life I saw as at last on track. I was tasting the same sort of heaven I'd found time after time in meditation—and this time from *sex!* It was as if the multigigabit hard disk of a lifetime had been suddenly overwritten with new data.

Here was a nun of twenty years resting on my arm beside me in bed, bright-eyed, smelling of her favorite Blue Carnation essence, still as innocent as before I'd touched her, an angel of purity trusting me and loving me, as committed to God as anyone I'd ever met. My heart no longer had any doubt whatsoever that

God—as I still understood Him in those days, the God to whom Lori and I had vowed our lives—was rejoicing on the edge of our bed as we snuggled in it. Neither of us understood yet how true that was or why. One day, years down the road, we would.

I knew in a way above and outside my familiar database of dogma and theological formation that somehow all was well, very well. I was prepared for how my church was going to judge the situation, but I knew in a deeper part of me that the glow I was feeling was different and greater than just the satisfaction of what it called an animal appetite.

I no longer saw the chastity I'd vowed as a thing of total abstinence, but of total right perspective. After all, you don't have to throw the gold into the ocean when all you've been asked to do is not make a golden calf out of it.

During all the time Lori and I roamed the freeways and back roads of northern California, only once did we ever get lost, and that was on the way to our own wedding, 8:00 P.M., December 19, 1969. We'd left Berkeley in plenty of time to make it to the ceremony in San Jose, but freeway construction had riddled the route with interminable detours through back streets and along county roads. As my impatience mounted at the lack of signs to help us back on track to where guests would soon be waiting, Lori turned on the radio to check the time, since neither of us had worn a watch. Instead of time we got Dionne Warwick singing her current hit, "Do You Know the Way to San Jose?" Our problem suddenly had a new perspective. We laughed, relaxed, and eventually arrived with time to spare.

It was a small coincidence, but we saw it as a divine gift of lightness to carry with us into our new life together. That lightness has remained. As Mark Twain said about his own life, the worst things in our life together never happened. And we've never been lost again.

I had gone "off to the world" twice before, but by getting married I did it this time with bridges in full flame behind me. I no longer had any options whatsoever of returning to the cloister, and henceforward there would be no support at all from a wealthy Church. My die was indeed cast.

I found I loved it.

I'm surprised, as I look back, that I wasn't intimidated by this new self-dependence. The challenge even proved to be invigorating. In sermons I'd often used the theme that life is an adventure, and now I was beginning to experience it as exactly that every day.

More than a thousand pages of spiritual introspection in the abbey had taught me that one significant breakthrough does not necessarily mean that problems are suddenly and permanently resolved. I knew that I still had much work to do—more work than just finding a job. Only during the first month or two of marriage did I even momentarily have a fantasy that I might never be faced with inner doubts again. I was certainly not the first newlywed to discover that old habits manage to survive even the most ecstatic of honeymoons. I was feeling better than I ever had, but there were still moments when all was not well. I may have discovered significant new parts in myself, but I still didn't like others that remained.

Even so, life was better now than it had ever been. If problems of self-criticism and doubt lingered, at least now I knew loneliness was over. Lori would always be there. Right from the first I sensed I could share with her even my darkest moments.

Some Catholics in what was still a largely Catholic city, San Francisco, let me know that their doors were henceforth closed to me, but in Berkeley and with the professors and graduate students at USF, Lori and I were still welcome and frequent guests.

Friends told me over and over how much they liked my new wife. I particularly wanted to send pictures of her back to the monastery, but I doubted it would have been appreciated. When old Brother Stanislaus, whose spiritual director I had been for some years, did finally hear about the wedding, he wrote me a long and accusing letter. He recounted how unhappy his own marriage had been and how happy he had become as a monk after his wife died.

In less than three years the distance between Utah's Trappist monks and me could only be measured in light-years.

I'm not proud of everything about our wedding itself. I marked the occasion by consuming substantially more champagne than I was capable of handling. The next day I had to be told that we'd had a good time.

Wedding guests who came by the next afternoon regaled my aching brain with how I had indignantly insisted to heads far cooler than my own that I personally drive my bride back to our new apartment in Berkeley. I finally agreed to let someone else drive only after Fred Aigner authoritatively pronounced it to be an ancient tradition (created on the spot by himself, he later admitted) that a groom never drive his new bride anywhere on their wedding day. "Well, why didn't somebody tell me?" I asked indignantly. Then, refusing help, I struggled into the back seat of my car—*our* car now—as though over yawning chasms while climbing a mountain, and collapsed in victory on the back seat. Lori climbed in beside me. I dutifully put my arm around her and fell sound asleep until mid-morning the next day, when I awoke to a singing wife bringing me a tray with a flower, toast, and a cup of badly needed coffee.

Fortunately, my drinking that evening proved to be the exception. I was much too involved with an exponentially accelerating life to want to escape again into the alcohol I'd known so well in high school and my first year in the navy.

Late in the afternoon, after the well-wishers had gone, Lori and I made it back to bed together again, this time as a married couple. At last—now that all the logistics of satisfying consciences and getting married were past—we could throw all restraint to the wind and make a great game of it. I would almost claim that sex with Lori has always been more a thing of fun than the act or art of love. I'm convinced that sexual intercourse is supposed to be fun first of all, a game between two lovers, a release, an exercise in freedom that makes it achieve, in that approach alone, its wonderful and eternal purpose. If offspring sometimes result from this dance of two bodies, that only contributes another dimension to the magic. In this perspective, children will always be seen as the result of lighthearted play and never as the outcome of some hush-hush ritual. Sexual love making is ideally and essentially two individuals enjoying their incarnations in an intimate, supremely pleasurable, outrageously playful way. How organized religion has managed to screw that up with guilt and befuddlement!

Whenever Lori and I have had rough moments in our relationship over the years, our problems have been routinely absolved, dissolved, resolved as soon as we make love. At that moment there is no longer any right or wrong, no substance to opinions or hurts. Bumps are forgotten on playgrounds. The old liturgical line about two persons becoming one flesh has much truth in it, and in more ways than a celibate clergy could ever theorize, fantasize, or understand.

A year or so later, one late afternoon as Lori and I were watching the sunset out over the Pacific from the hills in neighboring Marin County, we found ourselves discussing how things were going between us. I was feeling particularly low and guilty about having for the first time raised my voice in impatience with her a couple days before. Somewhere in our conversation we came to understand marriage in a new way. The monastic rule of Saint Benedict told monks that a monastery is a "school of the Lord's service," and we decided that we would always look upon marriage as a *"school of love's service."* Marriage is a place, we agreed, where we would *learn* to love one another, not a place where love could be presumed to be forever already enshrined in all its fullness. Two persons, like ourselves, who had grown into adulthood with no close loving relationships certainly needed lessons in love, and we knew it. We were committed students, and we decided to see marriage henceforward as the site for our continued training in that which we held most dear of all things: our love for each other.

I wondered out loud how I could have thought previously, as a celibate, that I knew what love was all about. How could I possibly have known anything substantial about married love without this daily practice of living with someone and having to strive to be more careful in patience, sensitivity, concern? I am embarrassed, and the Catholic church should be even more so, at the egregious answers Catholicism teaches its priests to pass out to married persons in the confessional and during marriage counseling. How could a married man teach a monk the finer points of honest celibacy? But, equally, how can a celibate teach the finer points of marital love? In the years that Lori and I have spent together, circumstances have often shown me how very little I knew before marriage about the practice of dependable, daily sensitivity and care.

Because we were willing and alert, Lori and I learned early that what makes a loving companionship work is that, besides being fun and containing repeated physical ecstasy, it demands constant attention. We were honestly in love, but from the start we didn't take that to mean that we didn't have to continue to work hard to demonstrate our love with consistency and care.

Later during the years I was a licensed marriage counselor, I frequently found myself reminding couples with scarcely veiled impatience to quit prattling on about "loving" each other when what they needed to be concentrating on was how to show appreciation and sensitivity to each other in one small way after another, one day after another. Lori and I decided early that that was how we would prove our love to be real.

Learning to Manage

At the time of our marriage, Lori's Danforth Fellowship and my Veterans Administration grant both continued to the end of the school year. That gave us five months of assured income. After that, we'd be on our own. I felt sure no church job, at least no Catholic-church job, would ever be offered me again, and I wasn't sure what else I could do. As it turned out, my first job out of the priesthood came looking for me before I went looking for it.

In mid-May 1970, two weeks before graduate school was out and before I'd even started looking for work, the secretary of a re-tired army colonel called me from San Francisco's Presidio and said her boss wanted to see me as soon as possible. Joe Burke, director of education in the army's Presidio, had been on General Patton's staff and still had much of his former boss's style. I had met him two years earlier when I moonlighted teaching speed reading to soldiers at his center.

It was a crystal clear May morning as I left Berkeley and set out across the Oakland Bay Bridge to keep my appointment in the Presidio, near the south end of the Golden Gate Bridge. Dumb monk: no job, no known prospects for one, windows down, wind in his face, music blaring, and not a worry in the world. I remem-ber listening to Herb Alpert's "Tijuana Taxi" as I resolved I would not return to the Education Center just to teach speed reading.

Without even announcing me or knocking, Joe's secretary walked me into his office as soon as I arrived. The conversation that followed was without frills, typical of most I would have with military officers with whom I would work for the next fifteen years. They definitely were not the insensitive war mongers often caricatured during the Vietnam era. It wasn't the military, after all, who begot and fostered the Vietnam war, but industry-controlled political animals without conscience in Washington. If I observed any apparent insensitivity in military men as a class, it was their exaggerated concern to conceal their gentleness and warmth in a subculture where these were often seen as weakness.

"I hear you got married, Father George."

I laughed, surprised that he knew it, and, since I knew he was Catholic, a bit uncertain as to what would come next.

"How'd you find that out, Joe? And, please, call me George."

"So it's true?"

"Yes."

"Got a job?"

"No."

"Want one?"

"Doing what?"

"Counseling our men in Project Transition."

Transition, he explained, was a Department of Defense effort to help Vietnam returnees reenter the job market or continue their education. I'd never heard of it.

"Sure."

"When can you start?"

"Lori and I were hoping to take a break after school's out the end of May so I could introduce her to my family. How about the middle of June?"

"Be here June 15. Want to go to the Officers' Club for lunch?"

That was Joe Burke, and that was my first job out of the priesthood and out of the Catholic church. It was timely, as they all have been since.

———

In the twenty-five years since marrying Lori, I've had eleven different jobs, she an equal number, and we've lived at eighteen addresses. Neither of us has ever been fired from a job, and we've never been evicted from where we lived. Each time we moved, it was our deliberate choice.

This footloose style has exasperated both of our families and finally surprised even us. We eventually found ourselves standing back and asking what all this job wandering implied. Were we, perhaps, as irresponsible and naïve as our friends and families not so subtly suggested?

It would have been comforting had we been able to reassure them—and ourselves—that all along we'd had some master plan clearly in mind, some wisdom received from on high or predesigned in our heads. The truth is we weren't even aware of how atypical and "risky" our life together had become until we were almost thirteen years into it. Until then, we simply called adventure what our friends were calling instability.

Today, all those jobs and addresses later, we're glad we didn't become concerned about our rootless habits early on. That could have scared us and cost us the freedom of spirit we each now have. Had we recognized early and been frightened by our seeming indifference to careers and home equity, we might never have come to appreciate what a lifestyle of trust could do for us.

Many persons who have never been near a religious convent or monastery don't recognize that they, too, have walls to scale if they are to come to freedom. They may not cling to religious dogmas and tradition, but they do cling—just as tightly as any cloistered monk ever clung to his dogmas—to fear-driven rules about making it economically and socially. Lori's and my experience in counseling others suggests that many individuals have compromised or forgotten their need, first of all, to find inner freedom if they are to be whole and truly happy.

It makes no difference that individuals have no stone walls to scale if, in fact, they live as slaves to favored positions, to the drive for impressive home equity or a profitable portfolio. Many people live so completely oriented to tomorrow's retirement that they never learn to live today. When retirement comes, they have neither the skills nor lightheartedness to enjoy what they've saved. Such people have lived enclosed by walls higher than those of any monastery. They will have to leave their own brand of cloister if they are to be free.

Lori and I may have entered the job market late in life, unaware of many rules of the road, but we entered it already alerted to the need to keep first things first, freedom and lightness of heart before all else. Because our cloisters had been visible, we remained unrestricted by new ones of any kind.

As a result, we moved blithely forward as opportunities presented themselves until, while living in Virginia in 1983, a first real perspective on our employment history became apparent. It was a thoughtful Sunday afternoon in the spring, and we were sitting together with cocktails on the brick garden patio of our suburban Fairfax home. Neither the summer heat nor summer bugs had arrived yet, and the sweep of countryside before us added to our sense of well-being and abundance. We were relaxing after a weekend of guests—friends who had always been critical of our lifestyle. We were rerunning some of the conversations we'd had with them. For the first time we realized how our history of career hopping had looked to others, despite fourteen years of successful marriage and financial abundance. Our visitors had helped us finally see how unusual our attitude toward jobs, investments, and equity actually was. We talked about it for a while, but ended up deciding we didn't repent of any of it. We had never gone hungry, had always lived in nice places, and, most of all, were happy and still much in love. We decided we must be doing something right. Job bouncing apparently came from something we'd been sensing intuitively.

Our spiritual goals in life together had not changed from what they were when we lived as nun and monk at opposite ends of the country. Now, moving about in what we once referred to, at times contemptuously, as the world, we were still as oriented to *inner* evolution and fulfillment, to freedom and joy, to working for the good of all, as we were when back in our robes and cloisters. Moreover, we didn't now just pray for the world and, in Lori's case, teach Catechism to its children; we were out on its streets, contributing money, energy, and both political and social responsibility to the solution of its problems. And in the process, we had preconsciously taken it for granted that we would never stay with a job, place, or situation after it had lost its potential to serve our growth and thereby make us better, more useful citizens of the world. We saw that we had gone through jobs exactly as we went through clothing: out it goes the minute it doesn't fit or feel right.

We ended our cocktail hour by deciding that the way our jobs had always come to us seemed to support our conviction that as long as one remains truly dedicated to a path of spirituality, the universe will always be there to help. It certainly had been for us.

With school finally out and before reporting for my new job, Lori and I took off in our Grandé once again, this time not just around California, but in a great circle through six western states. My family was anxious to meet the nun I'd married and who, as my stepmother put it, "has done us all a great favor."

They all loved my new wife immediately, although it was evident some of them weren't quite sure at first how to act with a former nun in the house. My father and mother, who had met her six months before at Christmas, had no such problem and simply continued to dote over her. They loved having her in their home. She endeared herself still more, and in language Montana farmers understand well, when she showed herself to be a fine cook. She represented just about everything my parents had wanted for their oldest son for the past twenty years.

My father and I had many long conversations, still skating carefully around the few patches of thin ice that lingered from our past. He told me many times again, as he had at Christmas, that he was certain I had found the most perfect wife in the world.

When we had come to spend Christmas with them six months earlier, they met us at the Salt Lake City airport, and Dad asked me to do the driving back to Logan so he could sit in the back with his new daughter-in-law. He spent the long trip with his arm around her, more pleased than he could explain. I understood. I had come a long way. He had come a long way. *We* had come a long way.

During this second visit, as we had at Christmas, my parents and sibling families, who one by one showed up to meet Lori, routinely sat up until well after midnight playing pinochle in a gala-like togetherness that we had never before experienced as a family. It was a heady moment, a moment when everyone, apparently, had decided that I was an acceptable member of the family after all.

Each time we closed the card game down in the wee hours of the morning, I could not help thinking of the monks of my former abbey, not many miles from us up in the Wasatch Mountains. As we went to bed, they would be rousing themselves to the wake-up bell and be off to chant the night office. When I shared this musing with others, no one saw any special significance in it. I did. I would not have traded places with the monks for anything in the universe, but I missed the choir, the chant, the silence— and, most of all, those doing the chanting. They had been my brothers for seventeen years.

When I showed up bright and early June 15 for my new Presidio job back in San Francisco, I found a paycheck covering the first two weeks of June waiting for me. I took it to Joe to explain the mistake, and his Irish eyes twinkled as he told me to put it in my pocket. "We'll take it out of your hide around here soon enough, *Father.*" And then, with dutifully wrinkled brow and to justify his wedding present at Uncle Sam's expense, he added, "Besides, it's too complicated to undo mistakes like that in this damn government."

I later found out that he had started me at the top pay scale he had in his power to grant, eleven dollars an hour, a hefty salary in 1970. Lori and I soon found our first home, near the ocean in San Francisco's Sunset District. With our new credit cards, we had it beautifully furnished within weeks.

I began my new job in a crowded government-issue cubicle, and it took me by surprise to see how hard it was for me to accept this. No nuns were pampering me now, as at the Lake Street convent a couple miles away. No morning staff meetings and hobnobbing with doctors as during my just finished intern year in counseling. No parishioners or counselees clinging, confiding. Nobody looked up to me or called me Father anymore. Instead, I found myself side-tracked into the last available cubicle with a dingy metal desk whose drawers squealed in pain each time I opened them. I was left alone for several days with interminably dull manuals on the Transition program that Joe asked me to "learn all about."

I ended up working hard at the Presidio. I let the young men and women returning from Vietnam get close to me, and they did so readily, once they decided they could trust me. In Project Transition we didn't see those with the most severe physical, mental, or emotional damage, but we did deal daily and intimately with those who came back with varieties of emotional trauma, hurt, and not infrequent rage. I was left with the image of fat, vulgar, lascivious, and powerful old men, Washington politicians, flaunting the law they had on their side, lining these young people up in their beautiful youth, and giving them a pep talk about the pressing need that they now be violated for the glory of both God and America the Beautiful, then ordering that they dutifully bend over so they could be roughly, often savagely—but officially, systematically, and routinely—raped. Not for one day, but for 365 days. The grossness of this image be damned! The inner pain I saw and dealt with daily for five years was more savage, more gross, more offensive than this shocking image could ever represent, simply because many of these rape victims came home feeling betrayed, psychologically damaged, and not infrequently missing arms, legs, health, and buddies.

It's too easy when we limit our outrage to what is officially designated as outrageous. The Inquisition and Crusades were never so designated, but they were and remain significant crimes against humanity all the same. The rape of a generation of young people in

Vietnam, immoral but wholly legal, is a horror I could never have imagined had I not watched so many men and women try to recover from the betrayal by their parents' generation.

Infantry personnel often refused to talk about Vietnam at all. Some wanted to and kept trying. I learned to be silent. Hollywood has subsequently tried to recapture the reality of Vietnam in several films, but as one returned soldier recently told me, "They can't catch the smells or heat or big bugs or snakes or tiredness or pain of lost buddies or what it feels like to accidentally step on a stinking body part. Those fuckin' films suck. They make people think that's what it was like. They should spray everybody in the theater with shit and blood and throw rotting body parts around and turn the heat and humidity up to a hundred and then play those fuckin' films."

The above is not an attempt to editorialize a gross political crime. That's been overdone, usually badly. I write this simply to continue my own story and to share in two dimensions what my tears let me experience in three and some of my young confidants told me in twelve. I spent five years with a savagely violated generation of young men and women. I spent five years watching some of them dare reach out to me for help in reentering a world that frightened them because it was one that had betrayed them, a world they could no longer trust, one they had been jerked out of just as they were beginning to feel a bit grown up and comfortable in it. They were all trying to forget, and a few to forgive.

Many times tears ran down my cheeks with those who wept in my office. Once the door was closed and after they chose to trust me, stories came out that were beyond my wildest images of what it must have been like. It was easy to love them, and I did so easily. They knew that and loved in return. That's what made my job for the army special.

When I left the Presidio five years later, I had earned a number of promotions and had served as assistant education director, then as interim director, and, last of all, as director of the Education Center at nearby Letterman Army Medical Center. I was well on my way to a management post in army education at SHAPE Headquarters in Belgium.

When the possibility in Europe came up, I began investigating what employment possibilities would be available for Lori there. Surprisingly, because her years of teaching as a nun and as a campus minister at Purdue University all had to do with religion, there seemed to be no opportunities for her with the army in Europe. She could find a clerking job in a military exchange, but that would not have been satisfactory to either of us. She had held various positions in San Francisco, including for a time one as counselor to Vietnam returnees, and, ultimately, as administrative assistant to a senior officer in a corporate headquarters in San Francisco's financial district.

While the stress of our dilemma about what to do was under way, I suggested that Lori fly to Seattle to spend some days with Earl and Eleanor LaBerge, who had completed their work in Berkeley a couple years before and moved to the Pacific Northwest. While there, Lori was offered not one but two jobs, either of which she felt would be exciting.

I made a quick decision. Women had followed men and their careers around for centuries, so why shouldn't it work the other way, too. I was on a plane to Seattle within the week to see what kind of job I could find for myself there.

Many advised me that the Puget Sound area was a hopeless place to look for employment in 1975. I learned they were right. My first trip was completely unsuccessful, and it presented no glimmer of hope whatsoever that any future search would be any different. Lori came along on a second trip, and after some days of searching it seemed we were going home empty-handed again.

And then the universe played its trump.

We had lunch in downtown Bremerton just before folding our tents and heading for the Seattle-Tacoma airport. As we emerged from the restaurant, I noticed a sign directly across the street: Puget Sound Naval Shipyard Employment Office. We crossed the street and, with little expectation, I thumbed indifferently through the navy's employment opportunities in a looseleaf binder handed me by an attendant. Nothing looked promising. I'm not a qualified engineer of any variety, not a riveter or a laundry technician. I wasn't about to ask those behind the counter if they had any jobs for former priests.

Near the end of the book the lights went on. The new Trident submarine base on nearby Hood Canal wanted an administrative officer. It sounded dangerously like a glorified secretarial position, but it would be a beginning. Who knows where it might lead.

I asked for the forms, filled them out, dropped them in the mail, and we flew home to San Francisco to wait. Our wait was a short one. Within two weeks the Trident base personnel office sent me a ticket to fly up for an interview. I did. Another week back in San Francisco, and they called to say I was hired.

Lori accepted the better of the two positions she had been offered, and we sold our home in San Francisco and moved most of our things to Bremerton, where her job began immediately. I returned to my job and a bachelor's apartment in San Francisco to await notice of when to report to the submarine base.

Notification didn't come and kept not coming. We alternated commuting back and forth almost every week for several months, and then, when I was in Bremerton for Thanksgiving, the Trident Personnel officer called the day before the holiday and asked me to report as soon as possible. The next Monday I was back in San Francisco resigning from the army and beginning a long round of farewells.

The army had been good to me, but it was not difficult to leave. The only hard part was leaving the men and women with whom I had been working for five years. But even they had accustomed me to separation, passing through as they always were.

Leaving San Francisco itself, however, turned out to be more difficult than I had foreseen.

The day before I left, I took a long drive by myself in my new 280Z. I drove through the Haight-Ashbury, now in shambles, past and around the USF campus, past the convent where I'd been chaplain for two years, past Holy Names College in the Oakland hills where I had taught, and then around Berkeley. My eyes were teary most of the time—teary with gratitude and, probably most of all, with simple sentimentality.

Two days before Christmas 1975, I reported as administrative officer, code SPB51, to the navy's new Trident submarine base west of Seattle on the Hood Canal. I didn't know it then, but I was entering a completely new world. I had no forewarning at all of what a change that job would forever make in my life.

The first person to welcome me aboard when I reported for duty was the personnel officer, Shirley Raudstein, wife of a retired military intelligence officer and a totally unforgettable person in her own right. She made a tremendous impression on me and continued to do so all the time I was there. A lady of consummate culture, she sported a three-carat diamond on her finger that her husband had brought her from what was then the Belgian Congo and that she told me she wore not as precious jewelry but as a happy memory. Meeting her should have alerted me to the kind of place I was joining.

22

Nuclear Weapons and Other Kinds of Power

The new Trident submarine base and the Trident program as a whole were as full of energy as they were challenging when I joined them in 1975. I watched later as governmental hairsplitting and expanded military bureaucracy from Washington, D.C., eroded much of the spirit of the place, but for most of my time at the base, the experience was dramatically upbeat. It was there that I learned to respect myself and to recognize my abilities in external matters for the first time.

As the newest facet of the nuclear deterrent forces of a wealthy nation that saw itself locked in a dangerous cold war, the Trident submarine system was one of the best-funded government programs in the 1970s. Soon after my arrival at its only submarine base, I told a San Francisco friend on the phone, "This place is Jesuit all the way." Like the Jebbies, it seemed to be on the cutting edge of everything. We simply had to ask and we were given whatever it took to get a job done. Such a ready availability of assets inevitably led to abuses, but it also helped give a think-big, can-do dynamic to the whole enterprise. It was dramatically unlike the shuffling confusion that characterized so much of what I had just come from in army education, where sometimes our budget wouldn't permit us to buy notepads for soldiers just back from Vietnam who were working toward a high-school diploma.

Something else I told my San Francisco friend may have sounded pretentious. I said Trident was the first place I'd ever been that had as much of an "of-course-we-can!" attitude as I do myself. Right or wrong, pretentious or not, that's how I felt within a month of beginning my new job. I felt as if I'd been waiting for this place all of my life. The frustration of the army's attitude of "rules first, what makes sense next" was suddenly replaced by routine staff meetings aimed precisely at finding out what *did* make sense—and then how to get around whatever bureaucratic nonsense might be standing in the way.

I had just come from a place where I was a recognized manager. Suddenly, for yet another time, I was low man on the totem pole. It took me a month to learn the acronym-saturated lingo people use in defense industry, but I realized that once you learn them, acronyms are an oral shorthand, a way to say a lot in few syllables. It's a vibrant language, and I had fun with it. I was a long way from the monastery—and I was loving every minute of it.

After a couple weeks on the job, someone confided that managers around the base were watching in apprehensive amusement to see if I could survive the staff I had inherited with my new position. My first duty, my predecessor had warned me concerning this staff of four secretaries, was to "fix 'em or kill 'em." I wondered at his coldness, and then spent my first days sitting at my desk studying Trident usages and realizing he might be right. The four women kept circling and talking about how they intended to do things now that they no longer worked for "that asshole," my predecessor. I knew there had to be a message in there somewhere for me.

As administrative officer, I had responsibility for an office that had been mismanaged in the extreme. Its four secretaries used significant amounts of their time to express hatred for one another, joining forces only against their former boss and now and then against one of themselves who had been selected as target for the day.

On my second day there, Lady Number One walked over to clinch an argument with Lady Number Four—who happened to be handicapped—by running her arm across Lady Four's desk in such a way that all of her newly typed documents and everything else on her desk went flying across the room. Lady One had composed an appropriate text for the occasion, which she now intoned in her untrained contralto: "Take that, bitch!" Then she whirled to look at her new boss, me, as if to dare me to say anything against the justice she had just meted out in so deserving a manner. It was too early for me to take sides, so I rose from my desk, walked over as close as I dared to her adrenaline-filled quiver, and looked her gently in the eyes. "Give me, please," I smiled, "something better than that with which to fill your evaluation report when I write it at the end of this quarter." Then I winked at her. We looked each other in the eye for just a second—as long as I dared. For an instant I thought I detected a smile of amusement or some evidence of appreciation on her face, but she quickly regained her noncomposure and snorted in disgust as she whirled to stomp back to her desk.

After a few days I no longer blamed the four secretaries for their conduct. Their former boss, who had stayed on for a week to help me get started, exhibited about as many people skills as an abused bull with a bad headache. These ladies didn't know it, but they were exemplifying an old monastic dictum dating back at least to medieval times: *Quantum abbas, tantum abbatia*—"As the abbot, so the abbey." Monks, and civil servants, it turns out, tend to model on the leadership given them.

I ended up concluding that my predecessor deserved everything he had received from his staff. They had learned that the only way to survive around him was to give as good as they got. He was openly disdainful of them, and they of him. I walked in as a former priest and they didn't know whether to like me, hate me, or drop a desk on me.

During my first couple of weeks when I tried to greet my coven each morning, I got back silence and grunts in a dissonant chorus. One morning Lady Number Two saw me coming down the hall and, making sure I was close enough to hear, announced to the others: "Put the arsenic in the coffee, girls. Father Sweetie Pie is about to make his grand entrance." As I passed her I whispered, "Thank you very much, and do please bring my coffee right in, but I take cream in it and don't care for either sugar or arsenic." She, too, almost smiled. I can only fantasize what the response would have been today when serving coffee is no longer something secretaries do. It causes me to tremble.

My secret clearance had not yet come through, so Lady Number One, who possessed that level clearance and was in charge of the vault of classified documents, made a great show of making sure I didn't walk too near "her" vault. It's not that I tried, which, I think, also bugged her. She so wanted a chance to belt me a good one in the interest of national security.

Three of the four ladies and I eventually became fast friends and often later regaled ourselves about "the good old days." The fourth secretary had to be sacrificed on the altar of threat, which, as planned, caused her to resign—it being far too difficult to fire a civil servant in a more civilized way. But even she, months after the sacrifice, met me one day in a store in downtown Bremerton and told me that being forced to resign was the best thing that had ever happened to her. Then she introduced me to her new fiancé, a handsome and genial young man who obviously was able to teach her what others could not.

As my birthday approached a year later, Lady One collected money from the then greatly expanded staff so that "we can give the boss the most poisonous insect we can find." On the morning of my birthday, she led a group of employees into my office with great ceremony and delivered a glass aquarium outfitted with sand, crickets, rocks, and a large tarantula spider. That was her way of admitting finally that we had become friends. But that was later. My task those first weeks at Trident was not to eat anything they offered me.

————

These beat-down and troubled secretaries were not at all typical of Trident. From the very first staff meeting I attended, I felt its high energy and loved it. At these weekly meetings, the commanding officer, executive officer, and five department heads sat at a huge central table with about seventy division heads and other supporting persons sitting in chairs circling the table. As a minor division head, I initially sat in the outermost ring. I could not have imagined or hoped that eighteen months later I would be sitting at the central table as head of a department of four divisions. Still less could I have foreseen what the experience would mean to me.

What I remember most, and most warmly, about that dynamic place is its commanding officer. He set its tone and kept it on pitch. Dan Piraino was a brilliant, up-front Italian-blooded navy captain. He and I got along famously from the first time I spoke up in a staff meeting to explain something from my division to his satisfaction. About a year later I told him, to his amusement, that had he been my abbot, I might still have been a monk. I think I almost meant it. Rome, of course, would never have permitted him to head an abbey. Piraino would have been banging on the pope's door within a month. He was never known to conform when conformity didn't make sense.

Captain Piraino was commanding an organization called by the navy, in its own special way of abusing tolerable English, Strategic Weapons Facility, Pacific, more commonly referred to by its acronym SWFPAC (pronounced swif-pack). It was being prepared to provide and protect Trident nuclear missiles. He had been selected as commanding officer because of his reputation for getting things done on time. The missile aspect of the Trident program had significant and broad problems that a few years downstream would, if not corrected, result in missiles not being ready when the first Trident submarine, the *Ohio,* was ready to receive them. Dan was sent out from Washington to manage the base's Get Well Program. He succeeded famously. It was the biggest adventure of my life to watch him, and, much more, to help him do so.

All of this is past now, but it's a significant part of my story.

When I arrived at SWFPAC I was an ex-monk who a few years earlier would have imagined he would be afraid of his own shadow in such a rapid-fire, high-stakes environment. At SWFPAC I was given a significant piece of the action, a huge budget, and a confident endorsement to "Go do it." To my surprise, and lasting lesson for the future, I did it.

Moreover, I needed the modeling of a man like Dan Piraino in my life. I needed to witness first hand someone who was gentle, gentlemanly, cultured, reasonable, and, when the need changed, fierce as hell and explicitly demanding. I had long mastered how to be gentle, gentlemanly, cultured, and reasonable. Dan showed me the side of the coin I had completely missed: a hellish fierceness when honesty or any other need demands it.

A bit more than a year after coming to work for him, he promoted me to be manager of one of his five departments. It had four divisions, including the administrative one I had been hired to head in the first place. One of my new divisions had responsibility for planning the security of nuclear weapons. It was managing that division that took most of my attention and gave me my best experience.

Nuclear weapons are unfortunate at best. A great case can be made that they should never have happened, certainly never used. My job at Trident, however, was no longer as a priest who dissertates on the ethics of nuclear weaponry. It was to make sure that no idiot with doubted manhood for emotions and semen for blood ever got hold of one. That sounds straightforward enough. It wasn't.

The specter that faced us daily was the informed realization of what could be done in the world—*to* the world—if a nuclear warhead were ever to fall into the hands of a zealot or psychopath or the uncomprehending. Our purpose was to design a storage place that no one could penetrate and from which, should that impossible thing happen, no one could ever get out of with even so much as a pencil stub.

In this new role, my secret clearance had to be upgraded to top secret, a security clearance that was approved for me in record time, Washington explained, because of my years safely tucked away in a monastery. I was at last ready to be properly prepared for my new position and was shipped off to several classified training sites around the country. I also visited an assembly plant where I watched the nuclear warheads themselves being nursed together with all the finesse of brain surgery on what looked remarkably like operating tables.

All of this I took in stride, but, for whatever reason, and probably because I had been a student of cultural history for many years, it was a visit to a top secret nuclear-weapons museum that brought me face-to-face with the enormity of what I had been hired to do. There in front of me were the prototypes of the bombs dropped on Japan. And over there were representations of most of the increasingly sophisticated weapons subsequently developed.

My meditations that evening and again before leaving my hotel room the next morning for more classes were longer than was usual for me in those days. It was as if I had been shown the first crossbow the day after it was invented. With that sight came what seemed like a primordial feeling in the heart of a far simpler man of a far simpler age—awe at what a terrible weapon lay before him, one that would completely change the tactics of warfare. Only today I was looking not at crossbows, but at nuclear warheads.

Technology is forever surprising and then terrifying us with the realization of what we humans can do. Only after we have invented or discovered something do we set about finding the wisdom to use our breakthrough devices safely. Many early pilots died between the time humankind learned to fly and later understood the niceties of aerodynamics. Many people died when miraculous medicines were used before all their side effects were adequately recognized. And, God forgive us, Hiroshima and Nagasaki happened before we understood what we were doing.

I came back from my nuclear training filled with new knowledge, and more committed than ever to my job of helping to keep nuclear weapons secure in a world where the consciousness and conscientiousness of many of the world's decision makers are not much different than that of screeching chimpanzees fighting over bananas.

To help us in our task of designing nuclear-weapon security, we had the support of the best technology in the world. It supplied us with all sorts of wonder-filled "black boxes." There were motion detectors that could distinguish between a flag waving and anything not that usual. There were footstep detectors that could discriminate between an elk, a bear, and a man. There were wire-disturbance and clipped-wire detectors and classified devices more exotic than a previous generation of sci-fi writers could have dreamed of. It was our job to figure out how any or all of these marvels could be fit together in our given circumstances, and then to make sure that our final configuration of them worked. The most interesting part of our job came last of all when, after designing the most secure building or site we could, we would try to defeat our own design.

We wondered sometimes if we were exaggerating our concerns. Military intelligence in Washington, D.C., repeatedly told us we were not.

I had a group of young officers and contractors working for me but, unfortunately for everyone concerned, besides the complete support of the SWFPAC commanding and executive officers and this dedicated staff, we also had the "help" of hoards of people sitting around far-off tables in the Pentagon and Crystal City. They were forever telling us what to do, even though many of them had never visited SWFPAC. It seemed to us—only a bit unfairly—that they must have a sandbox in which they played with Legos to design what they imagined to be the perfectly secure universal nuclear-weapons site. Their headquarters-inspired model—confused by them with divinely inspired—was supposed to serve equally well in the deserts of New Mexico, the rain-drenched Pacific Northwest, and anywhere else in the world where nuclear weapons might one day be found.

The irony of the situation was that should a warhead eventually be compromised as a result of *their* unrealistic and mandatory design, people in the field—*we*—would be the ones going to prison. Our primary challenge became working around directives coming from afar that made no sense whatsoever in our actual situation in Puget Sound country. By the time my conflict with a few powerful individuals in Crystal City finally hit the fan, I had surrounded myself with a go-get-'em civil service, military, and contractual staff, and we seldom failed to achieve our goals.

In the spring of 1979, my conflict with Washington had come to a head, and I risked everything by standing up in a Pentagon meeting to oppose openly a decision people there had made that would severely impact our work at SWFPAC. I had prepared well and ended winning the point. I came home victorious and very tired—very fed up, actually. As it turned out, that victory was my last major undertaking for Trident.

I learned at SWFPAC to feel my own ability in nonchurch, nonspiritual, work-a-day matters. SWFPAC undid layers and layers of old habits nurtured in a self-doubting past. It was a time of finding power on the inside as I experienced myself managing it successfully on the outside. This was an experience I had never had before. Lori kept telling me how tired I seemed, and I knew she was right, but over the weariness I maintained a nonstop, almost youthful exuberance.

I knew failures, too, of course, and significant ones. My enthusiasm was not always softened by those habits of self-restraint that come from seasoned self-confidence. One immediate result of this was that I simply didn't know how to play the game by the rules, and, worse than that, as I openly told the senior civil servant at SWFPAC, I wasn't interested in learning them. He had come up through the ranks of civil service and lived, what seemed to me, a plodding, overstaffed approach to everything from planning for nuclear weapons to sneezing. He was, though, a fair man, and expressed appreciation that I often got things done ahead of schedule. He never failed, however, to wring his hands and remonstrate with me that I wasn't following the rules in doing so. My independence in achieving goals perturbed him endlessly, and he had his point. I was a loose cannon on his deck, and now I realize that a bit of temperance would have made me even more effective by winning more of his and others' support. I had come to recognize and use personal talent and power, but I had not yet learned how to do so wisely.

A far greater problem for me, and one that I many times injudiciously ridiculed, was the antagonistic attitude that many military personnel harbored for civilians. We civilians sometimes wondered if they understood that nonmilitary types were Americans. SWFPAC was a place of extreme bigotry: military versus civilian and, less often, vice versa. This conflict frequently made it difficult for me to get a team effort going on important projects when I could not keep the two "groups" in my divisions either gainfully joined or realistically separated.

One immodestly self-important senior military officer, a fellow department head, was a particular problem to me. His contempt for civilians, and particularly for those of us who did not stand in awe of his rank and presumed to speak to him as to a peer, was the single biggest challenge I had while at SWFPAC. Unfortunately, it was only after leaving the place that I saw the value of what he had contributed to my life. His attitude toward me had been a high-profile caricature of what my own attitude toward myself had been most of the years of my life. My resolve not to be bothered by his foolishness needed, I saw, to be matched in my life by not paying attention to my own similar foolishness.

It sounds vain to say that I greatly enjoyed the center table at weekly staff meetings. I am confident, however, that I enjoyed it not because of what I imagined others might think of me as I sat there, but because of what—for the first time in my life—I began to think of myself as I sat there.

The army had given me one award, but by the time I left SWF-PAC, the navy had given me three. And then a year after I was gone, they included me in a unit citation and commendation medal sent to them from the Department of Defense.

In retrospect and at the bottom line, I'm not sure if my Trident adventure says more about my native ability or about my intemperance. At any rate, intemperance about both work and alcohol there certainly was, and it started causing problems in my relationship with Lori.

I still loved her, and these needed to be solved.

23

First Things First

Almost in proportion to the success I was having on the job, Lori and I began to experience problems in our marriage for the first time. This was not surprising since "success" for me at SWFPAC equated to absorption in work (most of which was classified and could not be shared with her) and to being away from home. I was putting in long hours, traveling often, and, most distressful of all to her, abusing alcohol more and more. Lunches at the Officers' Club always included cocktails, and whenever the SWFPAC community socialized, which we did often, it was with cocktails before meals, wine during meals, and after-dinner drinks into late hours. I didn't hide it from Lori that on my frequent trips to meetings in DC, it was standard practice to end a workday with Defense Department friends in a bar.

At Trident social events, Lori was never content to be just one of "the wives," as spouses were called. Most of these women either busied themselves chatting about their children and homemaker preoccupations or sat dutifully by and listened silently as their husbands talked in the foreign language of acronyms about sub base matters. Lori had always pursued a professional life of her own, and found little in common with most of the other managers' wives. Our dilemma became that when my Trident friends were having a social event, she had to come along and be bored or I had to dissociate from them or we had to go separate ways for the evening. None of these alternatives was acceptable.

I could not dismiss Lori's growing dissatisfaction. I watched week by week as the big bright eyes I'd first noticed across the seminar table in Berkeley grew more and more sad. We were still honest and grateful lovers, but clearly something was going awry.

The restlessness I saw in her helped me become aware of my own unrest, one that my frantic pace was keeping fairly well hidden from my consciousness. The challenge and power I was enjoying were persuasive reasons to try to believe that all was well, but even they couldn't camouflage the clear signs I saw in Lori and that she helped me see in myself.

I began to roll and toss at night, and in my third year at Trident I returned to a meditation that for almost two years I had shortened always and skipped increasingly. I soon realized it was time for me to leave my power trip behind and move on.

The clincher was when Captain Dan Piraino retired from the navy. With his leaving, the management style he had established at SWFPAC was filleted. The spark was gone. The fun over. He had succeeded in making the SWFPAC portion of the missile program healthy again, and the base was up and running, but with him gone, bureaucracy began to take over.

I submitted my resignation to SWFPAC, and, yet again, started saying good-bye.

The last image I have of my days in the Trident program is at a final cocktail party. Across the room I saw Lori, five foot three inches, beaming, sparkling in a new evening gown, and talking animatedly to the leading admiral in the Trident program, visiting from headquarters in Washington, D.C. Well over six feet tall, he was leaning over and listening intently to her above the din.

Several people asked me "Whatever is Lori saying to Admiral Wertheim?" I had no idea, but on the way home she told me he had asked her why in the world I would want to leave the Trident program in view of the position I now had. Lori said she told him how much I appreciated what his program had done for me, but that I had an opportunity to open my own engineering firm to help local industry design security for its computers. She told him nothing about my growing dissatisfaction.

If Trident was a time of learning, the eight years that followed was a time of sorting—not painful, but often disappointing—until, that is, I found myself teaching spirituality again, this time without the obstacles of any organization's presuppositions. The chief difference between Trident and the other jobs I held afterwards was that SWFPAC had always been a positive challenge and almost always made eminently good sense. When I finally founded my own organization, Trident and Captain Piraino would remain as models. Nor have they ever let me down. They continue to inspire and energize.

The chronology of my first eight years after SWFPAC, 1979 to 1987, is simple.

At the start of this period, I did, as Lori had told Admiral Wertheim, join two former naval officers in founding a security-design corporation. It lived for thirty months and had blossomed into twenty-eight employees, when it died suddenly as a government agency with which it had twenty contracts, Health and Human Services, withdrew its funding for computer security planning.

Then, for a somewhat stressful period, I worked for a Los Angeles firm that had worked for me at Trident. Dan Piraino, who never liked them, was right; their only energy came from my pressure, and when the shoe changed feet and they were calling the shots, nothing happened beyond their incessant exchange of inner memos. They seemed to be forever getting ready to go to work. I resigned after two years when I sensed they were about to fire me for my honesty about their do-nothing habits. The organization has since disappeared.

Within twenty-four hours I went to work in Alexandria, Virginia, for their chief competitor, Taurio Corporation. The contrast between the two places was as refreshing as it was dramatic.

Taurio was a dynamic place, and I was full of energy. We should have been a good match. The simple fact is that my heart was no longer in industry.

I had originally come to the Defense Department as an expedient when the Catholic Church would no longer let me function as a priest. This move had proved helpful in more ways than earning a living, but by the time I got to Taurio thirteen years had gone by, and I had learned what I needed to learn. It was time to get back to doing what I really wanted to do and was primarily trained to do.

My fully restored meditation was making me feel more and more like a fish out of water. Every day fellow workers were in my Taurio office talking about this or that personal problem, this or that spiritual hunger, and several had asked me to help them learn to meditate. I seemed to be always finding yet another excuse to set work aside as national marketing director and talk to them about spiritual matters. Restlessness came to a head one day at a staff meeting when I bolted upright in my chair as the question formed in my head, "What in hell are you doing here?" My decision was really that sudden, that simple. Lori said she had been waiting for it.

Within three weeks, she and I were driving across country back to the Pacific Northwest. She had found a job with Eleanor LaBerge's artsy cottage industry in Gig Harbor, and I soon found another as a bookkeeper at a nearby middle school where Earl was principal. The LaBerges once again proved to be special friends.

When I received my first paycheck at Kopachuck Middle School, the reality hit me that I had taken about a 600 percent cut in salary. That was acceptable because, as I honestly reported to all who asked, I was also aware of what felt like a 10,000 percent increase in job satisfaction.

Officially, I was bookkeeper, but before long I became an unofficial counselor to the more maverick students, "toughs," who, for some unknown reason, gravitated to me. A few weeks after I arrived, this mystery was solved. Word had gotten around the school that I had been a monk, and to middle-school student boys that could only mean that I had been a Ninja monk. As a Ninja monk—known in comic books and Hollywood, at least, as one who is a night stalker, wall climber, and stealthful killer of those who need killing—I was an overnight hero to my street kids. Several times in moments of quiet exchange, one of them asked me if I would not please confide to him how many people I had killed, "if you can remember." My denials were interpreted as part of some Ninja code, which, of course, I would never betray. The whole misconception unraveled for them one day when, now able to trust me, three of them asked if I would teach them how to throw Ninja "stars," the sharpened little weapons that were forbidden in school, and which I had to confiscate from them. I loved those kids and the school, and the principal told me they loved me. Even the two official counselors, who could have been miffed, had they been more insecure types, and I got along famously. It was an especially happy year.

My time at Kopachuck only lasted one school year, however, because I was offered a job by the United Methodist church as their campus minister at the University of Washington in Seattle. They seemed to care not at all that I was neither a United Methodist nor about to become a United Methodist. The pay was not good, but it was twice what I was making at the middle school. Even had the pay been less, working at a major university held great excitement for me. The university would give me a chance to talk with young adults about what I had been learning in meditation for the past thirty-eight years. I knew that the campus was dominated by fundamentalist churches competing to gain the students' commitment to the externals and fears of institutional Christianity, and I looked forward to giving as many as would listen another option: the *inner* side of religion, a broader grasp of the world's reach for God.

Before returning to the Northwest from Washington, D.C., an experience had outfitted me to survive with humor what was about to be my final two years in institutionalized religion. Every place I have been in life seems to have provided at least one special gift to carry away as I left. The gift I took from Washington, D.C. and the defense industry, one that would prove helpful as I moved back into organized religion and then out of it, turned out to be as significant in my life as had been the snake-handling incident in the monastery hay fields many years before.

24

Orange Resurrection

I stood transfixed. An observer, had there been one, might have asked if I were breathing. The rising sun, deep orange on a smoggy horizon, was just beginning to set fire to the gleaming white marble of the capital city's Lincoln Memorial, at which I had just arrived. I found myself standing in a pile of blazing orange marble and staring up at the enthroned figure of Abraham Lincoln as if I were a miniature man come to a moment of final judgment.

As it turned out, in a way I had. In this case, though, I was to be judge as well as defendant, and the verdict was going to go decidedly in my favor. I was about to try, and then convict, a problem that had needed adjudication all my life. Recent evidence was in from a host of new life experiences, and it was time for the retrial of something on which I had found myself guilty a thousand times before.

That morning on the Mall, a few months before Lori and I left to return to the Pacific Northwest, shall forever remain indelible in my memory. Lincoln's white memorial, flaming orange in the sunrise, was unforgettable in itself, but in my memory banks it remains but a dramatic backdrop for the far more unforgettable *inner* events that took place at that moment.

An experience came to me there at the feet of Lincoln that summarized many years of insights and breakthroughs and served to give me, finally, the experience and consequent energy to put all my theory about individual inner worth effectively into practice in my life.

The event of which I am writing has become a permanent point of reference for me. Like so many moments on the road to wholeness, here was yet another of those incidents that come to move us along the way.

Lori and I had lived nearby in suburban Virginia for almost two years, and the Mall had long since become one of my favorite haunts, especially for my morning jog. This particular day I slipped out of bed early, despite Lori's protests, and drove there for a good run. There were two hours remaining before I promised I would be home for brunch with our houseful of guests from New York. I had time to dawdle. This visit to Lincoln, a longtime mentor, had not been planned, but here I was staring up into his wise and patient eyes.

The previous day in my Alexandria office had been more than ordinarily difficult. It had cast me into gloom, and my night had been restless. At the first sign of dawn, tired as I still was, I almost gratefully got out of bed. Running helped me think—or, more accurately, quit thinking—and I felt I really needed to get in some time alone before turning into a Washington tour guide for the day. Getting up early and jogging in an uncustomarily quiet great city has always been a special adventure.

It worked. I wasn't far along my path when my spirit began to lighten. The fellow worker with whom I had clashed in the office and to whom I'd had to concede because of his higher rank, and despite his lack of pertinent information, seemed suddenly less important.

My pressing thoughts were questioning—for the millionth time—what it was that disturbed me so much when I had to deal with men like Jack. I knew enough about psychology to know that it was more than either this man or any individual encounter with him that was upsetting me.

It certainly was not that Jack was unlikable. Quite the opposite. Everybody liked him, including me. What I saw in him that bothered me were his power and advantages and the obviously exaggerated high profiling of both. He was reasonably athletic, reasonably good looking, paid an unbelievable salary, but, worst of all, brimming with a self-confidence that his store of either natural or acquired talents did not justify.

The special irritation about him, I was honest enough to admit to myself, was that he conducted himself self-confidently in ways that I could never manage. He habitually spoke with firmness and conviction, even though often missing the finer points in a conversation or staff meeting. At those same meetings I, too, spoke firmly and with logic, but inwardly I felt what others could not see: self-doubt. What got to me most was that Jack showed no signs of any self-doubt and openly bragged of having none. His self-confidence gave most listeners reason to believe him even when his presentation otherwise did not.

Why, I asked myself, should any of this bother me? If an overly confident man wanted to botch our strategy for some defense contract, and if the owner of the company seated at the head of the table was so wooed by his charisma as to permit it, any resulting losses would come out of that owner's pocket, not mine. And if Jack wanted to showcase his dullness by being outspoken, why should I care?

More than once I asked myself if I was simply jealous. I honestly didn't think so.

By this time in my life I had grown in objectivity enough to recognize that I was not a failure myself. Neither was I a physical slouch, as my just completed run from the Washington Monument and up the Lincoln Memorial steps had demonstrated. "Besides," I quipped to my ears only, "I still have more hair on my head than he has!"

The only thing I really lacked, I repeated again and again, was his feeling of confidence.

I had been too assiduous in practicing self-alienation and dependence on others during my life in Montana and at the abbey to develop even the beginnings of self-esteem then. The self-direction and leadership ability I had demonstrated since in my management positions clearly resulted from native talent *and acting ability,* I told myself, and not from genuine self-confidence.

Despite an education and diversity of life experience that my nemesis couldn't begin to match, despite being at ease socially, well liked, and successful in my employments, despite the awards and promotions that had come to me in the Department of Defense, I still *felt* less than others, and Jack seemed to have a special talent for putting salt directly into that gaping wound.

Those had been my thoughts during my restless night and as I parked in the Washington Monument lot and began running toward the Lincoln Memorial. As I sprinted up the steps to Lincoln's feet, I suddenly came face-to-face with the seated president in a manner than had never happened before. Perhaps it was that we had never been alone like this before. Finding anything not swarming with tourists in Washington is a rare moment, and probably only happens in these predawn hours. I found myself almost embarrassed, like someone who had accidentally blundered into the Oval Office, unannounced. My eyes swung nervously away from Lincoln's face and sideways over the inscribed texts on the surrounding walls, scanning words I long since knew by heart. Only then did my gaze come back to rest on the great man's downturned face.

The impact that face had on me at that moment could not have been greater had Mr. Lincoln actually just then lowered his stone head to attend to my troubled presence. In that instant—the instant our eyes met—I slid into an experience I can only compare to moments of prayer when experiential boundaries shift and cosmic dimensions overlap.

It was as if, instantly, all sense perceptions had been merged into a single point, as if all surrounding material realities were seen more clearly than ever before to be but One—yet retaining their distinctness.

I found myself watching—though I saw nothing of this with physical eyes—two finely detailed, rapid-pace scenarios playing out simultaneously to my inner eye. I saw Lincoln's life and my own, distinct and separated by more than a century, somehow paired into a strange unity, like two facets of a single gem seeming to blend as they reflect simultaneously the same ray of sunlight.

Out of unnamed recesses of my spirit I saw in an instant everything I had ever read, heard, or in any way learned about Lincoln's life. Equally, in the same moment, I saw everything I had ever lived in my own. The two lives were more than superimposed: they somehow melded while each remaining itself.

If my fear at the onset of this experience was completely muted, it was because an inescapable feeling was also being radiated in this blazing courtroom: "All is well!" It was more than the usual sense of the "I'm okay" that follows weekends at Esalen or Wintergreen. It was far higher and far deeper than any emotion-based high. It was more like a metaphysical dance hiding deep inside words that are customarily and too easily passed over as simply pious, like those spoken centuries ago by Juliana of Norwich from her own enlightened experience and which I had once felt so clearly at the Lady Altar back in the Utah abbey: "All is well! All is well!"

My faith in the ultimate, underlying benevolence of Reality that I had so long realized as applicable to the universe as a whole and to every individual unit in that universe—and thus, theoretically, to me—was somehow now, as never before, *experienced* as including me.

It was as if a whole slice of my doubting psyche had just been surgically removed and replaced by an implant of self-affirmation and a wholeness that had nothing more important to do than to dance.

I felt that a dam that had seemed to deny water to lowlands for half a century had in an instant irrigated every valley plant into bloom. Suddenly there was color everywhere, life and freshness and vigor. An overarching, overwhelming sense of benevolence seemed to preclude even the possibility of any lowlander's impertinent question about whether this bounty so suddenly materialized could possibly be real.

I seemed for an instant to see young Abe, prostrate, weeping on his lover's grave. Mysteriously, simultaneously, in the same frame, I saw myself, drawn and gaunt not so much by monastic fast as by my own self-rejection, lying on the grave of my manhood. Like so much in the inner realms, there are no images from our three-dimensional world to portray this scene adequately, but real it was nonetheless, and so the images are accurate as far as they can go.

Somehow the pain of both scenarios became one, and in that moment I also understood them to be completely without lasting significance. I saw two separate sleepers tossing through their long, lone nights of the past, for disparate reasons of disparate magnitudes, and their fears were now clearly the experience of but One.

Most compelling and startling of all, the agonies of those nights were strewn over with a gentleness and warmth so much greater than the pain that perhaps the best description of my reaction to the experience was one of joy, if not of actual mirth.

Standing there absorbed in this inner affair, but with so complete an awareness of my surroundings that I would have noted a passing insect in intimate detail, I felt for a fleeting instant the cold, near-absolute panic the minds of the insane must feel in their fleeting moments of lucidity. Was I going crazy? Had I snapped? As quickly as this panic came—and even more firmly—it left and took all doubt with it. The Benevolence, pressing home to me as the Warp and Woof of all things, made any considered doubt and conscious fear impossible.

The complete experience ended as gently as a kitten falling asleep at its mother's purring breast. I would have guessed an hour

had passed, but when I glanced at my watch I saw that I could not
have been standing there for more than two or three minutes. The
sun was still just as low on the eastern horizon, and the blazing orange marble all about me had not moved one observable bit closer
to becoming the blinding white that it would be within the hour.
I remember feeling a new appreciation of, almost an identifica-
tion with, the color orange that will forever carry for me overtones
of upsurging joy and special promise.

I felt totally grounded, natural, completely intact. Renewed and
almost on fire with the marble around me, I casually turned to go.
My problem had been solved. Jack could live. From this moment,
I would be peer to him and to all others.

Then I realized I was no longer alone up there at the feet of
Lincoln. A dog, a huge black Labrador with the sweet eyes of a
Golden Retriever, had come up the steps and was watching me,
ears up and head cocked slightly to one side. Had he seen with his
bodily eyes what I had seen with an inner eye?

Bending down, I spoke softly, and to my surprise he trotted willingly to me. I patted his head and he licked my nose. Protocol
complete, we sat down together on the top step. The dog sat close,
almost leaning into me, and I sat with my arm around him.

We remained there for perhaps half an hour, neither one doing
anything more than feeling how good it was to be alive and fellow observers of such a quiet sunrise. A couple times he spontaneously turned and licked my cheek as if to show appreciation for
the arm around him. I returned the passion of the moment with
a squeeze and continued to run my fingers through his coat. Over
on Constitution Avenue the early commuter buses were beginning
to roar their black breaths out into the stirring city, but for the moment the two of us sat still and close in a special kind of extramar-
ital affair.

When it was time to go, I stood up, respectfully ruffled the fur
on my friend's head a final time, and moved away. He didn't follow
me, but as I glanced back he wagged his tail as if to impart upon

me, with the dignity of a Roman pontiff, a blessing from the gentle hearts of his immaculate kingdom.

I turned and walked for yet another time, and with new freedom, back into the world.

Brunch was good that morning. That evening Lori's relatives told me I make one helluva tour guide to Washington, D.C.

25

My Last Church

It was a strange feeling to walk back into church work the day I reported as a United Methodist campus minister in August 1985. The University of Washington in Seattle was just across Fifteenth Avenue NE from the huge University United Methodist Church, where my office was to be located. I was primed to go across that street and onto a campus of more than forty thousand students to share the excitement for the human spiritual adventure that I had felt since my youthful days with Datus. It was an adventure I had by this time honed into an informed and critical enthusiasm. I had not been prepared for so exciting a job in Datus's day, but now I definitely was.

The big leather desk blotter that Lori had given me in Trident times for my then executive-sized desk swamped my new secretary-sized one and made me laugh as I saw it there. After unpacking the rest of my personal furnishings and hanging a few pictures, I sat down with a cup of coffee, feeling the need to let it register just where I was.

I wasn't a United Methodist, but, for their own reasons, that church sometimes invited individuals of other denominations to be their campus ministers. A distant cousin of mine, a nun, was at this same time a United Methodist campus minister at the University of Iowa.

It had been fifteen years and two months since I had last worked
in a church. Then I was a Catholic priest, and here I was setting up
shop as a Protestant minister. My God!—*me* a *Protestant*. Worse
than that: me a Protestant *minister*. If the abbot could see me now.
"Forgive me, Padre, for you think I'm sinning."

It gave me considerable satisfaction to recognize that I no longer
felt the smallest vestige of concern over what my former abbot
would or would not say. Not even what my former pope would
or would not say. What a long journey such inner freedom implied.

I sat looking around, wondering what I could do to transform
my gray office into a cheery place. As on the flight from the
monastery to San Francisco, I felt a need to review the changes that
filled my past few years, the interval between the last time I served
in a church and today. Here I was back in ministry, and much more
than my religion had changed.

The dismal basement office with its cobwebbed fluorescents
doing their inadequate best to cheer it up from a twelve-foot ceiling was a far cry from recent offices I'd known. It should have dis-
couraged me, but it didn't. I felt nothing but enthusiasm and
energy as I sat there ruminating on my journey between two disparate ministries and the exciting challenge that now lay before
me. Unlike before, I no longer doubted my abilities. I didn't feel
cocky, just confident. I recognized that I had something important to share and that I now knew well how to share it—without,
at last, the distraction of a frightened ego.

The span of time from when I was a Catholic priest in San
Francisco to now as a Protestant chaplain in Seattle seemed not unlike a planned vacation, or, better, a protracted seminar on how to
grow up in the many ways I had somehow previously missed.

How had I ever made it from day to day in the abbey, I wondered, with the fears and doubts that used to plague me? The answer was simple: church representatives had always been there to
tell me what thoughts to think and how to hold my face as I
thought them. I had found security in their reassurances that con-

formity was all that mattered, that my only important okayness lay in the future, in another life. Now, at last, I had learned to look for my security, fulfillment, and joy here in this life as a prelude and preparation for what is to come.

Fifteen years as what churches call a lay person had been good for me. The urge to escape that had driven me to a cloistered monastery in the first place was now gone. I was at last a man among men, a citizen of the world moving consciously and comfortably among peers. I didn't feel better than others, just equal to them. On this first morning back in church work, I recognized a certain wholeness in me, perhaps even a ballsiness, that had not been there when I was an active priest. I was thankful for it.

By the time I decided to go out and get some paint to give my office the resurrection it so sadly needed, I'd had time to marvel at Providence, to congratulate myself for the way life was going, and to wish my father were still alive so I could share with him what had happened to me over the years. Dad had died instantly and peacefully five years before, as his family gathered at home to honor him on the occasion of his ordination as a high priest in the Mormon church, following his serious turn to faith some years earlier. He and I had become very close, and he would have loved to catch up on his oldest son's ongoing story.

My starry-eyed idealizing of what I expected to be the open-mindedness of mainline Protestantism proved to be naïve and short-lived. On that first day as one of their ministers, I still imagined I would have church managers' support as I went out onto the campus to share a lifetime of insight with bright young students. As it turned out, the students exceeded my expectations and showed up in numbers to hear about spirituality and the inner side of religion, but United Methodism never did come to understand what I was talking about.

I had hit it off from the first day with Paul Beeman, the singularly personable senior pastor of the church where my office was located and the man who had hired me. He let me handle my ministry to students the way I judged best and was always there to help in any way he could, right to the end.

The group of ministers and laypersons whom Paul had represented in hiring me, and to whom I now made monthly reports, the Wesley Foundation Board, was also warmly appreciative at first, especially when, at the end of my first year on the job, student participants in their church's campus program called the Wesley Club moved from an average annual membership of 12 to 143.

But that was before they found out what I was telling the students.

They never thought to ask me what caused the dramatic growth in their club, and, in simplicity, I never thought to tell them. I had no suspicion of how completely uninterested they would turn out to be in what, all over campus, I was calling "the inner side of religion." I learned later that they had been ascribing the club's growth to my energy and easy presence with students. They were wrong. It wasn't I who was causing the burgeoning numbers; it was what I was teaching. The students were not interested in me; they were interested in what I was sharing with them. Had someone else come along and said the same thing better, they would have dropped me and the Wesley Club on the spot. As it was, more and more students showed up to participate in a class on spirituality and a related meditation service that I conducted as the core functions of the club. Significantly, however, less than five percent of these club members showed up for regular Sunday services with the congregation.

When the Wesley Foundation Board learned that what I was giving university students was theology and spirituality and not pep talks about church membership, tithes, and weekly attendance, they were unhappy, and our brief honeymoon crashed in flames.

The first sign of dissatisfaction was that the Washington chairperson of the committee coordinating all United Methodist campus ministries gently told me she considered my program to be "too intellectual." "You are still too Catholic, George. We like to see our campus programs involved more in fun times of food and games than in philosophy and what you call *spirituality.*" She had not the slightest inkling of what I was doing with and for the students. And she apparently saw no implication in the new membership numbers in her club.

A couple weeks after her guidance to me, a Wesley Foundation Board member expressed his church's concern still more candidly. He had read an address I delivered before a meeting of campus ministers in which I pointed out the distinctly spiritual hunger that I was witnessing in the more mature and perceptive students on campus.

"You must realize, George," he counseled me in front of the board, "that those you call the 'more mature and perceptive university students,' and to whom you are aiming your ministry, tend to leave the church eventually. Most of them will not be around in the church of tomorrow. We must use today's assets to cultivate the students—and maybe we have to admit they are the less mature and less perceptive—who will be there to support tomorrow's church."

I had never heard a more straightforward, honest statement of the very problem I was most concerned about: Churchianity as distinct from spirituality, institutionalized religion as distinct from religion itself, what Jesus taught as distinct from the institutional malarkey that has since adulterated that teaching.

Two others on the Wesley Foundation Board diplomatically agreed with the first speaker. It was clear that the board and I had totally different goals.

I resigned two days later, two years after arriving on the job.

More germane to my own story, this crash with the United Methodist church was a significant step on the path to where I find myself today: completely outside of all organized religion.

Lori and I thoroughly enjoyed the United Methodists. In our experience, Catholics tend to come to Mass, mew inaudibly and reluctantly through a few hymns, and then leave quickly through as many side doors as possible as soon as the Mass is ended. Not so United Methodists. Ten of them can out-volume a large parish of Catholics. Their singing and conviviality give a gala touch to every Sunday morning, and we found ourselves looking forward to it. Too, when the service was over, there was always the coffee hour, a time that never lasted less than half an hour and that was, in effect, a party to look forward to each week.

Unfortunately, that's not the complete story. Catholicism may be relatively asocial and depressing in its Sunday gatherings when compared to United Methodism, but it does have an orientation to inwardness and spirituality. Catholicism has its own huge dose of obsessively functioning Churchianity, but it has something else as well. It has an underlay of honest inwardness and at least a theoretical appreciation of mysticism and spirituality that remains unbroken with the past. United Methodism does have a singular degree of concern for social justice, a perpetually frantic busyness about many good things, and a wonderful conviviality in its functioning, but inwardness? Not at all.

Whether consciously realized or not, most individuals are deeply interested in spiritual (inner) growth because all people understand at least intuitively that only deep within themselves will they find dependable happiness, stability, and peace. Much has been written about today's spiritual renaissance, a phenomenon that is happening all over the globe. While many restless churchgoers, ex-churchgoers, and persons who have never had anything to do with organized religion will admit this interest, they will act on it only after they understand that this spirituality is not identified with institutionalized religion and the customary external observances that have grown up in it over the centuries. If organized religion wants to regain credibility with the masses, it will have to give evidence that its inner-directed priorities have been resorted, that *inner* growth and wholeness in *this* life (all of which is the basic content of spirituality) are once again its primary goal.

About half of the young people in the Wesley Club membership that grew up around my teaching were graduate students, so my critic in the Wesley Foundation Board was accurate: the new

Wesley Club was, indeed, composed of the more capable students. And, yes, repeated polls indicate that this type of person does frequently drop church affiliation.

It is significant that the only times younger and struggling students showed up in any numbers for Wesley Club functions were on those rare occasions when it was providing pizza or spaghetti or a movie. They were never present for our ventures into theology or the mystics. They never came to our weekly meditations late Sunday evenings in the monasterylike opposing choir stalls of the huge, darkened, candlelit church. They never came on our long weekend retreats at an old Victorian house by the ocean, where students and I routinely talked all night by the fireplace until time to prepare breakfast the next morning.

Was what I was teaching, then, "too intellectual" for their church, but not for the students? Apparently so. What were they seeking, those who came? What was I passing out that so interested them?

For one thing, I suggested the need for a critical reassessment of the role of churches themselves. I told the students—and openly stated in sermons when asked to preach to the University United Methodist Temple congregation—that churches are like schools and are supposed to provide people with basic religious insights on metaphysical, ethical, and moral questions and principles, *and* the encouragement to go out and make spiritually aware decisions and exercise spiritually aware leadership in applying what they've learned. Churches are intended, I suggested, to possess and share an appreciation for the history of *all* of humanity's reach toward the Eternal, not just that for their little roped-off portion of the Christian West. This perspective would deliver both people and institutions, I promised, from the parochialism, bigotry, and chauvinism of a thousand varieties that have led to centuries of religious infighting and attack on those of other understandings.

In so far as churches do these things, or even any significant element of them, I taught, they are helpful. In so far as they don't, they are counterproductive and an unnecessary distraction: a complete waste of time, much as if they were schools that no longer teach anything and only keep their students busy maintaining school yards.

Churches, like schools, are not ends in themselves. If the principal of a prestigious high school is so impressed with his school's reputation and traditions and with how safely it keeps its students off the streets that he won't permit them to graduate, that principal has forgotten his school's sole purpose. Either his priorities must be corrected or his school abandoned.

It's up to each of us, I suggested, to learn whatever we need from whatever source we can, churches definitely included, in order to awaken to our deepest reality, both as individuals and as members of the human community. This basic self-understanding is more important than any other goal in life. In fact, a proper comprehension of all other goals and realities in our lives depends on our coming to precisely such a self-understanding.

I offered students an exposure to—and an experience of—spirituality and theology, and they loved it. They were openly enthusiastic to make contact with the *inner* traditions of the race and its highest and most noble moments. Some of them told me they were gaining religious understanding and consequent convictions they had never imagined possible. These, in turn, they said, were helping them make sense out of life at last, helping them see their future in a more positive and optimistic way.

With an honesty students are noted for, and almost unanimously, they began reporting that they were finding their church not just a little laughable as its sermons prattled on in bromides and aphorisms that seemed to them as nutritious as yesterday's toast. They told me that they were not at all interested when I suggested that the state of their church was really a challenge to them, an opportunity to get involved and to foment a resorting of its priorities. They said they didn't believe that could be done, and, at any rate, weren't interested in even trying.

United Methodism had pushed an astonishingly superficial program onto its high-school students, and some now in the university told me that their high-school experience had forfeited whatever credibility their church might otherwise have now had with them. All the church had offered them was an assortment of group games, camping weekends, meals, and free Friday-night movies. And, most resented of all, shot through all of this were the ludicrously superficial "study guides" published by their church's Nashville headquarters, which I saw still being used with local high-school students. These publications—even for high-school-level students—were infantile, patronizing, and largely without spiritual substance.

And the powers that be in the State of Washington's United Methodism wanted me to offer more of the same to college-level students.

As one Ph.D. candidate told me, "I'm studying physics at a graduate level. I do highest mathematics in my sleep. And I'm supposed to come and listen to the same things I heard in grammar school and get involved in the same things I did in high school? Are you kidding?"

It soon became clear to me that while I was helping students, students were also helping me.

Their deadly candor helped me recognize how much I was compromising my insights and inner experience to fit in with organized religion. Their pointed perceptions and the courage they showed in shifting loyalties when their insights demanded it were good goads to me. I didn't tell them about it, but they helped me recognize daily how little hope there seemed to be that any substantial resorting or restructuring of priorities would ever be permitted in an organization as political and institutionally preoccupied as United Methodism. I had long since decided that the needed evolution would not happen in Catholicism, at least in the foreseeable future, and now I began to come to the same conclusion in a major and representative branch of Protestantism.

It was during my last weeks as campus minister that a young United Methodist minister in Nashville wrote an article in which he demonstrated from current demographic studies that at its present rate of attrition, the last member of his church will either die or withdraw from membership in the year 2011. I mentioned this study to several United Methodist fellow ministers, and they seemed to appreciate the possibility. But they admitted they had no inkling of what caused the problem. If they were willing to continue on the topic at all, and some were not, it was to express enthusiasm for new theories of church organization, building configuration, or multimedia recruiting techniques. At one meeting there was even a lengthy discussion about whether the answer to church attrition might lie in a need for more church committees.

When I resigned my position with United Methodism, I did it with a reluctant but relieved sense of final disillusionment with organized religion. When I quit that one church, I quit all churches. Every church I had ever experienced or observed closely at all had proved that while it had some good things to offer many, it had narrow horizons and pointless asides to insist upon for all.

During high school, Mormonism had proved for me to be pathetically impoverished, the best it had to offer being quotes from "authorities" in Salt Lake City and an alleged set of "new scriptures" that patently supported themselves by their own bootstraps. Its contempt for "the philosophies of men," by which label, I learned, it meant to include all critical human thinking about religion or philosophy, had made me shudder even as a high-school youth. Catholicism had much to share and taught me much, but it was at the price of individuation. United Methodism had now demonstrated that its highest priority is self-preservation. Last, and definitely least, the fundamentalists and evangelicals on campus, television, and radio clearly illustrated to what levels of silliness the human mind can stoop once it opens willingly to fear. During one week in The Hub, the university's student union building, a group from one evangelical church set up a booth with a dramatically colorful banner announcing, "Come and answer two questions and we'll tell you whether or not you're going to hell." It was a reliable gimmick: hook a person's fear, the standard tactic of Christianity for centuries, and you can get that person to sign on for almost anything.

Leaving organized Christianity meant I could now openly identify with the transcultural, supranational, universal reach of the complete human race for an understanding and experience of Eternal Reality. Jesus remained for me (and remains) one of the world's foremost spiritual masters. He came, as he said, to fulfill, not destroy, the Law and the prophets. He realized and then taught the inner dimension of a movement that had begun so long before with Abraham and that would become the inspiration of much of the West. Buddha had done the same in the East, Zarathustra in Persia for those lands that lie between East and West. Countless shamans and other masters had been doing the same on lesser scales throughout history all over the globe. From the plurality of all languages and all cultures, when this multifaceted reach of the human race is collated and refined of its variables, it is everywhere the same reach and the same finding about the same Eternal Reality.

After leaving United Methodism, I could say what the Sufi Master Pir Villyat would later say, "I do not belong to any church; all churches belong to me." I didn't need any of their tags around my neck to feel a religious identity, nor any of their reassurances to know I am safe.

Stated that way, my move out of organized religion sounds heady and ponderous. In point of fact, after I left my last religious institution, I found a lighter step coming into the dance my heart had been working on for years.

26

Monk at Large

From my start with Datus, through time in the navy and then college, the monastery, in San Francisco, and even with Louisa in Europe, I always found (or took) time for meditation. If it had not been for that slice of silence and inwardness each morning during those many years, I wonder if I would have survived. Five acquaintances have committed suicide; I could easily have been a sixth. If I chose to carry on, I'm confident it was because of the contact I made daily with a spiritual reality that, in the last analysis, must be spelled with a capital R, and that I always found to be bigger than any transient crisis.

After leaving the Methodists, I successively held positions as manager and comanager of two spiritual foundations, where, in both cases—as had happened in churches—the expectations of others complicated the straightforward message I wanted to share. I eventually withdrew from these foundations just as I had from churches and began identifying myself as a monk at large. I began offering classes in meditation, spirituality, and world mysticism, with seminars, speaking engagements, and personal spiritual guidance as options on the side.

I loved the tag monk at large as soon as it came to mind. It preserved the singleness of purpose implied in the term *monk*, while adding a flavor of irreverent independence. I soon began writing and publishing a biweekly newsletter on spirituality that continued for five years until a syndicated newspaper column demanded the time it had been taking. Before long I was facilitating groups of individuals who wanted to learn to meditate and become acquainted with the world's spiritual traditions. Experience with these groups helped me see clearly that the inwardness that works for me also works for others.

One lazy afternoon in 1983, over a beer at Chadwicks on the edge of Washington, D.C. in Georgetown, a senior officer in the Navy Seals, a man whom I admire at least as much as any other, shared with me how irritated he gets when he hears persons who did not fight in Vietnam presume to talk in any detail about the horrors of the war there. He said they can't possibly know what they're talking about, and, as a result, he'd like to make a suggestion: "If you haven't been there, shut the fuck up!"

He spoke with heat out of his concern for the sacred. He and his friends had lived for a time in hell. Great numbers of them had died in it, and he didn't need to hear the reality of that unbelievable journey being treated academically. I worked with enough young men and women returning from Vietnam to have at least an inkling of his sensitivity. I had learned to listen in silence about horrors I have only heard about while others have lived them.

Due proportion being guarded, Bruce's outburst is a useful comparison when others parrot prefab church judgments on my status as an ex-Christian and ex-monk-priest. I have had to ask them not to label my state before they have walked the path of meditation. Their anxiety to repeat the church line could keep them from hearing their own hearts.

Most Christians seem to take it for granted that I threw the baby out with the bath water. "How could you renounce the religion you once embraced so passionately and jettison God and any hope of closeness with him?"

Where did they hear I had jettisoned God? Questions like these make me want to quote Bruce: "If you haven't been there ..."

It's as if I were dancing with the most beautiful woman in the world and someone were to approach and ask if my dancing with this woman means that I now hate my mother. Where do you find words to answer questions like that? Anger comes easily, but the only adequate reply is sorrow and patient explanations for those who are willing to listen.

My heart will forever be full of gratitude for what I learned from Christianity. I have, indeed, graduated from it as it is preached and practiced, but I feel no need to burn it down any more than I feel the need to burn down the high school and colleges that once contributed so substantially to where I am today. I look at the alma mater of my spirit, organized religion, with feelings of honest gratitude.

Nevertheless, my heart is also full of sorrow because I know there is much more to the spiritual reality of religion than what the vast majority of church leaders know about or are able, consequently, to share, busy as they are with institutional preoccupations. As a class, they are absorbed in perpetuating the status quo. They fail to encourage their students to graduate into a deeper understanding and a greater freedom of spirit, primarily because they don't know these exist.

The same Jesus that Christian churches hawk so loudly is the very one who talked about a sublime joy that we can't imagine and a peace beyond understanding, both meant for all of us. Christianity, as it is practiced, gives little evidence of attaining or sharing that high experience, or that trying to do so has ever been much in the priorities of its managers. The only joy they are concerned with is the reassurance of being legally "saved," one they tell their followers will be had only by conforming to the local rendition of the Jesus-saves story line.

When I criticize organized Christianity, I'm not denying that it also does much good. Churches often feed the poor, help heal the sick, and visit prisoners. I recognize these achievements, but I refuse any longer to gloss over the harmful things they do as well. It *is* harmful to keep people preoccupied with institutional logistics and oriented to conformism as if these could heal either individuals or society. And that indictment does not yet mention what churches leave undone.

Institutional Christianity fails to offer help to those who hunger for the kind of fulfillment and inner bliss that Jesus and other spiritual masters told them they could attain. What about those who thirst for a peace that is unshakable? How about the prisoners who need liberating not from jails made of stone and metal bars, but from God-related fear and uncertainty or imagined personal inadequacy? Where is the church assistance that should be helping people move on to freedom of spirit? Why aren't churches giving people—*in a credible and convincing manner*—something that will prove more effective than troubled individuals' efforts to escape from despair by the abuse of alcohol and other drugs?

Where are the churches? Most of them are off taking care of themselves and squabbling about which one of them is bigger, better, and "right."

Religion has become for me, and can be for all, not a matter of observance, much less of frenetic logistics, but one of fire in the heart, deep understanding in the mind, unimaginable fun in the spirit. *That's* been the finding of every mystic in every world religion. It's what religion itself is all about. It's been the teaching of every spiritual master in human history.

Churches did not cause religion to open up this realization for me. It was done *in spite of* them, not because of them.

In direct opposition to institutionalized Christianity's orientation away from this world in favor of one to come, what needs telling—to all who show their readiness by asking—is that the world's common spiritual tradition is dedicated to "salvation" in *this* world. People want help to escape from despair, fear, addictions, turmoil in *this* life. What happens after death will take care of itself if we take care of what happens now. This is not a cavalier unconcern for humankind's ultimate destiny. It is the considered realization of millennia of spiritual persons who were not locked into seeing life on this earth as simply a trial. We're here to work at creatively, joyfully, peacefully continuing the unfolding of the potential in all of us and in everything around us. We're not here to spend our time groveling in repentance for an alleged divine debt as told in some ancient religious stories that were simply trying to get people's attention.

This shift of emphasis in my thinking and teaching had not come lightly or quickly. I arrived at it kicking and complaining all the way, having to struggle constantly against a conscience formed during years of institutional training as a monk and priest and the extreme timidity of one who had little or no self-confidence.

I have written before in this book of some of the breakthrough experiences that led me to realize that I could no longer believe what is, in fact, the foundation of Christian teaching: "You need to be saved." A deep part of me—or, more accurately, a deep *experience* in me—smiles quietly, "No I don't, and neither does anybody else!" That whole belief comes from religious stories of a much younger, a much less critical, and much more fearful race. To take these stories literally is no less foolish then to take literally those threatening ones about trolls under bridges or about falling off the edge of a flat earth.

There is a deeper meaning to the teaching of Jesus than the macabre form the teaching story took in the ancient world (the storyform) that told of an offended Divine King, his alleged demand for blood payment to atone for an offense to his Mightiness, and a hell standing by for those who would not accurately or adequately play his juridical game. Outside of this storyform, "You're flawed" is no more appropriate to explain our basic relationship with God than "You're a bad boy" is appropriate to explain the relationship of a human child to his parents when he falls while learning to walk.

The threat contained in a sin-salvation, heaven-hell approach to religion can, of course, serve as a starting point, a way to get listeners' attention. That's the only way that Jesus and other Hebrew prophets, speaking in their times, intended that the fear factor in their stories about hell and an angry God be used. Fear always remains only a beginning, an attention-getting expedient, and a *very* small part of the total myth with which they were trying to explain the race's intuition of Ultimate Reality. It's a teaching tool in exactly the same way that the wildly unrealistic story of Santa Claus driving reindeer through the sky and sliding down chimneys is a tool to teach small children their first lesson about generous giving and the rewards of right action.

Studying spiritual masters and the experience of meditation led me ultimately to realize that, like Santa on the rooftop, Christian doctrines were built on a central storyform: "There's this big offended God, you see, and after our original parents deliberately stepped on his toes, we had to go and step on them yet again ourselves. Boy, are we in trouble! We have to pay a price for these dreadful offenses, but since we can't manage the needed infinite reparation for our infinite offenses, God sent his Son Jesus to do it for us." All this is nothing more than a concocted teaching tool to get the attention of a young human race in the West, exactly as a previous story— the creation of the cosmos in six days by an artisanlike God—had once been used to make the idea available to the unsophisticated early members of the Hebrew race that there is an intelligent Source behind everything we see around us. Unfortunately, huge organizations quickly built themselves around, and vested themselves in, both stories.

There is a vastly deeper consciousness in the religious experience of humankind than the powerful-artisan tale of the Bible. A more developed level of insight, witnessed to by the mystics and spiritual masters of the race, tells us that we are invited to grow beyond all such storied details as sin, threats, blood payments, unending fire, pearly gates, golden streets. Both Santa Claus and salvation stories have deeper meanings than what they deliver when heard only literally. I am no longer willing to stop at institutional Christianity's "Come and be saved" presupposition. I would suggest something more along the lines of the spiritual tradition of the race: "Let's get beyond all these religious stories and wake up to see and experience Reality as It is."

The only thing we have to be saved from is what Hindu thought calls maya, what Buddha called our sleeping, and what *A Course in Miracles,* representing as it does the inner dimension of the Judaeo-Christian tradition, calls our illusions.

Christians need to be reminded to read more carefully the repeated statements in the Bible that "Fear of the Lord is the beginning of wisdom." The word *beginning* is the important word. The Bible never once says this fear *is* wisdom, but only that it is the *beginning* of wisdom, the launching platform. The threat of a spanking can be a useful expedient with small children who keep rushing out into a busy street, but it's only a small step toward the adult care they must eventually develop concerning pedestrian safety around traffic. To make threats a lifelong basis for traffic safety would be ridiculous, but no more so than what institutionalized Christianity has done with the "get-saved" story about relating to God.

A creek, the Pondera Coulee, runs through the ranch where I grew up in Montana, and when I was very young I fell into it and very nearly drowned, they tell me. Mother and Dad subsequently tried to keep me away from it and threatened various kinds of punishments if I should disobey them, but to no avail. In desperation, Mother finally composed a story that would get my attention: "Don't you realize there are goblins in creeks?" I never went near it again without an adult alongside me. Mother did what biblical writers and writers of myths did. She thought up a storyform that would get her message across. If today in my mid-sixties, I still believe there are goblins in creeks, I'm a fundamentalist. I've kept the literal message of the story, but have never got through to its only intended content: don't be careless around water or you may drown. Mother wasn't teaching me anything about goblins, but about being careful with my life.

Biblical writers weren't telling us anything about God's six-day work week or about trees talking or the sun standing still in the sky or whales swallowing men or about God being offended and hypersensitive concerning his rights. Like my mother, they were trying to get the attention of too-often disinterested people. And they had every right to hope, as did my mother, that as we grew up we'd get beyond the literalness of the stories they wove.

No word of Jesus fascinated me in the monastery as much as one ascribed to him in chapter 16 of John's story of his life. John has him telling his followers, "I have more to tell you, more than you can now bear...." The word *more* was what hooked me.

The thought of this "more" drove me inward to think and study and meditate in search of it. What could he have meant?

Another time, when his closest friends asked him why he taught people in stories (told in chapter 13 of Matthew's account of his life), he explained that the "secrets of the kingdom of heaven" were not yet for everyone.

So there are also secrets, deeper meanings. I wondered what they are.

Jesus was saying that he couldn't share his deeper realizations as freely as he'd like because the people he was talking to—representing the development of the human race in the West at the time—couldn't yet handle insights that were so advanced beyond what they were used to hearing.

In direct contradiction to the common Christian teaching that he gave us the full story on how the universe works, Jesus himself said precisely the opposite. He said that as the race grows up, it will become capable of understanding more than the material details of his stories. He explicitly said there is "more."

In proportion as this became clear to me, religion made more and more sense. The mystics of both East and West have claimed that they have realized a deeper side of religion. They tell us that in their meditation something more has been shown them. Even

Christianity's favorite legislator and defender, Paul of Tarsus, wrote to Jewish citizens in Corinth that he had been taken up to some place of high consciousness—"whether in the body or out, I don't know"—where he "heard things that are not to be spoken, that no mortal is permitted to repeat [in the society of his day]." Like his young mentor, Jesus, before him, he was saying there's a "more" and a "not yet."

Despite differences of expression, the information of the mystics is essentially identical in East, West, and everywhere else in the world where persons of deep inwardness have reported their experiences and highest realizations. In widely varying storyforms that rise from different cultural frames of reference and different languages, they share what they have seen and experienced, and it all comes out to be the same experience, the same insight. What they report is striking in its similarity. From their common human spirit, a common spiritual hunger broke through everywhere to a common awareness.

Astonishing to me, this enlightenment turned out to be what I had for years been backing into myself.

For my last few years in the cloister, I felt so guilty about early intuitions of this awareness of the mystics, which tradition calls higher consciousness, that I often found myself rushing off to confession to ask pardon for "sins against the faith." I would later see that those early "unorthodox" insights, intuitions, intimations—I would almost call them suspicions at that stage—were actually first breakthroughs into high consciousness.

They were not "sins against faith," but sins against my church's reduction of religion to dogmatic formulas and literal adherence to the stories in its Bible. My insights were out of sync with the least-common-denominator teachings of the church and so seemed scary to me at the time. But they were urgent invitations nonetheless and were not about to be turned aside by my timidity. Jesus had said that the time would come when "the spirit will lead you into all truth," into what he had just referred to as the more. It took me many years to dare to recognize that that more was exactly what I was being shown.

While neither Catholics nor United Methodists play the "devil-may-get-you" game in the explicit way that evangelical churches do, that is only because they are less logically thorough and courageously honest than their fundamentalist neighbors. Jerry Falwell and his type of evangelical literalists may be objectionable, but they should be granted this much: they take institutionalized Christianity to its logical end, and that in the face of a ridicule the pope and mainline church leaders are careful to avoid.

The core doctrine of Christianity is identical throughout its many organized forms. Catholicism and mainline Protestantism may dodge or camouflage the fact, but essentially they don't move any further beyond basic Sunday-school stories about an offended and potentially dangerous God than do their more forthright evangelical neighbors. They are simply less transparent about what really underlies all they teach. Take away their central doctrine that we are all in need of being saved from some alleged awful fault, and what remains of church practice or teaching as we know it?

The pathos is that none of the branches of organized Christianity teaches the deeper meaning, the more, that their Leader told them was there for all to realize eventually. To do so would be to compromise the functioning and purpose of the churches as they have evolved over the centuries. To organization leaders, that horror is unthinkable.

Teaching the inner side of religion is what I've set out to do as a monk, now at large in the world and no longer behind walls built of institutionalized and vested thoughts.

I used to ask myself how I would have reacted had I been a loyal Christian in northern Germany in the sixteenth century when across town a young Augustinian monk with a doctorate in theology, a certain Father Martin Luther, nailed his revolutionary ideas to a cathedral door? It's easy now, on a Monday morning almost five hundred years later, to recognize how important his game plays were—his condemnations of the corruption of Roman practice and his variations on the Christian theme. But how would I have reacted *then?* Would I have offhandedly rejected what he said simply because it wasn't familiar and because it was unacceptable to top management in Rome? Or would I have been among those gutsy types who dared listen to him and overnight found a new vitality in their lives?

There's a still better example I used to examine the courage of my convictions. Suppose I had been a temple-practicing Jew about the year A.D. 30 in Jerusalem. Would I have been willing to stand up against my relatives, friends, local synagogue, and whole nation by listening to a radical young teacher from Galilee named Jesus? His teaching could only have seemed far-out, unorthodox, dangerous to most people of his generation. Would I have dared give his insights a fair hearing and perhaps, as a result, have to update my practice of the religion of my forebears? Jesus did not have the remotest intention of jettisoning Judaism as such ("I came not to destroy, but to fulfill"): a second and third generation of his later followers did that. All he was doing was cleaning house in exactly the same way that many previous prophets, his predecessors, had done. He was just pulling back from the industrialization of the religion of Abraham and the patriarchs. Would I have dared go along with him? I can easily imagine hearing monks and bishops and ministers I have known complaining, "He talks with Samaritan women and is kind to hookers and extortionists!" Would I have been willing to take him seriously anyway?

One of my deepest joys during these years of change is that Lori all the while was reading and meditating as well, every bit as assiduously as I. I have often wondered what would have happened to our marriage if she had not been passionately involved with her own spiritual journey. What if her reading and meditating had only lasted for a few months out of love for her husband and then she had returned to the Catechism and Rosary?

I didn't have to worry. As it turned out, we moved along parallel paths and have come to the same insights. Lori has gone on to lead seminars, teach classes, and develop her own practice of counseling spiritual seekers. One day, perhaps, she will write her own book about her own experiences. She already has a title: *My Side of the Dance.*

Yet another realization came to me in those first days out of organized Christianity. I came to understand that every individual is on his or her own cutting edge. I have no right to doubt that all are seeking peace and fulfillment as consistent to their insights as I try to be to mine. The urge to help others see more and experience something more enlightened than the external preoccupations of the churches has to be contingent on their expressed or clearly implied desire for help, their clear desire for greater peace and joy and sense of security. It could never be based on any implication that they are "wrong" in what they are now doing. If this or that individual sees things differently than I, that doesn't imply that he or she is any less honest or using any less energy in pursuing that vision than I am in pursuing mine.

The question is not who is better or more honest, but who will gain more freedom from all fear, who will gain the peace and joy that the masters have spoken of. Who will find bliss even here in this life.

The churches are on another path. I don't have to be on theirs, nor they on mine. I can—I must—speak up about there being more paths than the story-bound one they teach, but I must leave the church path to those who choose it.

Having at last found peace myself, I was now able to leave others in peace as well. A great calm settled in my heart. Buddha smiled. Jesus nodded. Zarathustra chuckled. Lao-tzu winked. Babaji nodded knowingly. My angels did flips.

And I? I was ready to get to work.

27

The Rest of the Family

Why did I, raised with considerable exposure to Christianity and later trained in it far more than most, reject it as the only path to God and embrace a worldwide spirituality instead?

Sometime in the first few months out of the monastery and while I was still in San Francisco, I realized that I had still another cloister to leave. This time it was going to be more like leaving a ghetto, a racist and chauvinist club, a tribal village that looked upon neighboring tribes as inferior, less favored by God, outsiders to be conquered and put in line. This second cloister was a thing of the mind, the core Christian presumption of being unique in the world of religion. I saw that I had to get beyond this bigotry completely if I hoped to join the rest of the race and respect it with an honest heart, if I wished to have the advantage of their insights and wisdom and not be limited to those of my Christian heritage.

It's one thing to break out of Christian dogmatism, doctrine by doctrine. It's quite another to back off far enough to see the complete Christian movement in perspective. Early in 1968 I followed an intuition—as always, way out in front of my understanding—and began worshipping with Hindu monks, meditating with Buddhist monks, and, most rewarding of all, associating myself with the Jewish community. A new perspective on Christianity was quick in coming. It was *not* a pretty picture.

What in the world, I asked myself, had Christians been doing in and to the human race all these centuries? Ensconced in their "we're-right-and-you're-wrong" doctrines, they had fought self-righteously among themselves from day one, as witnessed in their New Testament itself, and had then moved out to persecute others. They openly despised and persecuted *every* other faith and outsider they contacted. And they did it all with the conviction that it was for the glory of God.

Down the centuries this more-blessed-than-thou, master-race attitude led to bloodshed not by way of exception, but routinely. Being sure God was on their side (and, by implication, on no one else's), they judged that no holds were to be barred in imposing their brand of truth, their interpretation of reality on everyone else. In medieval Spain they gave the Jewish people the options of becoming Christian or being put to death, and eventually kicked them out of their homes and country. In foreign missions when they had rice and indigenous people had none, they told them to be baptized or starve. Everywhere, they patronized and treated non-Christians in ways as contemptible as they were contemptuous.

The severity of this overarching error is revealed in the fact that for the most part Christian leaders encouraged it with good conscience. A sincerity of purpose in religious persecution is more painful than when such crimes are openly driven by avarice or other temporal connivance. Openly identified motivations of greed and lust have certainly played their part in fueling Christian arrogance, but they have not been the primary push. Had they been, they might have been recognized earlier and condemned. What was particularly dangerous in Christian self-righteousness down the centuries is that people were trained to believe honestly that what they were doing was a holy thing. As though to flaunt all this, the Roman department that managed the tortures of the Inquisition was called the Holy Office, whose fundamental guideline was that there need be no constraints on a work, howsoever bloody, when it was announced to be the work of God.

————

It is a monument to how well I had learned my Catholic lessons when discovering genuine spirituality outside of Roman Christianity took me by complete surprise. I was dumbfounded, and at first openly skeptical, to find books of substantial spirituality written by Protestants. I remember the first one that crossed my path: *The Dark Night of the Soul* by Georgia Harkness. How could this be! A book by a Protestant sporting the very title of an earlier one by one of Catholicism's greatest sixteenth century mystics, Saint John of the Cross? I was honest enough to recognize Harkness's sincerity and depth of spirituality, but it says much about my training that I was surprised to see such qualities in her.

If discovering that Protestants possess a genuine spirituality surprised me, finding a still higher level of mystic consciousness—and a much deeper spirituality—in *non*-Christian places astonished me vastly more.

Unlike many in the sixties and seventies, I did not feel a need to rush to the East to find spirituality or to join one or other of the oriental religious movements that had been transplanted to the West. I knew we had no lack of mystic wisdom in the West. The problem, I understood, was that the West's high wisdom lay eclipsed under institutional priorities. When I did turn to the masters of the East, it was not to find a mysticism, but to enlist their help in better understanding the rich store of Western mysticism that lay deeply camouflaged in doctrinal wrappings. I wanted to understand the full gamut of the mysticism of Isaiah, of the author of the psalms, of the young Jewish prophet Jesus, of Teresa of Avila, of John of the Cross, of the Catherines of Siena and Genoa, and many others. The East turned out to be a capable teacher.

All that I initially knew at this period in my life about Hinduism, Buddhism, and Taoism I had learned in the seminary in bits and pieces and in almost forgotten ways years before from Datus. I had forgotten it, but in 1946 Datus had already introduced me to the fact that high spirituality does exist outside of Christianity.

Increasingly suspicious of the objectivity of my seminary training, almost as soon as I arrived at the University of San Francisco in 1967, I began reading broadly in Eastern religious traditions. What I found out about non-Christian spirituality in those early days in San Francisco provided only initial clarifications, but even these were enough to astonish me.

During this time I took a class in yoga from four young Americans who had been drug users, and now had become yogis. Their poise was astounding and almost a spiritual experience even to see. They were totally without affectation and made a deep impression. While I was working with them, I had my first conscious realization that genuine spirituality might not have to deny the body after all.

More than any other influence during this period, however, was my dawning recognition of the gentle spirituality in Judaism: dedication to God through dedication to human beings. This insight ran completely contrary to what we had been taught in seminary training about the so-called heartless legalism of the Jewish religion. Getting to know and appreciate the Jewish people in San Francisco was, probably more than anything else, the wedge that finally broke down my spiritual snobbery and broke open my Christian ghetto walls.

The city's largest synagogue, Temple Emmanuel, stands on the corner of Arguello and Lake streets in San Francisco, three blocks from Saint Anne's Convent where I was chaplain from 1967 to 1969. Within a few weeks of moving into Saint Anne's, I ventured into the large courtyard that is at the center of the temple complex. People were friendly—and seemed not at all interested in jumping on me with handouts proclaiming I should become one of them. I wandered unconfronted throughout the institution in open admiration of its immaculate appearance.

Opening onto the south side of the inner courtyard of the vast complex there is a small prayer chapel, perhaps thirty by twenty feet, and I fell in love with it on that first visit. I sat in it and tried to absorb its dramatic beauty. It had windows only on the south wall, and these were made up of huge, irregularly thick chunks of richly colored glass twelve inches thick in places. This rich elegance of deep color was matched by everything else in the chapel's elegant appointments. I remember thinking that it had to be one of the most beautiful places I'd ever seen.

I sat there a long time feeling the peace of the place. Eventually, and I suppose largely from habit—or perhaps simply from mechanical association with chapels—I surreptitiously recited a Rosary, keeping my hand in my coat pocket as I fingered the beads. "God knows what a scene these Jews might make if they caught me saying a Rosary in their synagogue," I thought. Now, of course, I know they would have smiled in patient compassion, as I now do myself. And had they, in fact, asked me to leave, it would have been with the graciousness and quiet strength I have come to know in them so well.

About this time I enrolled in a course on the Torah taught by a rabbi on faculty at USF, another new experience. Rabbi Bernard Ducoff and I got along famously. He introduced me to Jewish literature and scholarship in areas beyond that of the Torah. Looking back, I realize this gentle, older man was no great scholar, but he was a true gentleman as he patiently tried to represent another style of belief and life at what might be called a preeminent bastion of Christianity, a Jesuit university.

During this period I went to see a French documentary, *La Nuit et le Brouillard* (Night and Fog), a film including much actual footage from the Third Reich of their concentration camps and human-experimentation labs. It is difficult to know how to share the complex facets of what that movie did to me, and for me. Perhaps I can best share its impact by comparing it to an incident back on the ranch in Montana when I was still a child.

I had raised a lamb from the moment my father gave it to me after its mother died during its birth. The lamb learned to look to me for its milk and later meals and learned to trust and want to be close to me. It seemed to remain confused all its life about why it was stopped at the kitchen door and was not allowed to follow me into the house.

Eventually, when it was fully grown, my father quietly told me it was time to include the lamb among those that were to be butchered. After all, a ranch is not a zoo, not a place where the long-term maintenance of animals is the point, but where their production for slaughter is the point.

Long story, but, finally, bowing to the logic of the situation, I agreed, and one day upon returning from school I found myself looking at the severed head of the lamb who had so often nuzzled me. It was not easy. Adult logic said one thing, my child's heart another. Logic had a hard time maintaining the tiller, and now I know it should not have tried.

What I will write now is almost blasphemous, but I'm only suggesting a comparison in which but a small portion of the compared parts are similar.

What I felt as I watched the French documentary was something akin to what I had felt when I looked at my pet lamb's severed head. Only vastly more so. This time there was no logic whatsoever in the situation to help me out. I didn't fall down. I didn't lose control. I just went deep inside and touched a part of my humanity that I had never consciously touched so completely before.

The eyes of naked Jewish men and women looking with embarrassment at German cameras filming them as they queued to walk into gas chambers they had been told were showers—these eyes will look into my eyes forever. The faces of individuals being roughly jostled into experimental labs where the cameras showed us concrete "operating tables" with center drains and restraining straps at their corners—the faces of these people will live with me forever.

My experience at this film was not personal psychic trauma. Its role was far more substantial. That evening in a small movie theater in San Francisco I joined the complete human race.

I didn't fully realize it yet, but I was no longer a Christian, no longer a white man, no longer an American. I was a human. Just that. Only that. Nothing more. From that evening on, that was all I ever wanted to be again, all I would ever again think of myself as. It would take me many years yet to absorb this fact into my life completely, but that night a new self was born.

Eventually, helped much by that film, I would come to ignore specific color or race or creed—especially creed—and every other specificity that separates anyone into any category other than just being human. Beginning that evening, I knew that if there is anything of greater worth for anyone to become, it is to become more consciously a part of the complete human race.

During my time in Europe later, I visited the caves outside of Rome where Nazis killed 335 prisoners in 1944, with many men and boys added to the truckloads of victims for no other reason than that they were Jewish. At the monument to those victims, there is a sarcophagus for each, and inlaid under glass on the lid of each is a picture of the victim inside. Once again, as in the French documentary, those faces looked back at me, only this time it was different. The faces were no longer accusing me of being one of the Christians who either stood idly by during centuries of pogroms or actively engineered and executed them. This time I was truly one with the gentle ones crushed there. I was Jewish by neither race nor creed, but I was, with them, human. I knew that I was by that time irrevocably dedicated to naming and undoing the anti-Semitism that had brought them to this cave, whether that anti-Semitism was carried out by Nazis during a few years or by Christian self-righteousness during many centuries. I knew that I would be shouting about twenty centuries of Christian anti-Semitism even more loudly than about the shorter Nazi's brand of it that had destroyed them.

What the Jewish people and their tradition had to offer went beyond a sensitivity to the realities of anti-Semitism. Rabbi Abraham Joshua Heschel, for example, had sublime spiritual insights to share. Anti-Semitism pointed out what was wrong; his message spoke of what was right. I already knew some of his writing, and one day when Dr. Heschel was to give a lecture at Temple Emmanuel, I had the good fortune to be there.

The room was filled mostly with older people, about equally divided between men and women. At one point during the lecture and interaction and in some way which I have forgotten, it became apparent that a sizable number of persons in the congregation were survivors of the German camps. With infinite gentleness and exquisite appropriateness, Rabbi Heschel suggested we sit in silence for a protracted time rather than use any words about the Holocaust, "for there are some events that far exceed the capacity of our words." There was not a dry eye in the room. No outcry. No loud weeping. Just silent tears beyond the possibility of analysis for those who had been stepped on by a self-styled superior race. As I sat there I became aware of a great anger in me about a far older, much longer, supercilious Christian religiosity that I felt, and still feel, must one day face the realization that it provided the model for the Nazis. By the time the Nazis began their "final solution," the world had, thanks precisely to organized Christianity, long become accustomed to feeling justified at having Jews as targets.

Rabbi Heschel was talking about the Eternal Sabbath—the peace of the Holy One—and the quiet faith we are invited to have in the benevolent Reality all around us. My monastic meditation was stretching, feet planted firmly on this earth now, and arms ever more widely spread.

The Jewish influence on my spirit was composed of living rabbis, masters of past ages, readings in Jewish literature of every age, poignant affinity to those who had perished in pogroms and the Holocaust. All of these were teaching me what the Jews had been faithfully saying for four thousand years: this world and its infinitely precious cargo of living people and gracious environment are to be safeguarded and cherished and cared for. No one is to be despised in even the smallest way in favor of some alleged heaven to come later on. As a favorite rabbi author, Leo Trepp, wrote in a book I was studying at the time:

By loving our neighbor we establish God as Lord of a united mankind. By loving our neighbor we love Him. The two elements—love of God and sustaining love of neighbor—are fused into one. Thus life becomes worship, every moment of it is hallowed.

I remember breaking out in laughter in a Jewish library one day where I'd gone to do research for a paper I was preparing for the university. I was reading a passage by a certain Rabbi Leo Baeck, who, after saying Christian monks are "vicars of romanticism," went on to congratulate any of them who are "willing to be influenced enough by the 'Old' Testament to leave their monasteries and their lives as egoistic hermits and go involve themselves in active care of the world." I was embarrassed for my outburst, but I knew that he had scored one and that somewhere he was appreciating my response to his words.

He excoriated medieval Christianity, and by then I completely agreed with him, for its dualism and its distinction of earthly and heavenly vocations, disastrously pitting one against the other.

Baeck was not implying—or, at least, I did not hear him implying and would not have agreed with him if he was—that it's a matter of either-or. We don't have to be either inner or outer directed in our lives. Both dimensions are essential aspects of our reality in this world. If some individuals forfeit peace and joy and live in turmoil because they ignore the inner dimension of themselves, others (like Christian monks, Baeck was saying) err in the opposite direction. They play the charade of already having left this world, or they perpetrate the dangerous error of treating the world as if it were beneath them. This world and this body are the means through which each one of us is to find inner enlightenment, and—Baeck would have approved of this—where we must apply in practical ways the fact that we are all One.

Baeck had himself barely escaped the gas chambers by getting out of Berlin and to Cincinnati in 1939. Even so, I am not aware that he ever pointed out, as I was beginning to do, that the Christian dualistic distinction between earthly and heavenly "worlds" is what provided the mind-set behind centuries of pogroms and crusades and holy wars, and, ultimately, of the Holocaust.

There might be nothing inconsistent for a thirteenth- or seventeenth-century Christian to let "outsiders" starve because they refused to embrace Christianity, but this attitude was as totally inconceivable in Jewish thinking then as it is now.

Their duality of focus upon two mutually exclusive worlds explains how Christians "in good conscience" could officially call fellow human beings "perfidious Jews," as the Good Friday liturgy of Roman Catholicism did until the revolution of Pope John XXIII in the mid-1960's.

Some members in congregations and audiences where I've spoken have become angry at hearing the accusations I'm making here. When this happens, I simply step aside and let history speak for itself. Neither my audiences nor I can change history, but I am determined to learn lessons from it and to present others the same opportunity.

It's interesting to note, and should be remembered with embarrassment and pain by every Christian, that in the mid-1960s even Rome's revolutionary Second Vatican Council decided by majority vote *not* to exclude the word *deicide* (god killing) from charges leveled against the Jewish people.

When I heard of that little caper by career church politicians, I shook my head in dismay. It would take me yet a few more years to become aware enough of the deeper message of Jesus and countless other spiritual masters to break completely free of the Churchianity that deals in such truck.

Politics, bigotries, and angers aside, my burgeoning awareness of worldwide religious thought began adding a vital dimension to my spirituality and to my life from the day I arrived in San Francisco onward. I began realizing that a profound involvement in the world must be a valid part of any conscientious religion, even of any valid high mystical experience. In the end I had to realize that it was *non*-Christian spiritualities that had forever freed me from what stood revealed as a totally silly Christian duality, an imaginary conflict between "worldliness" and the highest levels of human consciousness.

Wherever life would take me from now on, I would be there as a citizen of *this* world, consciously part of a vastly greater spiritual *and* material universe.

My heart and mind and spirit had been learning to dance from my earliest meditations with Datus. With the help of Jewish and other non-Christian religions, I finally found my dance floor: this world.

28

Beyond Stories

What was it that I learned in meditation? What was it that I found beneath the surfaces of various religious traditions, their multiple languages, and widely differing storyforms? Since Buddhism, Judaism, Christianity, Islam, and other belief systems believe such widely divergent "truths," what was it that I learned both from study and in meditation that makes me say, as I have in this book, that the same common religious insight and experience are there at the heart of all religious traditions?

The study of the differing beliefs and rituals of world religions is not new. Courses in comparative religion have been available in most universities and some high schools for many years. Countless books have been written on the topic. Unfortunately, however, most of them deal with where and how religions differ. They deal mainly with the relatively accessible variables—rituals, architecture, doctrines. Most have not searched for the elements that are held in common beneath what is different.

In the past few years there has been more effort to study the spirituality, as such, at the heart of all world religions. The most popular efforts in this regard have been the study of the religious myths of the race, a study popularized, for example, by the life work of Joseph Campbell. His book and television series, *The Power of Myth,* have brought an unprecedented awareness of this underlying central reality. The unbiased study of myths comes closer to a clear realization of what I am writing about and what has been my experience in meditation than academic comparisons of the doctrines and rituals ever could. Myths can reveal more than doctrines because they spring from a human intuition and unconscious awareness that are not limited by words and their connotations. Myths do not speak, primarily, from mind to mind, but from spirit to spirit. Myths born in Borneo, Africa, North America's Great Plains, and Central Europe, or in a Lucas film studio in California, may vary in how they are ultimately translated into words, but the best ones initially spring from a common transcultural Source and express a supracultural Reality.

Just as I have only understood my own life by looking back and seeing its beginnings and subsequent paths, so, too, the religious landscape of the human race, with its many and apparently contradictory belief systems, can only be understood when it's seen in historical perspective. Only by going back to the origins of religion and following its development can we understand its pluralistic profile today.

Humans do not trace back to a single couple, as the Hebrew storyform tells it in the book of Genesis, but they do trace back to a point in the evolution of an increasingly conscious species when reflective thought and words appeared, undoubtedly over an exceptionally long period of time and during which personal consciousness was initially as rare as cosmic consciousness is today. At some point, the race found itself greatly dispersed and ensconced in isolated valleys, on different sides of mountain chains, even on opposite sides of oceans. As awareness and mental ability evolved, completely different families of languages slowly made their appearance. An individual in the steppes of Asia felt the need to name his spear, for example, just as did as an individual in the rain forests of Africa. They, obviously, would come up with totally different sounds for what Anglo-Saxons—and we—would eventually call a spear.

But it's more complicated than just needing to name things. Separate societies, divided by thousands of miles, also had to talk about what they had named. Whether they said "Don't throw the spear" or "Please pass the butter," not only did they use different sounds (words) to do so, they also used different associations of thought and varieties of grammar and syntax to get their ideas expressed in meaningful combinations of those words and on their way to a listener. As anyone who has studied languages will agree, translation is much more complex than a simple matter of substituting the words of one language for those of another. There is the way ideas are put together, the great variation in thought processes that must be taken into account. One language, for example, may not simply say "Please pass the butter," but "I would be happier if I had that butter down at the end of the table for this bread that I am holding." The idea is the same ("I want butter for my bread"), but the way that idea is expressed differs both in the sounds used and in the way they're used.

If various people in different parts of the world had to find words for spears and grandmothers and rivers and stars, they also had to find words—and concepts—to handle the death of grandma, the birth of a baby, the strange feelings they felt when a bright and clear spring morning burst upon them after a night of lightning and thunder. They had to find a way to share their thoughts about intangibles and, ultimately, their intuition that there is some kind of Ultimate Reality that is the explanation for all that is otherwise too mysterious and, so, frightening. Just as various valleys and geographical areas thought up different ways to dress and to prepare food and to talk, so they eventually all came up with various myths and word-laden statements containing their best intuitions and explanations of the unseen. And how they did this varied from valley to valley, continent to continent, just as their foods and words did.

It is no more surprising that there are plural religions in the world than that there are plural languages, cuisines, styles of clothing and shelter. The important reality about clothing around the whole world is that, whatever it's made from and looks like, it has this in common: it protects human bodies from the elements. No matter what the many cuisines of the world look like, smell like, or are composed of, they all nourish. In the same way, no matter how many explanations of life, its purpose, and Source there are, they all, like food, clothing, and languages, make life livable.

Unfortunately, the logical application of the simple historical dynamic of the same basic thing happening everywhere in multiple ways gets more complicated when someone tries to apply it to the appearance and development of religion. One can argue, of course, and probably get by with it, that the metaphysical and religious explanations that various isolated areas of the world worked out were as disparate as were the languages and cuisines they worked out. But if one then goes on to say that religions contain a universal, core realization, a whole new level of consideration arises: pride and fear. It's acceptable to say that all cuisines nourish, all cultural garbs protect from the elements, all languages communicate ideas. But to say that all religions also have a common purpose *and achievement* is to step on all sorts of vested—and frightened—toes.

There have always been parochial, cloistered minds who "know" without any hesitation that their native language, food, dress, architecture, weapons, and everything else are better than those of any other people. Imagine, however, how fervent their contention will become (and usually does become) when what is being spoken of are the insights that have given one's people its sense of security and direction, its peace and bit of joy. Suddenly the cloistered mind is not defending the superiority of his language or food or weapons, but his understanding of God, his very philosophy of life, the very thought system that permits him to feel secure. To ask him to alter this is vastly more unthinkable than to ask him never again to eat the foods of his native land or speak his mother tongue.

Unfortunately for the cloistered mind, however, like it or not, just as all cuisines nourish, all native garbs clothe, so do all religious traditions approach, intimate, and reflect a deeper core intuition possessed by the human race everywhere. This intuition may struggle for expression in widely varying myths, may have totally different rituals connected with it, and may be worded in widely divergent belief systems (which is not surprising, after all, since formulated thought always depends heavily on local cultural variables). Nonetheless, despite these evident differences, *there are common realizations in all cultures from which every belief system emerged.*

This is so because human minds worked everywhere upon one identical world and human life cycle, and always by starting from the need to explain human experience. Tribe X may have understood death and the hereafter in one way, for example, and Tribes Y and Z in other ways. But all three had to handle birth, death, and so on, and did, in fact, devise ways of dealing with them. In all three cases there were identical elements: human beings, human experience, and a need to understand it with the best intuitive thinking (and then worded statements) available. And because words could never quite contain what the shaman or priest or wisdom woman was trying to share, humans composed myths to share the insights more accurately.

As these efforts were bearing fruit all over the world, all that was available in any one given place was what that given place had realized. In primordial times, one local valley, one side of the mountain, one side of an ocean possessed only what it alone had produced, whether in clothing, food, languages, or religion.

Once a society has formulated its workable set of understandings with which to handle life's unknowns, it will find great comfort and a sense of security in these reassurances. Obviously, it will be a major disturbance if someone comes along and announces that people on the other side of the mountain believe something quite different and have a completely different set of religious stories.

"Does that mean we're wrong? Are we in danger, after all?" The next step will be either to attack such enemies of the "truth," or send missionaries to them and give them a chance to be "saved." "Who do they think they are? Let's protect ourselves from their errors. Let's attack them, because, you know how it is: one rotten apple can spoil the whole bushel." Or "Let's pray for them and send missionaries to them so they will come to the 'truth' as we, rightly, of course, know it."

Today there are no longer any separate valleys or mountain sides, no safe havens for one single food or language or religion. The cloistered mind must twist in fear as it sees its previous clarity muddied by all sorts of other ways of seeing and then explaining the world. The immensity of the shift in presuppositions that is newly called for can be overwhelming now that communication and transportation have caused all peoples everywhere to know what all other peoples everywhere believe and think. Other cultures' foods are suddenly thrust before us, and we're expected to expand our taste and like them. We see all sorts of weird styles of clothing on the street, and we're expected not to laugh. We are urged to show other peoples the respect of learning to speak their languages.

And, then, horror of horrors, we one day realize how out of touch and inadequate our xenophobic fear of religious pluralism has become.

Some "doctrines" about the world and its Source and functioning that various elements of the race have come up with are so gentle and comfortable to the human spirit that they don't need much external assistance and tend to spread by themselves, like Buddhism. Some have within their insight a reason not to seek propagation, and they remain forever the joy of the few, like Taoism. Some are so sure of themselves that they give special honor to being militarily aggressive about their special insight, as Islam once was. Some are deliberately unformulated and so humble that they run the risk of being forgotten, like the spirituality of the Sioux. Some are so defensively withdrawn that they will always be limited to a specific few, like Hasidism. Some are so grand in scope that they will forever confuse most people by the rich variety of their content, like Hinduism.

Christianity has been repeatedly redefined in such exquisitely refined and often contradictory doctrines and is so totally juridical (reflecting the Roman Empire's legalism in which it took its birth and where it developed into independence from its Mother Judaism), that it must stand in a category all by itself. It squabbled badly and bloodily for its first four centuries, but by then its management system of bishops was so sure of itself that when it gained the support of the Emperor Theodosius I, it simply from that point on told people what they would believe and *that* they would believe it, willy-nilly, for their own good, of course.

Suddenly the rest of the religious world was wrong. All other storyforms, all content of all myths, and all human intuition of all human cultures were erroneous except in so far as they agreed with the tenets of Christianity. All human religious experiences were thereafter to be measured against the verbal formulations of Christian managers.

With some notable rebellions and splinterings along the way, the same state of affairs remains today. Christians may bicker among themselves about the details, but they all agree on the basic storyforms that originated in just one small segment of the human race. All other racial religious data are to be minimalized, missionized, felt sorry for, and brought into the fold of "truth" one way or another. The end is all that matters.

With greater objectivity and independent of vested biases, what is the basic insight and experience at the core of all religious traditions? What lies beyond religious stories, beneath diverse doctrines, at the heart of all myths?

It is what mystics and poets have tried to share from their highest moments: the simplest fact that everything is a facet of an ultimate One. Things are many, but they are all expressions—outpressings—of One Being, One Existence, One Life.

Logic can play with this realization, but it cannot demonstrate it. The only way it can be known is by being experienced. That is why most theologians, who deal with words and logic, and the managers of institutionalized religions, who have made their primary task the guarding of familiar myths and formulas, deny that the underlying basis of all religion is humankind's effort to recall and touch the One. They disown such a realization because it comes only from an inner experience, one that they have not taken time to search for and find.

This experience, nevertheless, awaits everyone and will one day be the universal realization of a grown-up human race. How it came about in one person's life is the story of this book.

29

When the Curtain Parts

All things have turned out well. More accurately, I realize now that all things were well all along. My days pass in gentleness and humor, and dawns are consistently bright at last.

If the degree of my youthful confusion and delayed maturity embarrasses me in the telling, as friends warned it would, the degree of my present healing and joy makes me chuckle in the face of that embarrassment.

Years of self-attack, they tell me, made certain cells in my long-despised body hear the rejection in my mind and rebel from me as cancerous. I was diagnosed with cancer in November 1989. Helped by the best of today's medical science and with a new realization of my inner reality—or, as the mystics say, of the One Life I share—my body seems to have turned in time to join the healing in my mind and heart. But my days would remain bright and lighthearted anyway.

I have come to understand that when the mystics of the race, Jesus included, tell us that we are all One, they are not speaking in metaphor. Almost immediately after I realized this, after I took them seriously, my life changed dramatically. The happiness and peace that spiritual masters speak of as surpassing understanding and being beyond our imagination became tangible realities in every day.

I've learned to listen inside in meditation, and I've come to understand that all of us, whether now or in another time, and without exception, will necessarily come to the realization of our ultimate and absolute security. If personal and worldwide horrors continue in the meantime, it's only for as long as the human race continues to forget its shared Divine Life, only as long as it's not capable of the universal love that this shared Life involves, only as long as it thinks itself poor, in danger, and in need of competition. All people will eventually find bliss because they will eventually remember their Nature.

My final step to the beginning of freedom and bliss, to this happiness that surpasses anything I could have otherwise imagined, came with the realization that God is not at all what I had been told "He" is. The God I sought to know and serve through many years turned out not to be, after all, an Archruler, a bookkeeping Lord, or even a Benevolent Benefactor. Nor does He reside somewhere out across a universe. He turns out to be *here*—the Life and Existence of all things.

He turns out, too, not to be a He or She or It at all. Much of the human race has called God *He* for no more insightful reason than that human words stumble about so badly in topics they can't reach around. God was seen in the West as He only because the early lessons we inherited about the Ultimate were mostly managed and disseminated by males who wanted to ensure that the highest and best were always portrayed as masculine. We can believe they did this honestly, perhaps, because in that earlier era, height of stature, physical strength, and reach of sword arm were the most recognized indicators and assurance of power.

In a deeper sense, of course, this Source Being *is* a He, but also a She, an It, and all things else.

Nor did the One I found turn out to be a father as I'd also been told. That was just another metaphor, dreamed up long ago when the race was young and a need was felt to temper the image of God as a powerful and potentially dangerous, vindictive King. *Father* is an improvement on *King*, but it still doesn't reach around the

Reality it is intended to represent. If we were told we might confidently address the great Creator King as our Father—and in some deeper cultures also as our Mother—it was simply a winsome way to compare God's begetting to humankind's best moments of love and the parent-child relationships that sometimes result from these. To make God less frightening and more available, Its "outpressings" were compared to human children, and It to a parent.

I've learned we must not burden metaphors with greater loads than their makers designed for them. Eternal Being is something like a father, yes, and something like a mother. But that's because we are left with only comparisons to call on when our hearts and minds return from touching the Incomprehensible.

Nor did the Source turn out to be a "creator," as if It had invented all things from something else or even "out of nothing," as the traditional phrase puts it (an irrational notion from the moment of its dull conception). The word *creator* is just another effort to help us grasp the Nature of Eternal Reality, this time by comparing It to earthly artisans who do make things from other things. Eternal Being is, indeed, the Source of everything that is, but It "creates" only in the sense of outpressing That Which only Is: Itself. It originates "other" things only in the sense of expressing—outpressing—Its Fullness in countless ways. For those who need such reassurance, biblical texts say all of this precisely: "Of His Fullness we've all received" and "In Him we live and move and have our Being" and "In Christ all the fullness of the Deity lives in bodily form, and you have been given [that] fullness in Christ." What we were taught to call "creation" is, more accurately, Eternal Oneness delighting Itself in countless varieties of forms.

Beyond all stories and metaphors, the so-called creation is Being's way to outpress in endless shapes and sizes. The ancients said "Good is diffusive of itself," and creation is precisely this diffusion of God's Being. It's how God expands the Bliss of Life: dancing into being whatever comes to Mind.

When I finally began to think about the Source Being without the constraints of the prefab thoughts called "doctrines," I realized that Eternal Existence, God, has nothing It can gain. What could God want for which It is not already providing the Existence? How could God seek to acquire what It already Is? The outpressing of Existence is done without even the slightest desire for, much less need for, the "glory" demanded from pulpits every week.

Nor has Being any place to go. Where would It go? Whatever exists in any place must exist there with the only Existence there Is: Its own. Aristotle implied it and mystics spelled it out clearly: Being is already present wherever It might "go."

I find great delight in realizing that the only thing Eternal Existence can do is to revel in being Itself. It is Eternal Existence and by its Nature loves to apply, to express, to outpress, to diffuse this Existence, this Life, this Being, endlessly and variously. Its process of outpressing in countless shapes and ways cannot be aimed at any gain (what could It gain?), except the delight of expressing Itself in countless shapes and ways.

Eternal Existence, Life, Being, God outpresses as color, light, and music, as love and trees and moons and a zillion things in a zillion styles, and then as intelligent beings to see the whole of it. And all of this *for no other reason* than to enjoy Itself as color, light, and music, as love and trees and moons and a zillion things in a zillion styles, and as intelligent beings to see the whole of It.

I have come to see this cosmic dance of Life as not unlike the dances we know on earth. We wouldn't go onto a dance floor and ask the dancers where they're headed with all their footsteps. We'd be equally foolish to ask them to demonstrate material gain for what they're doing. At best, they'd look surprised and say we've missed the point. The dance of "God" is just like that—no purpose but the joy.

Great traditions, raised on fear honestly veiled as love, will cry out in dismay to hear someone say that God's in it just for fun. That's too bad. Generations of spiritual seekers (and finders, the world's mystics) have long been telling us that Eternal Being is best known when seen as play and dance—the dance of One who has nothing to gain, nowhere to go, nothing to do but enjoy.

Most things that we were told about our early God were storied ways to teach, contrivances meant to lead us deeper and higher, ways to expand our vision and customary thought. They were small pathways intended to help us remember what each one of us most certainly must grow to one day realize: Eternal Existence is the core of all that is. Too bad if the purpose of these simple stories got lost along the way and the stories themselves retained as literal fact.

On the day when the race will have remembered what enlightened ones tell us we must remember, when ancestral myths and tales—the Bible included—will have served their role, they will be gently set aside. Stories are not needed when the Reality they were to remind us of has been found.

The God I've met is not a static Source somewhere "out there," or even a Source somewhere "in here." It's dynamically, actively the Core of everything, a Process unfolding outside of time, but still enough within our time to make us feel a warm new kind of joy, and to always make us laugh.

This Timeless Process is not some distant genius-God winding the clockwork of the stars, not some cosmic Artist painting clouds, designing horizons, and putting the spin on galaxies. It does all that, but from within. It's the gentle Architect of blossoms, designing them from inside and there becoming their texture, hue, and scent. It's the Archetypal Child pausing in play just long enough to prod all hearts to come join in the game.

The best that I could do at first was start in some small way to suspect some truth in all of this. Early in meditation, something of this kind seemed to be suggesting itself, but I couldn't grasp it. Intuition is always far ahead of clear understanding. Even now, words cannot adequately describe what I've found. If I were to say they could, I'd show I've missed the height and depth and light of It. As Lao-tzu wrote in his *Tao Te Ching,* "The Tao that can be described is not the Tao."

I understand now why mystic minds use myth and metaphor, stories and comparisons to tell us What they've seen. The best that they can do is just suggest the Fact of It. They want to share an experience that lies beyond our words, and so they create tales to talk about a God they cannot talk about. Words break down in realms like this, but inside of them there runs a happy smile that takes our breath away each time "God" comes into view: an instant's opening of the curtain, a nanosecond's glimpse of an iridescent hummingbird toying with the sun just outside the window of a dark and stuffy room.

But if God is not what I'd been taught, then neither am I.

Eternal Being is not found outside of me or even deep within me. It is my Life, my Existence. It is experiencing my breathing and my bones, my fingers and my feelings. It wasn't watching me or even present in me, but was there all along *as* me when I walked and laughed, cried and made love all those years when I didn't feel up to par. Despite my fears and throughout them all, I was all that while—already, securely, irreversibly—a Presence of the only Life there ever could be in any universe. Slowly I came to realize that my task is not to "practice the Presence of God," as traditional piety suggests, but to keep my attention and heart in the present where alone Life Is. Life is not something that I *have,* but the Something that I *Am.*

And there are implications in that.

The worst things in my life can never happen to the true Self of me. I am now able to mean the Bible's taunt: "Death, where is your sting?" The only role that's mine to play, the ultimate rule to keep, is to not forget or turn away, not to sleep through the dance.

Becoming aware of this single purpose is called *enlightenment,* what Buddha called to be "awake" and Jesus, with different emphasis, the Kingdom of God within. In this sense, awareness freed me at last to lighten up and join the Universe at play.

My house being now at rest, I've come at last to reach out honestly with my mind and heart to love all other people and all things. They are a part of Me, and I a part of Them. I know now why

Jesus and other masters said that every "other" is my Self, and that we each are one with each other. All of us are facets of a single Gem. To plumb the analogy, we're not even demarcated as much as facets are on the surface of a jewel, but are more as they exist beneath its surface. All history, space, and time are ours together. Space is where Existence plays as all of us, and time the measuring of Its game. History is the patient marking of Its way as our race awakens to What it Is.

Worth, okayness, and security depend not at all on the needs I felt as a child, youth, and anxious man. Now I realize that I didn't need to prove a thing and that there never was anything but appearances at stake. Nor did I need the smile of others to gain an acceptability that could only be based on appearances. The solitary thing I needed then, and still need now, is to remember none of what is real in me is passing, fading, fragile, aging. I am Eternal Existence expressing here as me.

I am not safe or adequate because of how I feel or what I possess, but because of what I Am. Emotional states and passing troubles are but weather passing over the landscape of my Mind.

And if the daily practice of my life has further purpose whatsoever, it is to help others awaken to Themselves, exactly as the Buddha said.

For years I watched poets circle this Vision with their mysterious words, and I listened as musicians wooed It with sounds that echoed Its dimensions. I studied hard the scholars who probed It with their games of thought and watched as preachers thumped their Book about something they'd clearly, mostly, long forgot.

And then one afternoon in 1986 in Gig Harbor, Washington, an experience showed me what lay within all metaphor and myth and beneath the stories and theologies of God. It is a day I remember as the day the Universe gently unrolled in front of me. I was playing with a friend's Doberman named Heidi, and as we wrestled, growled, and teased, she suddenly stopped, released my hand that she was gently holding in her teeth, and raised her head just long enough to lick my face, as if in gratitude for so much fun or to reassure me that she would never bite too hard. In that instant I saw colors I'd not seen and heard music I'd not heard. Unscheduled, not invited, not preapproved, and certainly without the fanfare I'd have planned for it, I felt the touch of God. The scene that opened before my eyes reached from ants crossing at our feet into the farthest galaxies, and yet everything was close, familiar, somehow one with both Heidi and me. What had still until that moment seemed theoretical knowledge of the mystics was suddenly now *experienced*. Existence-here-as-Dog had just touched the face of Existence-here-as-Me. In that instant I met a Oneness that would no longer play roles theology had assigned to It: Creator, Father, Mother, and offended, condescending King. It would be instead, now and forever, the simple Whole of everything.

Eternal Existence is no longer hidden when It becomes a peony in ballet with a breeze, a tiger's fur shining back Its own golden sun. I recognize it in Andromeda's pirouette and hear It as a whale's pure song sung softly through the sea. I laugh to see It as race-horse pride related to a mule, and in a royal lion's grimaced glance at a cousin alley cat. I wonder is It being impish or artistic when, as gems and crystal rocks, It fills Its hearts of solid stone with Technicolor light.

As Heidi and I paused in our play, my heart broke free, my mind went still, I smiled from deep inside at the overwhelming experience: *"This* is the 'more,' I've heard about, the bliss I've sought so long!" Life had come and announced, wordlessly, but with an unambiguousness surpassing words by far, "I Am the deepest part of you, dear one. You had just forgot. The wholeness you were searching for was here as you and all you met . . . outpressing just for joy!"

I'd been searching all this time for what had been not only mine, but *me!* Now, suddenly, with the Doberman tilting her head in curiosity at my sudden change of mood, I knew the meaning of words I'd read some years before: "You have nothing to acquire here, but All to realize."

30

Home

Coming home means more than returning to a bit of familiar geography. Home is a context that includes values, emotions, thoughts, special persons. Coming home to one's Self in developed spirituality means something similar: a returning to renewed familiarity with oneness, to conscious union with and love for everyone and everything.

Being consciously in touch with the One is to be immediately in touch with all things. This touch is not academic or abstract. It's a light in the mind, but also a feeling in the heart. It's an *experience* of the Spirit of all that is. There is not a single person's loss, pain, plea, or aspiration that is not now mine. There is no animal or tree or body of water—anything on earth or anywhere else—that escapes the reach of the love and concern that I now feel. I now know what Buddha meant about universal compassion. I see clearly that if there is a way to understand and categorize all agony—of the murderer as much as of the murdered—it is that yet for a time on earth the human race mistakes as real the nightmare of illusioned separateness. And that begets the greatest compassion of all.

It's been a long journey, but there is no bemoaning in that statement. It's simply a fact that it was a long trek to today from the

day of that frightened child's anxious reach for okayness in everyone's, anyone's approval, through a youth's compulsive sampling
of everything, to a young man's obedience to old men's fears. Now,
at last, the journey has brought me home to my Self where, all
along, fulfillment and bliss lay waiting.

In one sense, a person's journey never ends, for when do we ar-
rive at Infinity? In another, the journey ends the moment we realize that we never left Infinity in the first place.

I took the long way around to learn that spiritual masters were
not talking in metaphor, but meant literally what they were saying when they told us that the kingdom of God lies within us. The
place of our Source and fulfillment and bliss is only found within.
Heaven is not a place, but a condition.

Egocentricity, self-absorption, selfishness? Some will say so.
Many church managers will insist so. It *is* self-absorption, but the
Self that is centered upon in this context doesn't exclude or stand
apart from any other. It includes everyone and everything everywhere, for it is not the self of the isolated ego.

Our conventional understanding, built on appearances, is that
each of us is a separate being clawing and competing our way
through a precarious global bivouac. Some religions then add that
none of this really matters because all that is important is to obey
rules and one day give an accounting somewhere else for the success or failure of that obedience. Enlightened masters, however,
have been telling us for thousands of years that any understanding
we've had that we're here just on trial is only a passing and fictional
threat that was contrived to get our attention. I have come to see
they are correct.

Shreds of old habits linger, of course, and familiar emotions live on
to emerge again and again in my life. But they are greatly weak-
ened now and cause little distress. Lifelong habits of fear and self-
belittlement seldom bother anymore, and then only until they are
noticed. Our deepest Reality can never be qualified by human
thought or feeling.

The moment I began to recognize this outpressing of the One as being my truest Self, I began to sense in my heart the dancing that this book is all about. If I had to stumble about for a time with lingering habits of fear, it was nonetheless clear from the start that these hangovers were moving out of my life the moment I stopped taking them seriously. As they withdrew, the dance sped up, and new companions began arriving, companions of a brightness and lightheartedness for which there are no words in our human dictionaries—words created for material appearances, competition, trade, and fear.

I found that wholeness, happiness, and freedom are not pipe dreams, after all. Exactly as the mystics promised, bliss and rapture are available to everyone without exception, even to me, a fairly screwed-up guy and, by most churchy standards, a "sinner."

Slowly, the light in my life today has spread backward into all those painful and embarrassing periods of my past that I encapsulated with their pain and then tried (unsuccessfully) to forget about. One by one I have visited with today's consciousness these darkened capsules of personal history. And now they follow me no longer as a depressing chain of boxed memories that I'd rather slough off, but as a long train of glittering cars journeying with me across a starlit valley. My whole life, even in its painful parts, has been clearly just an adventure, a journey into the remembering of wholeness.

Like all the imagery used in this book, my image of a "long train of glittering cars" only inadequately represents what I'm attempting to express. Nevertheless, mental concepts and definitions would have done the task even less well. But, alas, even images and analogies have a limp about them. The best I can do is intimate and suggest, give an explanation in one place and paint a picture in another, and then, when the day of writing is done, return to that inner place where the dance will once again remind me that the touch of God cannot be shared, but only experienced.

Afterword

As I wrote in the Preface, this book is more about everybody's path than just mine. The circumstances and anecdotes of the life recounted here are mine, of course, but the path from fear to freedom, from trouble to peace, from dis-ease to healing belongs by Nature to everyone.

Everybody has a dance going on inside, awaiting recognition. Only the want of remembrance puts it off in the future.

It isn't, strictly speaking, even inside of us. Our dance is a part of us. It's been there living with us, *as* us, all the years we can remember—and, if we can accept this, for many that we can't.

This book is about everybody's dance.

Acknowledgments

I'm the type who chooses books carefully, but then reads every word of those chosen: copyright page, table of contents, footnotes, and down to the last word on the back of the jacket. There's only one section I always want to skip and sometimes do: the acknowledgments. "Yes, yes, we know you're overcome by gratitude, so drop the sentiment and get on with the book, will you?"

I've forever sworn I'd never write an acknowledgment page, and in a previous book did not. But this time, with my manuscript finalized and in the hands of the publisher, I realize how insensitive, even unjust, it would be to let this volume be published without acknowledging that, while it came out of my computer, it is, in fact, the production of many people. I understand for the first time that an acknowledgment page is a need in an author's heart.

The role of my wife, Lori, through months of writing, has dependably been everything one could hope for from a lover, keeper, and intimate confidant. Her gentle support has not dulled a bit in twenty-five years of marriage. She didn't have to remind me to keep at the task, but she did have to remind to let up, to eat, to take time for healing contact with fun and friends. This book is a monument to her love that never once lost its cool as again and again she had to pry my hands off my keyboard.

Second only to Lori, my special friend, Norman Ratner, also helped create this book. His spiritual—and substantial material—support for this project never once wavered. His kindness in reading successive drafts of successive chapters was as great in the end as it was the day I first told him, "I think I'll write a book about my journey out of fear."

Alongside Lori and Norman, my editor at Addison-Wesley, Nancy Miller, added her own top-drawer expertise from within the publishing industry. Again and again, she provided incisive insight to help me say what I was trying to say. In several significant places she saved me the embarrassment of gaps in meaning and chronology. Only another author can appreciate what it feels like to have a professional editor of Nancy's stature warmly endorse—and honor with insightful understanding—a writing project of this kind.

The litany is long, but several additional persons deserve to see their names here and to know their contribution is appreciated with love and gratitude. Joel Brokaw of The Brokaw Company in Los Angeles must head the list, and then Lena Williams of *The New York Times.* Both played special and unforgettable roles in the making of this book. So did Ellen Rolfes of Ellen Rolfes Books in Memphis. Jacquie Snyder from Puget Sound country was the one who first suggested—insisted—that I expand a feature article into an autobiography. Dyane Roth, Heidi Sewall, Bruce Kelley, and Connie Freeman read and reacted. Mark Breeding, Greg Smith, and Bob Dunn, Jr., were my rooting section and never let me take myself seriously. Dr. Dean Knoll and Dr. Paul Rosenblatt, both of Nashville, played important roles when cancer tried to rain out the game.

Last, but not least, there have been unseen friends whose lightheartedness and care made the whole process of this book a thing of joy . . . and not infrequently of outrageous fun.

About the Author

George Fowler is a nationally syndicated columnist on religious issues and is the coauthor of *Feed Your Soul,* a spiritual cookbook. He lives in Nashville, Tennessee, with his wife.